Praise for
Leadership in My Rearview Mirror

"A deep well of wisdom and experience in the realm of leadership. No quick-fix book here. No set of feel-good platitudes, to lie pale and empty when viewed in the full light of the next day's leadership challenge. This is a fully formed nexus of state-of-the-art leadership concepts and research, crafted into a highly useful and readable form, by a true master of the art of transformational leadership."

Lt. Col. Dave Grossman, USA (ret.)
Author of On Killing *and* On Combat

"A wonderful read. A master leader developer who uses storytelling to impart wisdom gained over a lifetime. Experienced and emerging leaders, as well as readers with only a casual interest in leadership, will find Dr. Beach's insights enriching and his stories moving and entertaining. An added benefit is the glimpse into how one of the world's greatest companies approaches leader development."

Col. Patrick Sweeney (ret.), Ph.D.
Executive Director, Leadershi͏   ͏ Gwinnett College
Former Deputy Head, Department of ͏   ͏s and Leadership,
United States Mili͏   ͏st Point, New York

"As a leadership educator, and leader developer, I ͏   ͏ read all I can on the topic of leadership—the good, the bad, and ͏   ͏ Beach's book is just plain good; a worthy read for anyone who wa ͏   ͏rstanding of leadership and leader development. The lessons ab ͏   ͏rk of compelling stories and smooth, easy-to-read prose. If you are p ͏   ͏ership who wants to be better, this book is for you—you will be ͏   ͏t more importantly a better person, for having read it."

͏   ͏euf (ret.), Ph.D.
Profes͏   ͏ of Management
Coach͏   ͏rship and Ethics
Fuqua School of Business, Duke University

"Jack Beach writes eloquently about the synergies resulting from trust, empowerment, collective leadership, and the vibrant power of engaged employees. *Leadership in My Rearview Mirror* is a splendid mix of profound—often paradoxical—leadership wisdom and wit that will enlighten and inspire leaders at any organizational level. It's a wonderful book and a should-read for any leader."

Lt. Col. Bill Adams (ret.)
Senior Faculty, Center for Creative Leadership
Greensboro, North Carolina

"A compelling read for senior executives or rising stars who desire to bring more of themselves to their leadership. Jack Beach clearly connects 'who leaders are' with 'how they lead' through the powerful medium of personal stories, critical moments, and the illuminating power of psychological principles. Jack models authenticity by sharing his own 'hard knocks' and victories on the path to leadership insight and understanding."

Col. Todd Henshaw (ret.), Ph.D.
Director of Executive Leadership Programs
The Wharton School, University of Pennsylvania

About the Author

Johnston (Jack) Beach is a Senior Leadership Development Consultant at IBM®, where he currently manages the Leadership Strategy and Research Group and has oversight of the Executive Leadership Development Programs. In that role, he has had a great impact on IBM's recognition over the past several years as the #1 corporation in leadership development. Prior to coming to IBM, Jack was a Colonel in the United States Army and a Professor of Psychology who helped to build the Department of Behavioral Sciences and Leadership at the United States Military Academy, West Point, New York.

Jack spent thirty years in the U.S. Army. His career started as a draftee in 1969. He was trained as a combat medic and served with the 101st Airborne Division in the Republic of Vietnam, where he experienced his first of many personal leadership experiences. He very quickly advanced from Private to a Sergeant. Commissioned in 1973, Jack spent nearly eighteen years in the Department of Behavioral Sciences and Leadership at the United States Military Academy, where he was a Professor and Director of the Psychology Programs. Before arriving at West Point, he taught at the U.S. Army's Academy of Health Sciences, where he was a key member of the team that created a course for training the military's paraprofessional counselors. He has consulted extensively on leadership development and leadership education throughout the world.

Jack received his Ph.D. in Clinical and Community Psychology from the University of Maine, Orono, and his B.A. in psychology from the University of Rochester, Rochester, New York. He is a graduate of various military schools, including the U.S. Army Command and General Staff College and the U.S. Army War College.

Jack Beach

LEADERSHIP
IN MY
REARVIEW
MIRROR

REFLECTIONS FROM VIETNAM
WEST POINT AND IBM

Jack Beach

MC Press Online, LLC
Ketchum, ID 83340

Leadership in My Rearview Mirror:
Reflections from Vietnam, West Point, and IBM
By Jack Beach

First Edition
First Printing—January 2012

MC Press offers excellent discounts on this book when ordered in quantity for bulk purchases or special sales, which may include custom covers and content particular to your business, training goals, marketing focus, and branding interest.

MC Press Online, LLC
Corporate Offices
P.O. Box 4886
Ketchum, ID 83340-4886 USA

For information regarding sales and/or customer service, please contact:

MC Press
P.O. Box 4300
Big Sandy, TX 75755-4300 USA
Toll Free: (877) 226-5394

For information regarding permissions or special orders, please contact:

mcbooks@mcpressonline.com

ISBN: 978-1-58347-353-5

To my wife, Maureen,
who endured many lonely hours while providing unfaltering support

And to all those who not only want to become better leaders
but who relentlessly pursue it

Acknowledgments

Ultimately, leadership and leadership development come down to an understanding of human behavior and the application of that understanding to the unleashing of human motivation and potential in service to the common good. Everything that I have written about, talked about, or done over the past several decades in the area of leader development can be traced to the likes of Sigmund Freud, Viktor Frankl, Abraham Maslow, Carl Rogers, B.F. Skinner, Albert Bandura, and other great minds who have offered principles of human behavior and insights into the human spirit. We in the field are all indebted to them.

More personally, there are two people who have had a profound impact on my life. Without them, the wonderful opportunities in my professional life might never have occurred. They are Howard Prince and Brad Scott. Howard brought me to West Point and eventually supported my application to become a tenured faculty member. When I was about to retire from the U.S. Army, Brad, who had reported to me at West Point, sought me out and recruited me to come to IBM, where we reversed roles; he became my boss. Both Howard and Brad faced some resistance to my being hired, but neither wavered in their support. I would like to think that I have justified their faith in me. My three subsequent managers at IBM—Carroll Connacher, Scott Whelehan, and Steve Bartomioli—have all given me incredibly interesting work and their full trust in getting it done. They have modeled empowerment.

A number of IBM's executives have allowed me to share their wisdom and insights: Mark Hennessy, Bob Hoey, Keenie McDonald, Dr. John Kelly III, Dan Pelino, and Mark Shearer. I have had the privilege of working closely with several of these leaders throughout my time at IBM. That experience has helped me gain an appreciation for the intense pressures under which business leaders work and for the great skill and personal demeanor it takes to lead well in such an environment. Private enterprise is not for the faint of heart. All these leaders lead well. They set examples for others to emulate.

Finally, I owe profound gratitude to my wife, Maureen, and my twin brother, Charles, both of whom not only helped to ensure that every "i was dotted and t crossed," but whose deep understanding of me often enabled them to help me express my thoughts better than I did myself in the initial drafts. Their dedication was out of love for me, more than the topic, but the text is so much better because of that love and dedication.

To all, thank you.

Contents

Foreword

by Howard T. Prince II

While there are too many books on leadership, there are still not enough good books on leadership. *Leadership in My Rearview Mirror* adds one to the short stack of good leadership books. If you are browsing the contents, buy it or borrow it for yourself. Do not put it down until you have drunk deeply from its wisdom.

Many men and women who have, expect to have, or aspire to have leadership responsibility are hungry, some even desperate, for a book about leadership that is written in the language of the everyday world. They seek guidance that has been found to work by someone with real leadership experience. Leaders of all kinds know they must lead better and differently now and in the future, but they do not know how. What they need are concepts that are rooted in a profound understanding of human nature and the realities of modern organizations that operate in an increasingly competitive, volatile, uncertain, ambiguous, and changing world. The leadership ideas in Jack Beach's book will work whether the setting is a competitive for-profit business organization such as IBM, a nonprofit helping organization, or even a government agency at any level of government, because any organization is just a collection of human beings brought together by some common purpose.

This book grows out of Dr. Beach's education as a clinical psychologist, his early experiences as a fellow ground-level leader in the U.S. Army during the Vietnam War, his almost two decades of teaching and developing cadets and officers at West Point, and, perhaps most importantly, from over a decade of teaching and coaching senior managers and executives at IBM.

After the Vietnam War and with the advent of the voluntary military service system, the need for good leadership became so deeply embedded in the culture of the military that it has become a place where good leadership is now commonplace. According to influential sources such as a November 2010 issue of the *Harvard Business Review* and *The New Yorker,* which in 2004 called Army colonels serving in Iraq and Afghanistan "the best leaders in the world," many units of our armed forces are already led in the ways described in this book, driven by the need to adapt to the realities and requirements of the harsh strategic environment of war and insurgency for the past decade.

But the greatest value to the reader will be to discover how the leadership principles and concepts presented here can be applied effectively and become a part of the culture of any organization that recognizes the critical need for good leadership in fulfilling its purpose. Dr. Beach convincingly demonstrates how a major business corporation such as IBM can develop leaders who lead others effectively in a changing world and a dynamic business environment. He shows us how to lead in one of the world's most successful business organizations that takes leadership development and practice very seriously, due in no small part to his influence on the leadership development programs for IBM, where he has served for over a decade. This is not a book just about military or corporate leadership. It is a book about the only kind of leadership that can succeed now or in the foreseeable future. So read on to discover its secrets.

Jack Beach's approach to leadership defies many common ideas and stereotypes that still persist for too many leaders in all kinds of organizations. Indeed, he shows convincingly why so many traditional notions about leaders and what they do are simply no longer useful, if they ever were. Dr. Beach also points out that leadership is not rocket science—indeed, it is much more difficult than that! Leadership, at least in free and open societies, is much harder than any physical science due fundamentally to the complex, emotional, sometimes irrational, and relatively unchanging nature of human behavior.

Dr. Beach sees clearly why we act and what we need out of the work places where we spend so much of our lives. Part of his grasp of human nature comes from his background as a clinical psychologist.

But Dr. Beach turned from the traditional focus of clinical psychology on abnormal or disturbed behavior to what has become known recently as positive psychology, or the good side of human beings. He knows that the deepest wellsprings of motivation and inspiration come from our social nature and from our strivings to find purpose and meaning in the places we choose to work or spend our lives. For him, leadership is fundamentally the means to helping others satisfy such basic human strivings by showing people how to connect their efforts to organizational activities that lead to individual fulfillment and organizational success. A very large part of what leaders need to do is help others develop their full potential to contribute to the larger purpose. Jack Beach decided long ago that his calling is to go through life doing what the fairy tale princess did a long, long time ago—kiss frogs and turn them into beautiful human beings. He has a large collection of frogs from people whom he has figuratively kissed and helped to become leaders in their own right.

Most people do not learn from their experiences—because they have never learned how. Lacking such knowledge, they just have experiences and move from one to the next without learning very much. Jack Beach is a major exception to this pattern, and his book is illuminated by sharing things he learned from experiences as a young adult, even before he became a leader in any formal sense. He began filing notes over 40 years ago on scraps of paper, long before he realized that he would turn his notes into a book about leadership. He shows us how to reflect on experience and to make sense of our experiences in ways that allow us to become more effective in future situations. This process begins when we notice something, assign significance to that observation, and make a record. After making a record of our experiences, we must take time to ponder the significance and meaning of what happened and be honest with ourselves about how well we did and why. If we were not successful, then we must consider what might have worked better. Finally, we close the process by generalizing to establish enduring truths and principles that can be recalled when facing challenges in the future. This process takes time, in part to allow our defensiveness to diminish so we can open ourselves to the possibilities of new truths, and for new insights to incubate and crystallize into important new lessons. The best leaders know they must continually develop themselves for a lifetime, and Jack Beach stands in that category as an exemplar.

In addition to his ability to learn from his experiences, Jack Beach is a great story teller. He understands that we remember and learn so much from good stories. In this book, he shares stories about such seemingly unrelated subjects as teaching a five-year-old boy how to fly a kite, describing an engineer who thought he had lost his identity, and leading a gang of teenage misfits to become a cohesive, high-performing unit in Vietnam.

Leadership coaching is a popular topic in many organizations today. I have often wondered what good leadership coaching might look like. Even after attending a session on executive coaching at a prestigious academic conference, I left still wondering what good coaching really was. Now I know what coaching for leadership development can be when it is done well, as Dr. Beach's descriptions of himself coaching senior leaders at IBM give a clear picture. Read how he assisted leaders to develop themselves as they grappled with increasing levels of responsibility in a constantly changing competitive environment. Discover how he helped IBMers as they tried to figure out for themselves how to apply some of the ideas they had heard him present in executive development seminars. In one of these coaching relationships, Dr. Beach reveals how to find experiences in the leader's past that help the learner grasp meaning as well as the vital importance of readiness for development on the part of the leader who is being coached.

Jack Beach and I first met as graduate-student peers completing a new kind of internship in community psychology instead of the more traditional clinical psychology internship. I believe the year we spent learning to consider other factors that shape human behavior besides our own inner struggles was a powerful influence on both of us when we later turned from clinical psychology to leadership and its development. We already knew from our previous military experience that leaders are a very significant source of social influence, but spending a year immersed in a setting that started with the assumption that human behavior is shaped by much more than what is inside each one of us helped us broaden our approach to understanding and influencing human behavior through good leadership.

At the time we met, we held different ranks in the Army, which had sponsored both of us to study and earn doctorates in clinical psychology. I am not sure anyone ever really understands interpersonal attraction, or "chemistry" between two people. But whatever it is, Jack and I had that from the first day we met. We had in common recent experience in the Vietnam War, I as a leader of an infantry company in combat and he as a combat medic in the same part of Vietnam where I had served two years before he was sent there. And we were both engaged in intense introspection about our Vietnam experiences, especially the very uneven quality of the leadership we each had encountered there. I was attracted to his personal modesty as well as his willingness to be very candid about what he did not like or think had been done very well during his year in Vietnam. He and his wife were both very open about the good and the bad parts of their previous military experience.

At the time, I was sure that Jack and his wife would not remain a part of the Army any longer than they had to. Even so, when I became the Head of the Department of Behavioral Sciences and Leadership at West Point, he was at the top of my list of people I wanted to help build a new culture and a new approach to developing Army leaders for a new era of post-war voluntary military service. Jack handled his role as my partner and military subordinate admirably. I only hope I did the same as a colleague and senior military leader for him. The thing I valued most about our collaboration was Jack's unflinching willingness to say what he thought was right, no matter how uncomfortable that might have made me or others. He kept me from making many mistakes, and he made me look back on those I did make in ways that often made me wish I had listened to him or others instead of acting as I had. He often led as a forceful follower! Long before he coined one of the major ideas that are central to this book, "360 degrees of trust," he knew that trust is the foundation of good leadership seen as a shared human enterprise that is about much more than just the person called the leader. I retired from the Army before Jack did, but he remains a trusted colleague with whom

I frequently discuss leadership ideas and practice. He and his wife are also among my dearest friends.

In the Epilogue of this book, Dr. Beach shares his own leadership philosophy, which I know he enacts and lives by every day. After his appointment to the permanent, tenured faculty at West Point, he was assigned to lead a team of officers that taught a required general psychology course taken by the entire freshman class. The military faculty members were not experienced college professors; they came to West Point to teach for three years and then returned to the larger Army. So I put Dr. Beach in charge of preparing them to be professors of a college psychology course. Previously, new officers had not wanted to remain a part of the faculty for this course after teaching it during their first year. They preferred instead to take over an upper-division elective course that would give them much more autonomy, and perhaps more organizational visibility, because these courses were usually a solo effort. But Dr. Beach and I knew that this course was one of two foundational courses that our department taught every year to each cadet. Along with a second required course taken by juniors called Military Leadership, it would have to become our primary way to contribute to the U.S. Military Academy's overall purpose of developing leaders of character for our Army and the nation. It was an opportunity to shape the way cadets would lead after they had graduated and become commissioned officers. If we did that well for a number of years, we believed it might have an impact on the Army—a large and important institution that had much room for improvement as it faced the aftermath of the Vietnam War and the end of conscription. We had found a noble purpose for our endeavors.

Dr. Beach was so successful in leading his team of instructors that within a very few years, no one wanted to leave his team for their second and third years on the faculty. He had shown them the importance of the larger purpose everyone at the Academy shares and made it so motivating to each officer that his instructors no longer preferred to teach electives after their first year. Dr. Beach already knew that he was responsible not just for developing college students to be future Army leaders; he was also developing young Army officers to become even better at leading at higher levels when they returned to the more commonplace military assignments. He taught them a new and very different kind of leadership than most of them had experienced before coming to West Point to teach. Dr. Beach is right when he asserts that leaders do not develop followers, they develop leaders. In leading and developing his team of instructors long before he had written it down, he was already practicing the kind of leadership you will read about in this book.

During the 1970s and even into the 1980s many in the military and elsewhere believed that "no-nonsense" leadership was the best kind of leadership. And that was definitely the dominant philosophy that Jack had experienced as a young draftee who had demonstrated the courage and a sense of personal responsibility to answer his country's call to duty during an unpopular war, about which he had some misgivings. The "no-nonsense" leadership as practiced in the 1970s and 1980s is but one of many false conceptions of leadership that still thrive among far too many leaders and organizations. Read on to learn some of Dr. Beach's lessons in how not to lead gleaned from his time as a young soldier and to be introduced to what is a much more powerful approach for modern leaders and organizations. Jack Beach convincingly demonstrates that "No-nonsense leadership is nonsense!" His focus is instead on understanding and developing leadership as a shared human enterprise, a coming together to pursue shared goals. To take root and become effective, leadership must be based on trust. It must be based not just on trust in leaders by others, but also on what Dr. Beach calls "360 degrees of trust." This means not only trust in the leader, for example, on the part of employees in work settings, but also among the employees themselves. Leaders enable people across an organization to trust in each other so they can be successful way beyond what is possible under any other kind of leadership.

Dr. Beach contrasts what he calls leading by conceptual controls with more traditional leadership based on rules, authority, and hierarchy. In doing so, he demonstrates convincingly why his vision of leadership is the only kind of leadership that can succeed in today's business environment, especially for a company such as IBM that is at the center of the "knowledge economy."

Leadership in My Rearview Mirror is a "must read" for anyone who is serious about leading well now and in the future.

Brig. Gen. (ret) Howard T. Prince II, Ph.D.
Loyd Hackler Endowed Chair in Ethical Leadership
Lyndon B. Johnson School of Public Affairs
The University of Texas at Austin
Austin, Texas
October 2011

Preface

This is a book any leader could write and every leader should write—although it is not the book I had intended to write. I am not sure where most books come from, but this one wandered in the desert for about forty years. I had always wanted to write a book about my experience in Vietnam and the events leading up to and immediately following my time there. It was not going to be an action story of heroic combat—not that I would have omitted heroics if I had some to claim. But I can claim no heroics, and the combat that I experienced would not have filled enough pages to call it a book. It was to be more a "coming of age" tale—followed by the movie!

Shortly after returning from Vietnam at the end of 1970, I jotted down some notes, but then there was graduate school and a dissertation to research and write. Over the years, I added notes and threw them in a manila folder. I would say "placed" them in a folder, but the process was not that orderly—they were scraps of paper with scribbled phrases that I just tossed in. At first I kept them together with a paper clip on the folder, but over time I had to resort to increasingly larger binder clips.

In 1991–1992, I attended the U.S. Army War College. I went as a "geographic bachelor." I was serving as a tenured faculty member in the Department of Behavioral Sciences and Leadership at West Point at the time and would be returning there after completing the nearly year-long program at the War College. Our youngest daughter, Emily, was in her senior year in high school, and after years of cramped quarters at West Point, we had been assigned a set that were more than acceptable. Maureen, my wife, was not interested in surrendering them, so I was off to Carlisle, Pennsylvania, on my own.

My expectation was that during the down time after classes, while my fellow students were out drinking and playing golf or spending time with their families, I would write. I was able to complete only about twenty-eight pages. What down time I had I spent playing research assistant to my daughter Amy (who was a sophomore at Dickinson College in Carlisle), commuting back to West Point on weekends, and trying to keep up with the extensive reading prescribed for the War College courses. A number of my colleagues counseled me, "Jack, it's only a lot of reading if you do it," but I continued to make the effort. I quickly came to the conclusion that *the book* would give me something to do when I retired. The twenty-eight pages went into the folder.

In 2003, a few years after coming to IBM, I received a call from David Kappos—who at the time was IBM's vice president, assistant general counsel for intellectual property, but has since become Under Secretary of Commerce for Intellectual Property and Director of the United States Patent and Trademark Office. He had been a participant in one of IBM's leadership development programs for high-potential vice presidents, which I had facilitated. He asked whether I would talk at his worldwide organizational meeting, which was convening near IBM's headquarters in Armonk, New York, where I worked. I would be their dinner speaker. He wanted me to "talk about leadership"—not necessarily the IBM Leadership Framework, with which most attendees would already be familiar, just "leadership." Flattered that David had asked me to speak and being incapable of saying no to any request to speak, I agreed and hung up—clueless as to what I would talk about.

After letting David's request incubate for a while, I remembered my folder, took it out of my desk drawer at home, and jotted down nine or ten of the incidents that I had noted as learning experiences. My idea was to talk about what those experiences had taught me about leadership. I called it *Leadership and Other Things I Have Learned Along the Way*. The talk took about forty-five minutes. I basically recounted, more concisely, what you will find in the first few chapters of this book. The talk was well received, and they asked me back a year later. For the next three years, the talk sat on my computer.

In 2006, I was tasked with embedding business acumen into our executive leadership development programs. Having no expertise in the area, I retained an outside expert to help. One of the suggestions we thought worth pursuing was to broadcast podcasts to managers. We met with Stacy Spiegel and George Faulkner at corporate communications. At the time, Stacy was in charge of communications for managers, so we got talking about leadership development in general. Some of the things that I said resonated with George, who suggested we get various ideas on tape. We discussed possible options, and I remembered the dinner talk that I had given to IBM's IP lawyers and offered to break the talk up into ten five-minute podcasts. Several weeks later, George and I met in the recording studio in corporate headquarters, and in a marathon session we recorded ten separate podcasts.

The podcast idea was strictly a skunk works venture between George and me. George had to edit the tapes, and he did it in his free time. It took two years before we were able to actually distribute the podcasts. At first, the podcasts were directed just to IBM's managers, but then they made their way onto IBM's main employee Web page. About a year later, I received a call from Steven Stansel at IBM Press. He and his manager had listened to the podcasts and wanted to know whether I would consider writing a book. I said yes, and Steve put me in touch with Merrikay Lee at MC Press. Merrikay was gracious and courageous enough to take a chance on the content of a manuscript rather than the celebrity or notoriety of the author. The result is the book you are now reading.

Now, let me tell you a bit about the book. When people talk about leadership development, they too often emphasize leadership and silence the development part. In this book I have tried to give equal time to development. Ultimately, leadership is not about accumulated skills, though skills are certainly required, but about human development. Leadership is about understanding ourselves and others. We must be in tune with ourselves to be in tune with others. Remaining in tune with ourselves and others requires ongoing examination of the frames of reference through which we view the world. Reflection is fundamental to this. This book strives to illustrate the importance of reflection in a leader's development.

Like many authors, I hope this book has mass appeal. I would like to think it is for people who aspire to be leaders, leaders who want to be better, and people who simply enjoy good stories. The book is not focused on any narrow field. It is relevant to business managers and executives and people in nonprofit organizations, government, and military service and parents and teachers and all the "ordinary people" who, by choice or happenstance, are in positions in which their ideas and character are likely to influence the thoughts and actions of other "ordinary people."

In addition to the stories themselves, I have attempted to incorporate a number of features to make the book more appealing to you, the reader. First, I have tried to provide quick bursts of leadership insights in a way that all readers can instantly "get it" and apply it. Second, when appropriate, I give the "other side of the story," the uncommon and seemingly illogical acts of leadership that influence human behavior for the better and lift the human spirit (e.g., trusting the untrustworthy, being influenced rather than influencing, not giving constructive feedback). Third, the book asserts that the primary task of leaders, especially senior leaders, is the creation of organizational climates characterized by 360 degrees of trust and deep engagement: organizations that recognize that leaders' development of a well-grounded trust in their people is as, or even more, important than employees' development of trust in their leaders. In service of this principle, the book illuminates the importance of *intrinsic motivation*, explores the concept of *principle-based leadership*, introduces tools such as *The 5 Trust Vital Signs,* and promotes the idea of *collective leadership*.

My hope is that this book accomplishes the above in a simple (not simplistic) way that neither insults your intelligence nor requires you to ponder too long to understand the points—yet will cause you to continue to ponder the lessons long after you put the book down as you gain your own insights and change your behaviors. Finally, the unspoken but pervasive theme is that leaders need to be humble. They must recognize their duty to improve continually; they must acknowledge that their success as leaders is measured by the success of other people's efforts; and they must understand that helping others to achieve success—to become better than they were—is the reason to lead in the first place.

The book consist of four sections: *The Reflective Leader: Leadership and Other Things I Learned Along the Way*; *Leaders in Search of Leadership*; *Leaders in Their Own Words*; and an *Epilogue,* in which I share my leadership philosophy and encourage you to write your own.

The Reflective Leader: Leadership and Other Things I Learned Along the Way is a series of autobiographical reflections. These chapters constitute a memoir, not a documented history. They are true to the best of my memory. I have generally used real names and will tell you when I have not. If I have not used real names, it is because I do not have permission and I fear that the people might think the text would reflect negatively on them. In a few instances, I use no name at all, though the words are accurate. In any instance where a quote is intended to reflect negatively, I use either a fictitious name or no name at all. First, this book is not about putting anyone down, and second, in all these cases, I do not know these people well enough to determine whether the quote is an aberration or a true indication of who they are as people. I suspect in most cases the former—these are most likely decent people who, at the time, were not living up to their better nature.

Leaders in Search of Leadership is a collage of executive coaching or mentoring experiences. There is a good deal of contrivance in this section. While the points being made have been made with various executives, I have packaged them in an effort to make the discussion more engaging and coherent in the recounting. In some cases, I have combined experiences with several executives into a discussion with a single, often fictitious executive. In another, I took conversations and emails over an extended period of time and put them into a fictitious sequence of scheduled sessions.

Leaders in Their Own Words presents a couple of stories based on actual quotes from executives. My poking a bit of fun at them is my attempt to use humor to make some serious points.

The *Epilogue* concludes the book. In it, I share my leadership philosophy.

I sincerely thank you for purchasing this book and for giving me the gift of your time as you read it. I know each of those decisions required choices about how you spend your money and time—and that there are a lot of things out there competing for both. I hope in the end that you find the book worthwhile and that you are the better for having made those choices. That would be wonderful for both of us.

Thank you and enjoy.

Jack Beach
July 10, 2011
Newburgh, New York

INTRODUCTION

Title Fight

"When God passed out opinions, He shorted some folks but not me, so here goes. That title sounds so boring, truly. I would run from such a book. The chapter 'Just Names' was very moving, and 'On Leadership and Kite Flying' was wonderful. I liked the tone: personal, warm, down-to-earth, and wise. Your book should be a big hit. But the title, can you take it up a notch?"

Nancy, a friend since childhood, life-long educator, and part-time writer, had tendered her not completely tender sentiments on some of the initial drafts of this manuscript. My twin brother, Charles, a retired corporate lawyer, had rendered a similar verdict: "Love the stories; the title makes me yawn." Both assured me that more "annoying" and "nitpicking" comments would follow should I continue to share the products of my literary labor. I did, and Nancy and Charles were true to their word.

Although generally defensive in the face of even constructive criticism, I valued their input and took their advice. I relinquished my original title, *The Reflective Leader: Leadership and Other Things I Learned Along the*

Way. At least I reduced it in rank. It does not appear on the front cover, but it has been given the not-so-shabby rank of section title. Whether you picked up this book because of the title or in spite of the title, let me say thank you, and I hope you, too, find the stories and ideas engaging and of value.

So, why *The Reflective Leader: Leadership and Other Things I Learned Along the Way*? Although I conceded and chose a different title, I rather liked my original wording. Let me explain—remember I said that I was defensive. But more than being defensive, I want you to understand several points essential to understanding leadership—and why I wrote this book.

At IBM, we believe that developing leaders is 10 percent classroom instruction, 20 percent on-the-job coaching and mentoring, and 70 percent experience. What we too often fail to do, however, is shed light on how our experiences change us. How do we learn from experience? Many assume that learning is automatic and uniform. Yet, we can easily find examples where two people have the same experience and different takeaways—and a third person may have no takeaway at all. Robert J. Thomas puts it more succinctly, "Experience by itself guarantees nothing."[1]

It is sort of like being a rat in a Skinner box. At first the rat inadvertently hits the lever and gets a pellet. But hitting the lever by accident and getting a pellet has to go on for a while before the rat does it with any consistency. Although the rat eventually learns that hitting the bar will result in a snack, I suspect the rat never thinks about how it learned to get the pellet or how to pass on that learning. We humans can conceptualize. So, if we hit the bar and a pellet comes out, we have the ability to make hypotheses about what links the events and put those hypotheses to the test. We can say to ourselves, "Hmm . . . I hit the bar and got a pellet. I wonder if it will happen again. Let me see." We can then try it again, and if it works, we get the quick "aha" insight rather than a more protracted learning sequence. We can then tell our

---

1   Robert J. Thomas, *How Do You Find What Matters in Experience: Becoming a More Effective Leader* (Boston: Harvard Business, 2008), p. 2.

colleagues how they can get a pellet. When it comes to leadership, however, most people are like the rat in the Skinner box. If we are successful at leading, we think it is because we are natural leaders rather than the more likely explanation that we unwittingly bumped into behaviors that worked and kept repeating these behaviors. Reflection helps us to understand these processes better so we can make our behavior more intentional and pass it on to others.

While experience alone may not guarantee that we learn from it, we generally do learn something from experience, even if we are unaware of the lessons at the time. By reflecting on our experiences, we increase our learning and our ability to articulate the lessons to others. By being able to give voice to our experiences, we can not only share lessons learned with others, but we can also accelerate our own development. Without reflection on experience and articulation of the lessons learned, our learning will be haphazard and incremental at best. Coaching and mentoring aid reflection and articulation, but we also need to learn to have private internal conversations about what our experiences have taught us.

Learning and development and helping others to learn and develop are essential and fundamental attributes of leadership. Leadership is about continually and effectively moving people into the future. That requires ongoing learning and development, not just mastery of the past and the present. In today's kaleidoscopically changing world, we must be agile learners.

From 2008 through the end of 2010, I had the privilege of leading a cross-organizational team whose mission was to decipher the competencies that will enable IBMers to make the rapid adaptations necessary to prosper in the volatile, uncertain, complex, and ambiguous (VUCA)[2] world marketplace so that the company can fulfill its goal of becoming the premier globally integrated enterprise. Although the competencies we defined are statistically independent of one another, they are laced with concepts such as "maintain openness" and "think and act shoulder to shoulder," all of which have to do with deciphering

---

2   Acronym used at the U.S. Army War College at the time I attended in 1991–1992.

and communicating the lessons that we individually and collectively learn from what we are experiencing. Behavioral scientists call this *sense making*. Emblematic of this goal of deciphering and sharing what we learn from experience are the competencies *continuously transform* and *act with a systemic perspective*.[3]

A partial description of *continuously transform* reads:

> IBMers are committed to building the future—a better world, and a better IBM. . . . Our intellectual curiosity and spirit of restless reinvention. . .infuse the enterprise with energy. Today, in a world where the future is far less predictable, IBMers actively seek what we do not know and haven't yet imagined. We cultivate an environment of openness to new approaches and experimentation. We rethink assumptions and ask probing questions—to grasp new situations. . . . We engage others whose background, culture, language or work style is different from our own. This is the heart of an IBM that can learn, adapt, and *continuously transform* [italics added].[4]

As this competency indicates, the need to make sense of experience often occurs in ambiguous situations created when we are faced with new experiences. Previous approaches may no longer work in dealing with new events. When we are confronted by the unexpected, we need to ask ourselves, "What's going on?" In the VUCA swirl that engulfs us, leaders must continually extract the relevant information and interconnected relationships that reveal patterns and distinguish them from the "noise." Sense making is what we do when we do not know what to do![5] It allows us to learn from new experiences. Leaders must not only engage in this search themselves; they must help others to do so. The competency indicates that leaders should seek to learn not only from their own experiences but also from the experiences of a

---

3   For a description of all nine of IBM's current competencies, go to Appendix I.
4   Copyright International Business Machines Corporation, 2010. Reproduced with permission from IBM.
5   This is a paraphrase of "What do you do, when you don't know what to do?" Korn/ Ferry International. FYI for Learning Agility™ (http://www.lominger.com/pdf/Final_lng_ agilitysellsheet_10510.pdf).

diverse group of others. The search may recall an old lesson from past experience or, more often, teach the organization a new lesson.

The competency *act with a systemic perspective* makes explicit yet another requirement of effective learning from experience: action. Learning from experience not only involves "turning circumstances into a situation that is comprehended explicitly in words" but "that serves as a springboard into action."[6] The description of *act with a systemic perspective* is as follows:

> IBMers are systems thinkers. We help our clients, our colleagues and the world understand and design the essential dimensions of any system—how it senses, maps and analyzes information, detects underlying patterns, and *translates that knowledge into belief and action* [italics added]. . . . This systemic view allows us to frame problems properly, and to take the right action in the right way at the right time. It also lets us anticipate the impact of our actions on others. Knowing all this, we act wisely while boldly taking the right risks.[7]

Note that this competency makes explicit a crucial, and often overlooked, mediating variable between new understanding and taking action: belief. As IBM entered its centennial year, an external team of business writers was commissioned to take a historical perspective on IBM and account for its ability to thrive for a hundred years—a rare feat among large companies. Interestingly, their conclusion was that: ". . . *acting*— actually changing the complex systems of our planet in lasting ways— relies most fundamentally not on data but on *belief* [italics added]."[8] In coming to this conclusion, the experts examined not only *what* IBM had achieved decade after decade but also *how* IBMers achieved it. They noted a consistent pattern of activity and mode of thought. What they

---

6   Karl E. Weick, Kathleen M. Sutcliffe, and David Obstfeld. "Organizing and the Process of Sense Making," *Organization Science*, Vol. 16, No. 4 (July–August 2005), p. 409 (http://orgsci.journal. informs.org/cgi/content/abstract/16/4/409).

7   Copyright International Business Machines Corporation, 2010. Reproduced with permission from IBM.

8   Kevin Maney, Steve Hamm, and Jeffrey M. O'Brien. *Making the World Work Better: The Ideas That Shaped a Century and a Company* (Upper Saddle River, NJ: IBM Press—Pearson, 2011).

uncovered was a five-step process: *seeing, mapping, understanding, believing*, and *acting (SMUBA)*.

Seeing happens in our mind's eye. It has to do with detecting the vast array of data out there. *Mapping* has to do with organizing those data. We frame the right questions and determine what data are connected, and how and if they relate to what we already know. *Understanding* means that we see something in a new light. Either it is something familiar that we see in a new way, or we realize that it is something we have not seen before. *Believing* is a combination of cognition and emotion. It is not faith in things unseen but rather "standing on the evidence."[9] Additionally, it is the optimism about the possibilities these new understandings have for the future *and* resolving to realize these possibilities. *Acting* is, simply, making things happen—taking steps to realize the possibilities.

Finally, it is critical to understand that learning from experience as described in both *continuously transform* and *act with a systemic perspective* is not simply an analytical exercise. It is not just breaking down a situation into its component parts and summarizing the relationships among components; rather, it is a process of synthesis. It is combining the separate parts and relationships into an orderly, functional, structured new lesson.

So again, why *The Reflective Leader: Leadership and Other Things I Learned Along the Way*? Effective leadership requires learning from experience, and learning from experience requires not only experience but introspection and reflection on our experience. As far as the "other things along the way," those are the lessons that reflecting on experience teaches us about ourselves, others, and how we learn—all vital to growing as leaders and as people. Indeed, the other things— who we are, how we learn and get better, and who others are, their needs and aspirations—constitute a firm foundation without which authentic leadership cannot be achieved.

The defense rests.

---

9 Maney et al.

The Reflective Leader:
Leadership
and Other Things
I Learned Along the Way

1

Out of Control

So, what got me reflecting on leadership? There were several things. First, my Ph.D. is in clinical psychology. I have been a student of human behavior for a long time. But the biggest impetus for me to look specifically at leadership was that I spent thirty years in the Army. Throughout that time, as I advanced from private to colonel, I had positions of increasing responsibility, and for the final nearly eighteen years, I was a professor in the Department of Behavioral Sciences and Leadership at the United States Military Academy at West Point. Since retiring from the Army in 1999, I have been a leadership developer with IBM, working mostly with executives and high-potential pre-executives. I have responsibility for overseeing all the executive leadership development programs and also manage the Leadership Strategy and Research Group. For more than forty years, my job has been to think in a self-conscious and disciplined way about leadership and how it is developed. But even before I became formally involved with leadership training, I would reflect on and try to dissect my experiences in an attempt to meet the leadership responsibilities entrusted to me.

In the pages ahead, I will be sharing some autobiographical stories and my takeaways from them. My organizing strategy is to present them, for the most part, in chronological order, starting with my earliest days in the Army. In fact, let's start with my very first day.

I entered the Army as an inducted draftee. I came of age in a time of an active draft—even before the draft lottery. I was twenty-four years old, which was old for a draftee. I was in my second year of graduate school when I was called to report. After petitioning the draft board for a delay, I was allowed to complete my semester; they postponed my induction date several months. Three days after defending my Master's thesis, I was in the Army. Things were happening quickly.

In the afternoon following my thesis defense, my wife, Maureen, and I loaded all our belongings into a U-Haul and moved from Orono, Maine, back to our hometown of Catskill, New York. Catskill is a small village of about five thousand people on the west shore of the Hudson River. The Catskill Mountains are just a few miles farther to the west. My parents had an apartment in their home where my father's widowed mother had lived, which they made available to us. Maureen's parents and family lived only about five miles away in the hamlet of Leeds, New York. Leeds was even smaller than Catskill, about four hundred residences at the time. Although Leeds was only about one hundred and twenty miles from New York City, Maureen had attended a three-room school through the eighth grade, at which time she and her eleven classmates entered Catskill High School, which is where we met. It seemed like being home was the best place for her as we waited to see just what Uncle Sam was going do with me for the next couple of years. While it was pretty likely that I would be headed for Vietnam, Maureen was not yet ready to entertain that possibility.

On July 1, 1969, I got up and headed for the draft board, which was on Main Street, across from the courthouse and next to the bus station. As I walked, my mind was not so much on the future as on the past. It was a clear day, and I could see the mountains. We lived at 9 Liberty Street in a large Victorian home that my grandfather had built in 1904. The particular location was chosen because it had a panoramic view to the west of the Catskill Mountains and the Catskill Mountain House[10], where my grandfather had been raised. One block to the east, the woods bordering the Hudson River began.

In James Fenimore Cooper's novel *The Pioneers*, which was the first of five books in his series *Leatherstocking Tales*[11], Natty Bumppo, the main character, speaks of a "second paradise." When asked where that is, he replies,

> "Where! why, up on the Catskills. . . there's a place in them hills that I used to climb to when I wanted to see the carryings on of the world. . . . You know the Catskills, lad; for you must have seen them on your left, as you followed the river up from York. . .the place I mean is next to the river, where one of the ridges juts out a little from the rest, and where the rocks fall, for the best part of a thousand feet. . ."[12]

And when he is asked, "What see you when you get there?" He answers, "Creation. . .all creation. . . ." As our high-school alma mater put it, we were "in the land of Rip Van Winkle, nestled near the Hudson's shores." Catskill, with the river and the mountains laced with waterfalls and swimming holes, was to me every bit the paradise Natty Bumppo said it was.

I thought of the hours spent along the river shore, having picnics, making bonfires, and on occasion camping overnight in the woods with childhood friends or paddling our canoe to Rogers Island on the far side of the river. I mentally reminisced about my brother and me hitchhiking out to the mountains with our friends to spend summer days basking on the sun-warmed rocks and diving from the cliffs into the cool clear

---

10 The Catskill Mountain House was the first major resort in the United States. It was built in 1824 and operated continuously until 1941. It was visited by Presidents (Ulysses S. Grant, Chester A. Arthur, and Theodore Roosevelt), authors (James Fenimore Cooper), artists (Thomas Cole, Frederic Church), and other elites of the day. My grandfather Charles A. Beach was raised by his uncle Charles L. Beach, who was the sole proprietor of the Mountain House for most of its years.

11 James Fenimore Cooper was among the most famous and prolific writers of the early 19th century. His *Leatherstocking Tales* and *The Last of the Mohicans* were among his best-known works. The exact place he speaks of became the site of the Catskill Mountain House.

12 Quote taken from *The Pioneers*, located at http://www.gutenberg.org/cache/epub/2275/pg2275.html.

pools that formed beneath picturesque waterfalls. It was an idyllic place to have grown up. It was no surprise to me that the fabled Rip Van Winkle would have spent so much time avoiding all manner of labor just to tread the wooded wilderness and delight in the vistas to which its pinnacles gave way or that Thomas Cole, Frederic Church, and other Hudson River School artists would have considered its magnificent landscapes as manifestations of God.

As I turned the corner from Liberty Street onto King Street, my reverie ceased as I ran into a friend, Eddy, who lived on the street one block down from Liberty Street. Eddy's house was the second house to the left when I looked off my back porch. As it turned out, Eddy, too, had been called to report. Greene County was not densely populated, and the draft board's quota was modest. Eddy and I were the only two being drafted from Greene County for the month of July. We proceeded down King Street, turned right onto Broad Street, and then left down Clark Street to Main Street to wait for the bus that would take us thirty-five miles up the New York State Thruway to the induction center in Albany.

As we crossed Main Street at the foot of Clark Street, we were face-to-face with the First Baptist Church where "Uncle Sam" had been a member. Samuel Wilson was a meat packer who supplied beef and pork to American troops during the War of 1812. As the barrels of meat were destined for the United States government, they were stamped "U.S.," from which the troops got Uncle Sam. He and his brother Nathaniel had a slaughterhouse and meat packing plant in Catskill. Also of interest was William Smith, a longtime resident of Catskill, whom local residents insist was the original model for the personification of Uncle Sam in a top hat, bow tie, vest, and striped pants. Photos dating from almost a decade before James Montgomery Flagg painted the well-known World War I "I Want You" recruiting poster show Mr. Smith in the iconic dress.[13] As Eddy and I walked the remaining few yards to our destination, I thought to myself, "You want me, old man—you got me!"

---

13 See photos of William Smith as Uncle Sam in 1908, eleven years before James Montgomery Flagg painted the famous World War I recruiting poster of Uncle Sam pointing and saying "I want you!" at http://www.liveauctioneers.com/item/3683666. See also http://www.catskillny.org/200years.htm.

We arrived at about seven-thirty in the morning and had been standing outside the draft board for a few minutes just chatting and waiting for the bus when I noticed Eddy was taking off his clothes. At first, I thought he had unbuckled his belt to tuck in his shirt, but the loosening of the belt was followed in fairly rapid sequence by his pants dropping to the sidewalk, then his shirt, and he continued until he was as naked as the second he had made his entry into the outside world. He then proceeded to walk back and forth, fist in the air, chanting, "Hell no, I won't go. I'm for peace, brother. I'm for peace!" The irony that Eddy's demonstration took place a few yards from the church in which Uncle Sam had worshipped years before has never escaped me.

Eddy's protest was clearly not something I had anticipated. Catching a glimpse through the window of the demonstration going on outside, Shirley, the clerk at the draft board, called the police. Meanwhile, I was walking alongside Eddy with my arm around his shoulder trying to reason with him—but to no avail. I am not sure that Eddy realized I was there. Although Eddy may not have felt my presence, I was acutely aware of his and Shirley's. Even a small village feels pretty crowded when you are walking with your arm around a naked guy on Main Street.

Within minutes, Harry, one of the local cops, arrived. Harry, Eddy, and I were the same age, give or take a year. We were also neighbors. Harry lived next door to Eddy. But they were not friends—quite the opposite. Harry pushed Eddy face first against the wall, cuffed his hands behind him, and took him away.

So, why do I tell you this story? What does it have to do with leadership? The episode taught me that sometimes we just have no control over events. We cannot always control circumstance, and we will not be able to influence some people. Such inability to control or influence does not undermine the importance of leadership; leadership remains important; but not everything is a leadership issue. I had little control over being conscripted. But I showed up ready to do my duty. And, as hard as I tried—and I definitely tried—I could not get through to Eddy. In the end, all I could do was fold his clothes, make sure he had his glasses, which he had also taken off, and see that Harry did not use excessive force. You do what you can with what you can control, even if you cannot control very much.

Not having full control is not an excuse for lack of leadership. In speaking to a group of new IBM executives, Lisa Su, who at the time was VP, Semiconductor Research Center, said, "As an executive I find myself looking at a situation and thinking, 'How can it get better?'" As a leader you may not be able to do all that you would like to do, but focus on what you can do—not what you cannot. And, in whatever ways possible, work to make things better.

So, what became of Eddy? With the help of a lawyer (and doctors), he was able to prove that he had psychomotor epilepsy. He was released and went back to college. He died several years ago. He was a kind and gentle soul. His friends, including me, will remember him for more than his one naked act of civil disobedience.

2

The Face in the Mirror

Soon after Harry had taken naked Eddy to the police station, the bus
arrived to take me to the induction center in Albany. In addition to
getting a cursory physical exam and raising my right hand to swear
to "support and defend the Constitution," I mostly waited around.
The induction center was full of inductees—one by the name of Bill
Cloonan. Bill had just completed his first year of law school when
Uncle Sam thought that he deserved a break from school. He was from
Kingston, New York, a city on the Hudson about twenty-five miles south
of Catskill. We quickly became friends.

By mid-afternoon, Bill and I along with the other inductees were
on a bus and headed for Fort Dix, New Jersey, for Basic Combat
Training. I had no idea what I was about to experience, nor did I have
much anxiety about it. The bus left us at the reception center. The
transformation from a lowly and flawed civilian to a noble soldier was
about to begin.

The first step in our journey from civilian to soldier was getting a
haircut. Even those who had tried to preempt the Army by shaving

their heads the night before did not escape. The act of sitting in the barber chair and having an Army barber spend a few seconds running his clippers over your head is a sacrament. Its outward manifestation is a flawlessly shaved head. The immediate mystical impact is that the person undergoing the experience no longer has any question about who is in charge.

If the haircut was the baptism that freed us from our old life as civilians and allowed us to be born again as soldiers, our transmogrification was completed by the removal of our civilian clothes and the donning of simple, green, not-so-holy raiment known as fatigues. Why they were called fatigues would rudely and clearly be revealed to us during the next ten weeks. (In recent years this uniform has become the battle dress uniform, or BDU. No longer solid green, it has a camouflage pattern. I suspect this change of name and color was a marketing ploy on the part of the Army.) Instantaneously, whether a person had been a "rich man, poor man, beggar man, thief, doctor, lawyer, merchant," or, yes, even "chief,"[14] we were rendered devoid of all trappings that might otherwise distinguish us from our fellow recruits. Who we or our parents were no longer mattered. Moreover, in the eyes of the drill sergeants, we all even shared the same name, *trainee,* signifying our membership in the lowest caste of the military. The playing field had not only been flattened, it had been turned into a pit, and for the next ten weeks our measure would be taken on how able we were to climb or crawl out of that pit.

Having shed our old selves and put on the new, we were again subjected to a physical examination, similar to the one we had endured just hours ago. One had to wonder what they thought could have occurred in the intervening hours, but they were taking no chances. Following the second physical, we took a battery of written tests that would in large part determine our "MOS" (Military Operational Specialty). Finally, before being assigned to our companies, one of the post's senior officers addressed us. He let us know that "in this era of nuclear weapons, rockets, guided missiles, and other modern tools of warfare, the most important element of the nation's defense is the man who employs

---

14 Josephine P. Peabody, *Rich Man, Poor Man* (http://www.readbookonline.net/readOnLine/12801).

these tools."[15] I have a sneaking suspicion that he knew that we were not going to be involved in nuclear war or even one all that modern, because he quickly segued from the technological to the primal. "Man's natural habitat is the earth, and in war, he must eventually defeat his enemies by struggles on the ground."[16] He concluded by making clear that he and the other officers and non-commissioned officers had a singular purpose, and that was to ensure each of us would be "thoroughly disciplined, technically qualified, and physically, morally, and mentally conditioned to survive on the battlefield."[17] We were then assigned and transported to our new companies, each convinced that we were on our way to becoming the ultimate weapon—the American soldier.

As luck would have it, Bill Cloonan and I ended up not only in the same Basic Training company but also as roommates. There were six to eight of us to a room. About two weeks into Basic Training, the drill sergeant switched one of our roommates and gave us a new one— Dickie Dickenson.[18]

Dickie was about six feet tall and probably weighed all of one hundred and thirty-five pounds—and was the biggest "tie up" in the company. He never seemed to know what he was doing or supposed to do. Within five seconds of the drill sergeant leaving the room, I had Dickie by the collar, up against the wall, and made it very clear to him that if he messed up in this room, he would have more problems than all the chaplains in the United States Army could remedy. Bill, who was sitting on his bunk, shining his boots, just looked up with a wry smile and said, "Jack, I am really impressed with all the psychology you learned in graduate school."

This one moment had an impact on me that has lasted to this day. First, I was incredibly embarrassed. My first and immediate takeaway was that I could be a real "rear end." And to this day, I have never raised my

---

15 Major General K.W. Collins, *The United States Army Training Center: Infantry* (Fort Dix, New Jersey, 1969). p. 3.

16 Collins, p. 3.

17 Collins, p. 3.

18 This is a fictitious name.

voice or been rude to a direct report or subordinate—I cannot say that I have been as considerate of peers, superiors, and bosses.

There were other lessons as well. One, we need to have at least one person we can trust to give us honest feedback—to hold a mirror up to us and say, "Do you see what you are doing? Do you see the impact? Is this what you intend to have happen?" At IBM, we call that *straight talk*.

Two, we need to be open to feedback. Straight talk is not only about giving it but also about receiving it—especially when the truth is personally disquieting.

Three, and perhaps most important, we need to take advantage of developmental moments. When we talk about coaching, people often think that it occurs on the third Thursday of every quarter. There is nothing wrong with scheduled coaching sessions; they are important. But coaching is also about who you are as a leader. Always be ready to take advantage of teachable moments. They generally arise unexpectedly, but if you are ready to take advantage of them, the impact will be far greater than that of many scheduled—and more detached—coaching sessions.

Yet another insight was that poor performance is not always improved by increasing motivation. Dickie Dickenson did not need more motivation; he was already doing his best. Leaders need to help a person's best get better. Dickie needed a helping hand. I was adding to the problem, not helping to resolve it. As leaders, we need to determine what resources and development people require and also figure out how to keep people at their optimal level of motivation. That is where we get peak performance. Sometimes reaching optimal motivation means backing off.

After my initial "coaching session" with Dickie, there were times when I literally carried Dickenson through Basic Training. Over the following weeks, the drill sergeant cycled other "problem children" into the room with Bill and me. His unstated expectation was that we would take these kids under our wings—and I like to think that we did. I might add that Dickie Dickenson had enlisted to be a computer specialist, which in the 1960s was pretty farsighted.

A few more words about the mystical power of shaving heads—even those already shaved. Like other rituals, that nonsectarian, sacred baptism was a common experience that created invisible bonds that connected the new recruits with each other and with all those who had come before and with all who would come afterwards. It gave us the sense that we were all on the same footing at a new beginning. Other than the haircut, there were going to be no shortcuts here. Instead of suggesting a rosy future, the ritual suggested a future that would be difficult and dangerous. Our training would not lead to monetary rewards but to the discipline and skills that we would need to survive and to carry out our mission, which was to protect others and to assist them to win freedoms to which we believed they were entitled.

I am not suggesting that companies shave new recruits' heads or issue them uniforms, but companies should think about the message that they send to people they recruit. How often do companies lure "high-potential" candidates by promises of shortcuts to the top and promises of financial rewards rather than offering them the opportunity to test their mettle and to achieve lofty goals? Too often we tell a certain few that they are "special" and offer them incentives that separate them from others and make them competitors rather than binding them to a joint mission with the entire organization.

In the short time that we had spent in the reception center—and most of us were *compelled* to be there, not lured to it—we left feeling that *we* needed to become the *ultimate weapon.* And, we were determined to do our best to do so. We were motivated not by monetary rewards (one hundred dollars a month) but by the challenge "to be all you can be" and being counted on to achieve a difficult mission that we understood would better the lives of others. While my view of the worthiness of that specific mission has changed somewhat over time, my view that leaders should challenge people to become better people, give them real responsibilities, and motivate them by the worthiness of the mission has not changed.

3

The Cost of Leadership

I graduated Basic Combat Training in September. I was now a private E-2—no longer a *trainee* but a *soldier*. Just before graduation, two of my fellow soldiers and I were brought in for "career counseling." Based on sociometric data collected from our fellow soldiers, we had been seen as having "outstanding leadership potential." Since I had both a college and a graduate degree, they offered me the opportunity to volunteer for Officers Candidate School (OCS).

"Private Beach, your fellow soldiers already see you as a leader, and with all your schooling, you could go right from here to OCS. In six months, you'd be an officer. The pay would be a heck of a lot more than you are getting now. What do you think?"

"Sergeant, would I be signing up for more time? Right now, I have a two-year active duty obligation."

"Yes, it would be an extra year, three years—but you'd be an officer, the pay is pretty good, and you'd get promoted in that time."

I appreciated that his tone was matter-of-fact. He was giving me information and not a hard sell. I cannot deny that the money was attractive. Only days before, Maureen had let me know that I would be a father in about seven more months. My current pay of just over one hundred dollars a month was meager for two. It would be more meager for three. Going to OCS would also delay any possible deployment to Vietnam for months. I might even be in the States for our first child's birth. However, since I had already begun to have reservations about the war, I was not interested in having a leadership position. In addition, I was eager to get back to graduate school and complete my doctorate.

"No, Sergeant, I want to get back to graduate school. I don't want to do more than two years," I replied.

"Well, Private, how about attending the NCO Candidate Course (NCOC)? In five months you could go from private E-2[19] to sergeant E-5 or even a staff sergeant E-6 if you were near the top of your class—I think you could do that. You have a lot of schooling. And it would not require any extension of your service."

"I am on orders to be a combat medic; would I still have that MOS?" This was very important to me. Although as a draftee I had no choice of what AIT (Advanced Individual Training) I attended, I was very comfortable with Uncle Sam's choice for me. As a medic, my main mission would be a positive one—to save lives. For a young man internally torn by my involvement in this particular war, that was a good solution to my predicament.

His answer was accompanied by throat-clearing and honesty: "There is no guarantee of that . . . [and] . . . it is unlikely. But it would not require any extra time of service."[20]

---

19 Private, corporal, sergeant, etc., are military ranks, and E–1, E–4, E–5, etc., are the pay grades that go with various ranks of enlisted soldiers. Officers' pay grades are noted by O–1, O–2, O–3, etc. NCO stands for Non-Commissioned Officer.

20 Though I did not know it at the time, all these graduates became sergeants in the infantry, and most were assigned to combat units in Vietnam.

Again, having a wife, and now a baby on the way, money was an enticement. However, in addition to my wanting to be a medic, all I could think of was having no experience, no skills, and being in charge of troops in combat. I did not see that having an inexperienced sergeant would be fair to those troops. I further suspected that sergeants who had worked their way up through years of experience would resent me for getting my stripes without proving myself and that the more junior soldiers would be peeved because they would see me as usurping a position to which they aspired and to which they had more right—not to mention their concerns about my capability to lead them in battle.

Looking back on my thinking, I know that it was less than objective. As far as I know now, graduates of the NCOC program performed well. But at the time, my thinking was prejudiced by the then-current term for sergeants who came out of the NCOC program: "shake 'n' bake sergeants." Moreover, the only shake 'n' bake sergeant I knew was one of the drill sergeants in the battalion, and he was not a man I wanted to emulate.[21]

Given the information that I had and the very few seconds to think further, I comfortably responded, "I want to be a combat medic. I'm not interested in entering the NCO Candidate program."

"Okay, how about attending the Primary Leadership Development Course (PLDC)? It will take two weeks; it will not involve any extension of your active duty; it will be at Fort Sam Houston, where you are already headed; and after graduation, you will start your medic training. While in AIT you will be either a class sergeant, platoon sergeant, or squad leader.[22] You will get some good training, and the Army will get to take advantage of your natural leadership qualities."

"I will still be trained as a combat medic?" I needed confirmation.

---

21 These were just thoughts running through my mind. To my knowledge, the NCOC program was a successful program, and most of the graduates performed well. Other than the one drill sergeant I mention, I have no evidence to the contrary.

22 These were temporary "acting sergeant" roles. These were not promotions; we were still privates and would return to that upon graduation from our medic training.

"Yes, you will have two weeks of leadership training before starting AIT. But it will all be done at Fort Sam, and you will be a medic."

"Okay, that seems good to me."

"Good, we'll amend your orders. You will leave on the same flight. I think you will find this PLDC program worthwhile."

What I did not know at the time was that while the Army was offering me an opportunity, it was also desperately trying to deal with a critical shortage of NCOs. The turnover of experienced NCOs was so great that there were not enough of them to lead an Army in the field. Not unlike IBM and other global corporations in today's expanding marketplace, there was a pressing need to accelerate the development of leaders at this level to ensure victory. The NCOC program was the military's solution. Had they told me that my nation needed me to become an NCO, I may well have agreed to do it. It was not something I would do just for money or rank, but I wanted to serve my country. They had pushed the wrong motivational buttons.

My orders were amended, and I was sent to the two-week leadership school before starting AIT as a combat medic. At the end of the two weeks when I started combat medic training, I was put in charge of other trainees. We were all privates, but I was an acting sergeant— basically a private with an armband with sergeant stripes on it. There were two rewards for taking this otherwise thankless job. One was that acting sergeants had Class A passes, which allowed us more freedom to move about and even, on occasion, to leave post. Freedom to be out of the barracks unsupervised in those days was extremely limited, so getting such privileges was a big deal. Secondly, we would be promoted from private E-2 to private first class E-3 upon graduation. My pay as a private E-2 was $110 a month; a private first class made about $130.[23] The promotion would mean about a 20 percent raise, so basically it

---

23 The figures are approximate. I should explain there are two levels of private, private E-1 and private E-2, and then there is a private first class (PFC) E-3. As a private E-1, I made $100 a month. As a private E-2, the raise was only about $10 a month. The raise from private E-2 to PFC was about $20 a month.

would amount to obtaining a 30 percent raise in less than six months. When you are as poor as Maureen and I were, every cent counted.

In the PLDC, we learned basic tenets of leadership, such as how to march troops and how to lead physical training (PT). I particularly liked marching my fellow soldiers and leading PT. The objective of drill and marching is more than just getting troops from place to place in an orderly and standard manner. It instills discipline, creates habits of precision, and teaches immediate obedience to orders. If a movement was done incorrectly, we would immediately repeat it until done correctly. In the PLDC, drilling our fellow soldiers also served the function of building emerging leaders' confidence through the exercise of command—giving the proper order in the proper manner and, as a result, experiencing people acting together to accomplish a task.

We were taught how to give orders. Commands generally have two parts: *preparatory* command and command of *execution*. The preparatory command signals that a move is about to occur and also often the direction. Commands of execution indicate the specific movement to be made. The command "Forward, March" consists of the preparatory command "Forward," which signals to the troops that they are about to take some action, and also the direction of that action. The command of execution, "March," tells them the behavior they are to perform.

How the command is given is nearly as important as the command itself. You do it with a "command voice." You need to project. Voice, enunciation, and inflection are all critical. The main instrument for integrating all the elements of a command voice is the diaphragm. The throat, nose, and mouth are amplifiers. Developing a command voice often requires developing the diaphragm. One method to develop the diaphragm is to take a deep breath, hold it, open your mouth, relax your throat muscles, and snap a rapid series of "huts" (i.e., "hut, hut, hut"). Expelling short puffs of air from your lungs should make this sound, and if done properly, you will feel your stomach muscles tighten.[24]

---

24 *The Marine Corps Drill and Ceremonies Manual* (http://nrotc.mma.edu/pdf/DrillManual.pdf).

Vowels should be elongated, and consonants and word endings terse and sharply clipped. We were told that "distinct commands inspire troops" and that "indistinct commands confuse them." To give a distinct command takes careful enunciation and inflection. The preparatory command should be delivered with a raised inflection of the voice, and the last syllable should be accentuated. Then, after a brief pause, comes the even higher and more sharply pitched command of execution. A good command of execution has no inflection but must have "snap." "It should be delivered with a sharp emphasis, ending like the crack of a whip."[25] Putting all the elements together, the command "Forward, March" would come out as "Fooore (slight pause) WARD (another brief pause), MARCH!" Finally, the person giving the command should be facing the troops and should have exemplary military bearing and appearance—command presence.

For me, the experience of giving commands all came together in leading PT. I would stand on a platform in front of the entire class—fatigues starched, boots shined—and call them to attention. All would snap to attention. Standing at the position of attention, I would announce loudly, in clearly enunciated clipped phrases: "The next exercise will be the four-count push-up. When I say 'ready,' you will assume the front leaning rest position. In the front leaning rest position, your palms will be flat on the ground, your arms will be extended, your feet will be slightly spread, and your back will be rigid and straight from your shoulders to your ankles. On the count of *one,* you will begin the push-up by bending your elbows and lowering your entire body as a single unit until your upper arms are parallel to the ground. On the count of *two,* you will return to the starting position by raising your entire body until your arms are fully extended. On the count of *three*, you will again lower your body as a single unit until your upper arms are parallel to the ground. On the count of *four*, you will return to the starting position by raising your entire body until your arms are fully extended."

I would then order the designated demonstrator to post—with a sharp "Demonstrator, post!" The demonstrator would stand on the platform with me at the position of attention. I would then command, "READY,"

---

25 *Manual*, p. 1004.

and he would assume the front leaning rest position. I would then, again, instruct the class, "Notice his arms are extended, his feet slightly spread, and his body is a rigid, straight line from his shoulders to his feet." I would then say, "One," and he would lower his entire body in the proper manner, and I would, again, draw the class's attention to the fact that his arms were parallel to the ground and that his body was still rigid. Next I would say, "Two," and he would return his body to the starting position; "Three," and he would again lower his body; and "Four," and he would return to the starting position, at which time I would more loudly declare, "ONE."[26]

Having explained and demonstrated the exercise, I would call the class that was already at attention once more to attention—"CLASS AaaaTEN SHUN!" and announce "READY," at which time in unison they would all assume the front leaning rest position, "BEGIN, One, Two, Three, Four, ONE! One, Two, Three, Four, TWO!" and so on until they had done ten repetitions, at which time I would announce "REST," and they would stop and momentarily lie on the ground, followed very quickly by the command, "On your feet." On that command, all would jump to their feet. I would say, "Shake it out," and all would shake their upper bodies to loosen themselves up again.

When marching my classmates and especially when leading PT, I felt a *rush*. It was exhilarating; but that surge of exhilaration was commingled with a twinge of anxiety. My motives and my values were in conflict— my *wants* versus my *shoulds*. The feeling of power that accompanied the immediate response to my every command was heady—and that worried me. I could see why Abraham Lincoln once stated, "Nearly all men can stand adversity, but if you want to test a man's character, give him power."

The source of my apprehension stemmed from my earliest memories. I vividly remember my mother and my brother and me sitting on our front porch and her talking to us about the Nuremberg Trials,[27] which

---

26 A four-count push-up really amounted to doing two push-ups for each one counted, i.e., ten four-count push-ups would equal twenty regular push-ups.

27 The Nuremberg Trials were a series of military tribunals held between 1945 and 1949 in which the Allies, victorious in World War II, prosecuted prominent Nazi leaders for war crimes.

took place shortly after I was born and in my early childhood were very fresh in people's minds. She had made clear to us that "I was just following orders" was not an excuse for doing wrong and that we had to take personal responsibility for all our behaviors and should never follow anyone, or any idea, blindly. I was now about to become involved in a war about which I was greatly confused, and at the same time, I was excited that in my position of authority, as minor as it was, people were following me blindly. I was concerned that I, too, was reacting or might react without thinking to orders that deserved thought. I resolved to heed my anxiety and remain vigilant.

I enjoyed being in the PLDC and graduated among the five honor graduates. I was made an acting platoon sergeant when I arrived at the Medical Training Center to start my training as a combat medic (MOS 91A10). My medic training company was on another part of the post about a mile or two away from where PLDC training had taken place. I was eager to start that training. In high school I had been on the junior ski patrol at Hunter Mountain, a ski area about fifteen miles from my home, and during summers while in college, I had been a lifeguard on a lake at a state campsite in the mountains. So, I already had some rudimentary first aid training and experience. And, as I have already stated, the idea of being a combat medic suited me. I was not only eager to learn some new skills that would be valuable throughout my life, but it went a long way to resolving my concerns about participating in the war.

I was not disappointed. Admittedly, some of the training, such as how to make up a hospital bed, was humdrum. And learning to give sponge baths, use bedpans, and take temperatures rectally was unpleasant. None of these routine tasks was part of the heroic lifesaving acts I saw myself performing as a *combat* medic. Learning to give injections and start IVs was more of what I had in mind, and the training on emergency battlefield procedures such as treating sucking chest wounds and performing cricothyroidotomies[28] I found fascinating.

---

28 A cricothyroidotomy is an emergency lifesaving procedure used to create an airway in a person whose airway has become obstructed. It is performed by making an incision in the cricothyroid membrane in the throat. Even under the best of circumstances, which are seldom the ones in which anyone would be doing the procedure, it presents a high risk for the patient.

In the fourth week, after our second exam, the battalion had been promised its first pass. At noon on Saturday, we could leave post and not have to return until Sunday at 5 P.M. Leaving post for that length of time was a huge deal. I had gotten a perfect score on the test, so I was allowed to leave on Friday evening. On Saturday, I was to link up with one of my acting corporals, Alfred Motarama, who had been in leadership school with me. Both his wife and my wife were flying in from New York. I had rented an apartment for my wife because she was going to stay in San Antonio even though we would be able to see each other for only a few hours each weekend. Alfred's wife was coming just for the weekend. It was the first time either of our wives had flown, and the cost of the ticket was over half our yearly pay. Alfred's wife was a schoolteacher, and mine had taught school the year before, so they were coming on money saved from their jobs. Keep in mind that we had not seen our wives for six weeks and had been allowed only two or three phone calls during that time—people wrote letters in those days. Over the three months since our induction, we had seen our wives only two or three times—and those visits were for a matter of hours, not days. This pass was a really big deal.

The company commander was Captain Weed.[29] Just before being released on pass, the company formed up for last-minute instructions, which generally amounted to a warning about all the things that could land us in jail. Unexpectedly, Captain Weed decided to have an on-the-spot inspection. He went through the ranks, checking brass and boots, and asking questions such as, "Who is the defense minister of North Vietnam?" No one knew what he was talking about. His response was to cancel all passes. The company found out about the cancellation when they went to sign out. There was a big, hand-scrawled note on the door of the orderly room that the company's passes had been canceled.

I received a call from Alfred, who was on the verge of tears. Not only would he not be able to see his wife, but he had no way of contacting her—there were no cell phones in those days. I told him that I would get the wives, to hold tight, and I would try to straighten things out. I picked up the wives and hatched my plan—a really poor one. My plan

---

29 This is a fictitious name.

was to have Alfred's wife call the company commander at his home and plead her case. That plan fell apart about a second after Captain Weed got on the phone. Alfred's wife broke into tears and could not talk. She handed the phone to me.

"Sir, this is Private Beach. I'm here with Private Motarama's wife. She's just flown in from New York for the weekend, and now I understand that he is not being granted a pass. I don't understand."

The first thing out of the company commander's mouth was, "We told you not to bring your wives down here!" He was correct. They had made it very clear that bringing wives to the area would be a mistake. In those days, the Army was 90 percent single, and the cliché that "if the Army wanted you to have a wife, they'd have issued you one!" was a reality. I repeated that I did not understand why the passes had been revoked. Captain Weed started to explain how badly the company had done at this on-the-spot inspection, and as a result, they did not deserve to have a pass. I countered with the fact that our platoon had come out first or second on the daily inspections for the last week and that as a squad leader, that performance showed that Alfred had been doing an outstanding job. Moreover, as an acting corporal, Motarama had been promised more pass privileges than others. This went on for a while until Captain Weed angrily said, "Beach, you and Motarama, get to my office—NOW! I'll be there in ten minutes."

The scene in Captain Weed's office was not pleasant. But taking my lead from Moses in Pharaoh's court, I persisted, insisting that what the captain was doing was not right or justifiable and that he should let Alfred go. Finally, the CO relented, but he also ended the session by getting up close and personal with me and saying, "Beach, I'm not going to forget this, and you better watch out. I will have your stripes before this is over." Needless to say, the word got out about the encounter with Captain Weed, and I had the best-performing platoon in the battalion for the remaining six weeks.

This incident taught me several lessons. First, I learned that sometimes it is better to have your people afraid *for* you rather than afraid *of* you. The men in my platoon understood that I had put myself at risk for one of them. They did what they could to protect me. It was a lesson in earning trust and gaining loyalty. Second, I learned that there is a difference between having power and being a leader. Captain Weed had power, and he used it, but he had not exemplified leadership. His arbitrarily canceling leave demonstrated his authority but did nothing to develop the soldiers under his command or further the company's mission of turning out qualified, motivated combat medics. The third lesson was the one that had the most immediate impact on me. Upon graduation, I was an honor graduate. I was in the top 5 percent of the class both academically and in physical fitness. However, I did not get the promised promotion to private first class. All other honor graduates and all other class leaders (and I was both) got the promised promotion. As is often the case, doing the right thing had exacted some personal costs. If doing the right thing were risk free and always turned out well, everyone would do it. Leaders must be willing to pay the personal costs inherent in leadership. Leadership is not for the faint of heart!

4

Values: It's All in the Feet

Just before Thanksgiving 1969, I was officially informed that I would be getting orders to the Republic of Vietnam following my Advanced Individual Training. This news came as no surprise to me, but Maureen had managed to convince herself that something would change before I got my orders. Her father, who had served in the Navy during WWII, had gotten orders to the Pacific. The war, however, had ended while he was en route, and he never got farther than California. Whoever said "the toughest job in the Army is being a soldier's spouse" knew what he or she was talking about.

We decided that we would inform our parents about my orders when we called on Thanksgiving to wish them a Happy Thanksgiving Day. It was going to be one of those good news, bad news calls because with the exception of Maureen's mother, our families did not know Maureen was pregnant. Just before coming to San Antonio, Maureen had told her mother that she suspected she might be pregnant. She told her because her sister had come down with spinal meningitis and was not expected to live—thankfully she did. Although Maureen visited her sister in the hospital, she approached the situation with much more caution than she might have under normal circumstances. She felt the need to inform her mother of the reason for her caution. She had not told her father or my parents. We planned to tell them before we returned for Christmas, when it clearly would no longer be a secret, and what better day than Thanksgiving? Having happy news to dilute the bad news made the timing even better.

We decided the best sequence was to share the more sobering news first and then leave them smiling. We also needed to figure out living arrangements for Maureen. At the time, she was living in an apartment just off-post. We had no car or network of friends, so staying in San Antonio was not a reasonable option. What made the most sense was for her to return to Catskill, where both our families lived. Fortunately, my parents had a large home with an apartment on the first floor. They would have to ask their tenants, a young couple who had just returned from a tour in the Peace Corps, to leave, but the couple unhesitatingly agreed. In December, Maureen moved in, and on March 9, 1970, she gave birth to a healthy son, Brandon Kirk Beach. The Red Cross notified me by radio. I did not see him until he was nine months old.

Maureen and I had been married for about two-and-a-half years, but this was the first Thanksgiving we had not shared with our families. Since I was not able to get home during the week, we had not discussed just what we would do for Thanksgiving. I had Thanksgiving Day off, so I was able to be with her Wednesday evening. When I arrived, I came up with the idea to get a turkey and have a few of my buddies over for a Thanksgiving dinner the next day. In hindsight, I am shocked that Maureen agreed. It turned out to be quite an adventure.

It was almost closing time for the stores (stores closed in those days), and we had no turkey, potatoes, stuffing, or anything else. Oh, and Maureen had never cooked a turkey.

As Maureen hurriedly made a shopping list, I called Brad Mau, one of my squad leaders, who happened to have a car. I told him that if he could get over to our apartment quickly, he and some of our friends would be having a home-cooked meal instead of eating in the mess hall. He arrived immediately. As the clock ticked, everyone went into high gear. We arrived at the supermarket and madly dashed up and down the aisles to find everything on the list. Everyone had an assigned task. I was to get the turkey. I had never purchased a turkey, and I was unprepared for the cost—which I no longer remember, except that it was a good deal higher than I had expected. It about exhausted our cash (no credit cards in those days). Checking the bill, I asked the cashier, "Isn't that pretty expensive for a turkey?" Her reply was, "Son, that is a hell of a price for a turkey, but you've got yourself a goose!" Whether the goose had inadvertently strayed into the turkeys or was right next to them I really do not know. Fortunately, the clerk permitted me to make the exchange. We left, the last customers of the day.

Now we faced another problem: how to defrost a twenty-five-pound frozen turkey in time to cook it the next morning. (Did I mention that we had never done this before?) For the next several hours, Maureen, my three or four fellow soldiers, and I took turns cuddling the frozen bird as we chatted. The combination of the warm attention we paid to the main course of our future feast and our soaking it in water thawed the creature enough so that Maureen could stuff it and cook it in time for a mid-afternoon dinner. There were eight of us. In addition to Maureen and me, Brad Mau, Stan Copland, Alfred Motarama, Jim Barnes, and two others whose names I can no longer recall were there. To this day, it is the best Thanksgiving I have ever had. When the meal was over, Jim Barnes, who was from the deep South, turned to Maureen and said, "Maureen, I have to be honest. When you told me you didn't have cornbread stuffin', I was really concerned—but this was delicious." Those words of praise are about all Maureen remembers of that day, and it still brings a smile. That evening, we all decided to go see *Butch Cassidy and the Sundance Kid*, a fitting ending to a wonderful day.

A few weeks later we graduated, and like Maureen's dad, I landed in California; however, unlike Maureen's dad, my stay lasted only three days before I continued my travels another eight thousand miles across the Pacific. My original report date was December 22, 1969. However, to avoid processing a large number of AWOLs (absent without leave), I imagine, the Army extended our report date to January 3, 1970.

Once in Vietnam, it took a few weeks to get to a company. We had processing and additional training to go through. I finally reached my company at night several weeks after I arrived in country. I was stationed in a beautiful spot in the very northern part of South Vietnam, just outside the provincial capital of Hue in Phu Bai Province. It was hot and very humid—everything seemed strange. I felt disoriented. But I will never forget reporting to the first sergeant. There were three of us: Brent Law, Chris Christopherson, and me.

I walked to the orderly room, where a fairly large first sergeant sat, and stated, as did the others, that I was reporting for duty: "Private Beach reports for duty." With that, First Sergeant Ira M. Rogers, from San Antonio, Texas, stood up behind his desk. The first words out of his mouth were, "I'm not only the first sergeant but a Baptist deacon. Let me tell you what I will and will not accept in this company!" That was over forty years ago, and it is still vivid in my memory. He let us know that there was only one color in his unit, and that color was green; that if we used drugs, he would do all in his power, of which he assured us he had a great deal, to see we went to jail; and that we were soldiers in combat with a mission to win a war, but that we were also representatives of the United States, and therefore, we would treat civilians with respect. First Sergeant Rogers not only talked the talk, he walked the talk. He ran a very disciplined company.

What I learned from that initial encounter with First Sergeant Rogers was to make values clear from the start, in your words and by your actions. Actions are imperative, but being open and up front with a clear statement of values reduces the time it takes for newcomers to discover what those values are. Values and norms must be purposefully instilled, promoted, and protected. If we do not set our values and norms, someone else will set theirs. Leaders must continually communicate the organization's ethical expectations. Employees should not be left to speculate as to what they may be. IBM is probably unique among companies in that our values were not handed down from on high. They came from IBMers at *all levels throughout the enterprise*. Nobody said, "This is what *you must* be." Rather we, hundreds of thousands of us, said, "This is what *we want* to be."[30] Having a company set values in that way is special, but it in no way lessens the responsibility of the company's leaders to state explicitly and exemplify those values, lest any confusion or uncertainty arise over what is, and what is not, permissible conduct. Rather than lessen leaders' responsibility to talk and walk company values, the method IBM chose to establish its values increases the leaders' obligation to instill and exemplify values because IBMers have told their leaders what *they* expect *their leaders* to be. Leaders have to make sure their people know they got the message.

So, how do leaders communicate company values?

First of all, leaders must talk to their people about company values. Such conversations should occur when people first come to the company or move to a new unit within the company. There should also be periodic reminders given to all employees. Even if employees know company values, leaders should ensure that their people know that those values are foremost in the leaders' thinking. Leaders have to take ownership of what the company stands for and see that their people personally adopt those values. As Nick Donofrio, IBM's former executive VP, technology and innovation, explained to a group of new executives and distinguished engineers, "If we are moving toward greatness, it is because you are. The values have to be *your* values not the company values or the values on the third floor.[31] The journey to greatness is not a corporate journey—it's a personal journey."

Sometime, early in the matriculation of people into a unit, the leader of that unit should let the new employees know what the company's values are and then help them see what those values look like in that organization. As leaders, we must tell our people what *we are doing*, what *the organization is doing*, and what we *expect them to be doing* to

---

30 In 2003, IBM undertook the first reexamination of its values in nearly 100 years. Through Values Jam, an unprecedented 72-hour discussion on IBM's global intranet, all IBMers were invited to come together to define the essence of the company. The result was a set of core values, defined by IBMers for IBMers, that shapes the way we lead, the way we decide, and the way we act. In the end, IBMers determined that our actions will be driven by these values: (1) Dedication to every client's success; (2) Innovation that matters, for our company and for the world; (3) Trust and personal responsibility in all relationships.

31 By "on the third floor," he was referring to corporate headquarters. The most senior executives have offices on the third floor.

live out those values. Leaders must also impress upon their people that *leaders* need feedback to keep things on track—and that they expect their people to provide that feedback. A number of years ago, New York City had a mayor named Ed Koch. He became known for stopping New Yorkers on the street and asking, "How am I doing?" Leaders need to hear how they are doing—and how they can do even better. Leaders not only have responsibility to make their people accountable for respecting company values; they also have responsibility to see that their people hold their leaders and each other accountable.

That the phrase "actions speak louder than words" is a cliché makes it no less true. The ultimate proof that we not only know the values but also believe in them is our behavior—we need to walk the talk. Set the personal example. Reinforce others who support the values, and correct those who do not. People in leadership positions cannot escape being role models. A few years ago, Keenie McDonald, IBM's managing director for WellPoint, was talking to a group of new IBM executives. She pointed her finger at them and said, "They talk about you at the dinner table!" Similarly, Dan Pelino, general manager of IBM's health care and life sciences, also talking to a group of new IBM executives, put it more graphically when he stated, "You are dinner fodder." Leaders at all levels are important in the lives of the people they lead. People pay attention to even subtle behaviors of leaders and take their cues from the leaders' example. What we do, or do not do, always speaks louder than what we say.

Values have to be more than a document. There are always two sets of values in any organization: those espoused and those practiced. There needs to be a high positive correlation between the two. Enron's values were Respect, Integrity, Communication, Excellence. But as one Enron employee put it, "We talked values. We didn't act on them." To paraphrase Aristotle, to determine a person's values, you watch his feet, not his mouth. Leaders walk their values.

It's all in the feet.[32]

---

32 The actual quote is: "Moral excellence comes about as a result of habit. We become just by doing just acts."

5

Leader of Rebels

In Chapter 3, I talked about not getting promoted to private first class out of my Advanced Individual Training—a promotion I had earned and deserved. Well, for people who like happy endings, I did get promoted very rapidly after I got to Vietnam—ahead of my peers, anyway. My next lesson came with my third promotion.

I was promoted to sergeant and put in charge of a platoon. At twenty-four, I had never been in charge of anyone but me. Admittedly, I had been an acting sergeant in AIT, but the promotion in Vietnam was for real. I had responsibility for about fifteen men. It was a small platoon—with less than a stellar reputation.

It was an ambulance platoon. In theory, the group's mission was to pick up the sick, injured, wounded, and dead; administer any emergency medical treatment that may have been required; and evacuate them to a proper medical treatment facility for more advanced care. In addition, we had to maintain the operational readiness of the vehicles. In terms of time and effort, vehicle maintenance was by far our primary activity, i.e., I ran a motor pool. For practical purposes, I was the "motor sergeant"—not very glamorous, at least in my eyes.

We had four rundown vehicles: two M70A1 front-line ambulances, one M151A jeep, and a duce and a half truck, all of which we had to keep running with very few tools and difficult-to-get replacement parts while operating in a tropical climate—and with no school-trained personnel. Why were none of my folks school-trained? Well, because with the exception of Arthur "Charlie" Brown, they, like me, were all trained as medics. We were also responsible for keeping the company's only generator going, and Charlie Brown was the generator operator. Charlie did his job well, but his greatest pleasure was periodically bringing the company to its knees by having a mysterious malfunction cut off what little electricity there was. If Charlie Brown was upset about something, the entire company was going to go without electricity.

Generally, within seconds of the "breakdown," the executive officer, Captain Alvin Short, would appear to see what was wrong and how long it would be until it was fixed. Charlie would look bewildered and remind him, "Sir, I was trained as a generator operator, not a mechanic. I can do only minimal maintenance." And, when asked what he thought might be wrong, Charlie would talk in unintelligible technical terms or, more often than not, about fictitious parts and systems that he made up as he went along. When Captain Short was sufficiently anxious, Charlie would tell him he was going to have to think about it for a while and see what, if anything, he could do. He always managed to get things back up and running—eventually.

I should be clear: Captain Short was as decent and conscientious a person as you would ever meet. He was seldom Charlie's intended target. Unfortunately, however, Captain Short's exceptional conscientiousness made him the one who suffered the most angst during these mysterious blackouts. If Captain Short had not been such a nice guy, the blackouts would most likely have lasted longer than they usually did. Charlie was very capable and generally figured out how to get the generator working again even when it actually did break down. Charlie also was a big help in keeping the vehicles running. He was from the Boston area and had been a machinist before entering the Army. He was good-natured—when not upset.

As challenging as it was to keep the vehicles operating, the platoon members were a greater challenge. A number of the platoon members were soldiers who had been transferred from other companies because of failure to perform or because of behavioral problems.[33] The only two people who had any formal training as mechanics had gotten it while serving time as juveniles—one in the California Youth Authority and the other in the New Jersey Juvenile Justice System. All these men had been in country longer than I had, and until I was made sergeant, they all out-ranked me. Moreover, I was sent to take charge of the unit because the person who had been the platoon sergeant had just been relieved for violating the Uniform Code of Military Justice and had been reduced in rank and taken out of his leadership position.

I was put in charge of this platoon because it was out of control and none of the existing members were seen as having the ability or inclination to get it under control. This platoon was commonly referred to by the rest of the company as the company's "armpit." Having me walk in as the new person in charge was not something they anticipated. Making the circumstances even more awkward, I had been a private first class in this platoon when I first arrived in country. About the only thing I had going for me was that none of the platoon members had enough respect for any other member that they wanted him in charge.

 In my first few minutes, I made clear that any personal problems we had within the platoon we would take care of internally. I was not going to be escalating problems to the first sergeant or asking the company commander to intervene. I also told them that we were known as the company's armpit, something they already knew and to which they responded, "We don't really give a f__ about what others think." I told them that in spite of what they said, everyone wants respect from others and most of all from themselves. And, that I was not going to try

---

33 If by any chance any former platoon members are reading this, I am most certainly talking about the others, not you.

to convince them that they were the heart or brains of the company but that maybe they were the liver. Not too glamorous, not very pretty. The liver deals with messy stuff, but it is absolutely vital to functioning: You cannot survive without it, and there is no duplicate. I reminded them that all of us were medics, that we could all take someone else's place in this unit, but no one could take ours. I pointed out that the company depended on us and that others depended on our company being able to do its job well. With very few bumps, by every internal or external measure, the platoon performed magnificently for the rest of the time I was in Vietnam. As one of the division's general officers noted after an inspection, with the possible exception of the transportation company, which had highly trained personnel, we were the best motor pool on Camp Eagle.

So, what did I learn during my time with the ambulance platoon? First of all, leadership is important. Because of leadership this platoon not only performed better than others expected it would—or could; it performed better than *they* expected they could. Second, sometimes leaders need to give people an uncommon response that forces them to think. It catches them off guard. These men had a lifetime of practice proving that no one could control them—and they were right. The question was, could they control themselves? I told them, essentially, that they were in charge.

Another lesson was the importance of having leaders trust the people who work in their organizations. Too often we focus on workers trusting leaders. While such trust is important, it is less important than having leaders trust their people—and showing them that trust. Perhaps for the first time in their lives, the members of the ambulance platoon were not in compliance mode. I did not tell them what to do or how to do it; I told them what needed to get done—and often I depended on them for that information, too. Integral to IBM's current strategy, and that of other companies, to compete in today's hyper-paced world is to become a more "horizontal" and adaptive company, not just with respect to IT infrastructure, but also with respect to leadership practices and the cultural transformation needed to bring about the required changes in those practices. Solving technical and technological problems is not all that difficult; making the shifts in leadership behaviors and shaping a new culture, which are essential for the continued success of a company, are the greater challenges. Authority must come from people's ideas, not just their position in the structural hierarchy. There must be cross-unit collaboration and decision-making power well down the food chain. The ambulance platoon's greatest need was the creation of an organization in which the people who needed to accomplish the work worked with each other in a climate of mutual trust and respect.

One of the messages from IBM's Values Jam in 2004 was that the center of gravity for decision-making within IBM had to be lowered. Part of the cultural change needed to lower the center of gravity was to recognize that leaders have to become *listening* members of their teams. The idea behind the design and implementation of "jamming" was the belief that anyone in the organization was capable of analyzing problems and coming up with imaginative solutions. The company would then be able to take these solutions and share them with people throughout the company who would put them into effect. When it came to the ambulance platoon's major tasks of maintaining the operational fitness of our vehicles and equipment, I could not tell them what to do or how to do it; I had to listen to them and then enable them to accomplish what *they* said needed to be done.

Lou Gerstner, IBM's former chairman and CEO, in his book cautions leaders that they should not just preside but participate.[34] Leaders sometimes have to be *in the middle of things*—not just *on top of things*. In a worldwide broadcast in 2004, Sam Palmisano, IBM's current chairman and CEO, said,

> "In today's business environment there are two alternatives: One is to create new management systems and exert tighter controls. This is a very real choice. We like bureaucracy. IBM is good at that. But there is a second alternative—and it's a better alternative. And that is to trust IBM employees. This will be essential if we are to be as adaptable as IBM needs to become to successfully confront the many complex problems it faces."

---

34 Louis V. Gerstner, *Who Says Elephants Can't Dance?* (New York: Harper Business, 2002), p. 199.

My experience with the ambulance platoon taught me other lessons as well. One was that we cannot always get the "right people" to do a job. Sometimes we have to help the people in those jobs become the "right people." And finally, a lesson that goes to the heart (or maybe the liver) of effective leadership is that leaders must help people find meaning in their work and then ensure that those people see how they are contributing. People will give their full effort to something that they find worthwhile and to which they feel their contribution is necessary. People have to feel valued. They have to understand that they are important to the mission and that the mission itself is important—and that their time is not being wasted. They want to feel like they make a difference. People must feel they matter.

6

Trusting the Untrustworthy

Being put in charge of the ambulance platoon was a watershed experience for me. The impact was both immediate and long-lasting. Let me back up a bit. I did not want this duty. First of all, as I stated in Chapter 3, I had great reservations about being in charge of anyone. I had turned down an opportunity to be an officer because by the time I had been drafted, I was having second thoughts about the United States' involvement in Vietnam, and I did not want a leadership role in an effort that I did not fully support. Having been drafted and sent to Vietnam, my personal mission was to be the best medic I could be and to return home in one piece. Furthermore, my desire was to be assigned as a medic with an infantry unit or to fly Medevac missions. That is what I had trained to do, and I thought I would be pretty good at it. Performing those tasks also fit an idealized self-image of who and what I wanted to be. I saw myself—or at least wanted to see myself—as a hero saving as many lives as I could, and now I was being asked not only to be part of a far-from-glamorous unit but to be in charge of it.

My being asked to replace the sergeant in charge of the unit happened very suddenly, which is not unusual in combat, but the need for the replacement was not due to a combat casualty. The first sergeant called me aside one evening and said, "Beach, you're not going to like this, but I need your help." And without giving me a chance to respond, he said, "I need you to lead the ambulance platoon. I'm about to relieve Staff Sergeant Vulcan[35] and transfer him down to battalion, and I need you to go down there and take over."

I was caught off guard; my mind was racing. I not only did not want to lead the unit, the assignment did not make sense to me. I knew nothing about vehicle maintenance, and several of the platoon members outranked me, not to mention (if you remember my friend Eddy who bared himself for peace on Main Street the day I got inducted) this unit was naked Eddy times fifteen. It was not a job I wanted to do, nor did I feel prepared to do it.

In as nonargumentative a tone as I could muster, I said, "What do you think the guys in the platoon will say? Some of them outrank me. Wouldn't it make more sense to send one of the sergeants from one of the other platoons down there?"

The first sergeant replied, "I've got orders already drafted making you a sergeant. I'll have them signed later tonight. As far as one of the other sergeants, I've been watching you since you arrived in this company. I need *you* down there, not one of the other sergeants. And as far as how the members of the platoon will take it, I'll talk to them in the morning—the rest will be up to you. But you will have my full support for whatever you think needs doing."

All I could say was okay.

He patted me on the back, chuckled, and as he started to walk away, he said, "There's one more thing. I looked up the regulations. I can get you promoted to sergeant, but you haven't been in the Army long enough to get sergeant's pay." He was not joking.

---

35 This is a fictitious name.

Not only was my self-image undergoing an assault, but my perception of my social role—both in my eyes and in the eyes of others—was in flux. I was no longer expected to be a medic. All those skills that I found interesting and exciting to learn and with which I was eager to prove myself were no longer front and center. I was now being asked to be the motor sergeant. No more the healer of damaged bodies, but a repairman—the head of the maintenance crew. I was disappointed. I felt that I was being compelled to lower my expectations, to pursue less lofty goals.

I went back to my hooch and lay on my bunk trying to sort it all out. In the morning, I would be walking down to the motor pool and would be expected to do something and to be something, and I had no idea what either of those would look like. My internal monologue jumped about. "I can't be the motor sergeant. I know nothing about vehicles! I have no mechanical skills or interests. But the first sergeant didn't say, 'I need you to be the motor sergeant.' He said, 'I need you to take over'; he had to know I was not going to be able to tell folks how to maintain dilapidated vehicles or keep an overtaxed generator operating—so, what does he expect? And he said he had been watching me. What did he see? I wish I had thought to ask. I'm going to have to lead this group and help them become effective, but how? *Lead!*" The word, which had come out with no conscious intent and gone by almost unnoticed, suddenly took center stage.

I knew I had the answer: I was to lead, but I was not sure just what that meant. I was seeing something I had not seen before and was gaining a new understanding, but I was still seeing "as through a glass darkly." The idea of being a leader helped uplift my sagging self-image somewhat, but I still was not at all sure just what that would look like. And I was going to be seeing it face-to-face in just a few hours.

I was enough of a psychologist to know that people have common perceptions about the positions occupied by each person in a group structure, that these perceptions allow the group members to anticipate their own behavior and the behavior of those with whom they interact, and that all members of the group expect each other to behave in accordance with the common perceptions. But I also knew that social roles do not exist in isolation. They exist only in relation to others, and I had to figure out how to change the current dynamic that existed in that platoon.

The normal processes that allow people to anticipate the attitudes and behaviors of others and help our everyday interactions run smoothly were not present to guide me. Our behaviors in many respects depend on our anticipation of how others will respond to them, and I was not fully clear as to how the fifteen members of the ambulance platoon interacted with each other, just as I was clueless as to how they would react to me. We tell jokes only when we anticipate people will laugh and be amused. We confide distressing personal problems to others who we expect will empathize and sympathize with us. If we do not think people will find what we say funny, we keep our jokes to ourselves. If we do not think people will share our pain, we withhold revealing it. What do leaders do? And what would this one do tomorrow morning when meeting his platoon of unruly soldiers for the first time?

Up to this point in life, I had assumed that good leaders just knew what to do and how to do it—how they knew, I was not sure. And, unfortunately, most of the people I had recently encountered in positions of leadership did not fit my current circumstances or self-image. Leaders were people others listened to and followed. They barked orders, often treated people arbitrarily, and used power to get things done. I knew how to give orders, but I had no demonstrator to post,[36] and I could not take these men through their tasks "by the numbers." I did not know the movements. Although I knew the mission, I did not know how to repair vehicles or perform the other tasks needed to carry it out. I was going to have to listen to the fifteen naked Eddies. I needed their help. That did not fit any concept of leader that I knew, but I had no choice, and I was determined not to fail. I had to stop fretting, and I would have to get the platoon and me positive about what we were doing, or the rest of my tour would be hell.

Now let's talk about trust. The traditional approach would have been to go down to this group, impose rigid discipline, and then ease off

---

36 See Chapter 3, "The Cost of Leadership."

after they understood *my expectations* had *earned my trust*—after *I* had straightened them out and *they* had proven themselves trustworthy. But I figured that approach had been used plenty of times before and to no avail. These guys had spent the last nineteen to twenty years proving that no one could control them. I had once watched them spend twelve hours working on a vehicle while an officer was literally standing over them, and all they had done was change the spark plugs. I was no match for them. So, the real question was, *could they control themselves* and take personal responsibility and ownership of their behavior? To find that out, I had to get them thinking differently. They knew how to counter what someone else said; they had to learn to set their own direction. My initial concept of leadership was now upside down.

Although I was unaware of it at the time, as I reflect on it, what at first seemed like an irrational act on my part made perfect sense. Taking a leap of faith is the essence of trust. And entrusting people with responsibility forces them to look at themselves. Think about the leap of faith the first sergeant had taken with me. He had a platoon that was vital to the functioning of the company. It was out of control—and he put someone who had never led anything or anyone in charge. It forced me to think about things that I would never have otherwise considered.

So, I got done with my little introductory speech to my new platoon[37] and said, "Let's get to work." Immediately, one of the guys piped up, "Hey, Jack, I'm going to the PX" (i.e., post exchange). There was a little trailer on base camp that served as a store. You could buy soda, cigarettes, toiletries, and other such things there. He was followed by three others who decided that they would be going, too. My first test—and a crucial one. I told them that they knew what maintenance had to be done that day, and they knew better than I how long it would take them—and to judge their time accordingly and to make sure that I had two drivers here at all times. They went to the PX—but they got the required maintenance done by the end of the day. We all passed the entrance exam.

---

37 See Chapter 5, "Leader of Rebels."

Again, looking back on my experience with the ambulance platoon, there was more to creating trust than my delegating responsibilities to these men. True empowerment is not just delegating responsibility. It is enabling people to be successful when they are given the responsibility.

I did several things. First, I mastered the procurement system. Getting parts was difficult. You had to know the system, and I set learning it as a priority. I took that as my task. I also had the ambulances dispatched from the motor pool instead of the aid station. There were at least two problems with having the ambulances at the aid station. First, it reduced the time the mechanics had to work on the vehicles. Second, in looking at the records, I noticed that the vehicles were averaging about four thousand miles a month. These were emergency vehicles, and the base camp we were on was only a couple of square miles in area. To have four thousand miles or even a thousand miles on a vehicle in a month meant that people were using them for other than intended purposes. I discovered that the officers—and others—in collusion with the drivers were using the ambulances as personal vehicles. Not only did this misuse risk the possibility that an emergency vehicle would not be immediately available when needed, but it also resulted in excessive wear and tear. By dispatching the vehicles from the motor pool, we cut the miles per month to four hundred. The increased time for repairs and the lower usage made maintaining the vehicles a lot easier.

Not surprisingly, the steps that I took to limit the use of the vehicles generated a lot of heat. The officers protested, but the first sergeant and the company commander backed me up. By removing obstacles, I was enabling the platoon's success. My actions also had an unintended positive impact on morale. The guys in the platoon saw the new vehicle restrictions as "sticking it to the officers." That was not my motivation, but that the platoon had the power to impose responsible use of the vehicles on the officers sent a message to everyone that what we did was important.

I also set up a program of cross-training so we could spread the skills within the platoon. Leaders not only remove impediments to success, they create systems that develop the organizational capability. Now, I am sure you are wondering whether I learned vehicle maintenance.

I tried, but when I went to change the oil and let the transmission fluid out instead, it was decided that I would stick to keeping the books and keeping the rest of the company off our backs and would delegate vehicle maintenance to others.

Although I never learned vehicle maintenance, I learned the power of trust, not only that the first sergeant and my people trusted me but, of more consequence, that I trusted them. We had 360 degrees of trust, which not only allowed us to excel but also inspired us to do so.

This experience fundamentally altered my understanding of leadership. I came to the realization that to a far greater extent than expertise, trust is essential to leading. We cannot lead people we do not trust. We can boss them, and we can micromanage them—but we cannot lead them. Even more significant, trust lifts aspirations and invigorates others to lead themselves.

7

"I Am—Somebody!"[38]

Trust and meaning are concepts that I address repeatedly throughout this book. The building of trust and instilling of meaning are so vital to leadership that they warrant repetition. Of course, "meaning" can have different meanings! In the Introduction, I talked about sense making, mostly in terms of coming to a cognitive and intellectual understanding of what is occurring about us. Meaning, as I referred to it in Chapter 5, is an emotional and visceral experience linked to our sense of personal purpose. I want to spend just a little more time with that concept.

In Chapter 5, I talked about the importance of instilling meaning in work. In that sense, meaning meant a positive and higher purpose, something that would spark constructive behaviors and generate the energy needed to do our jobs well. The little homily I described in that chapter about my unit being the company's liver and it being absolutely vital not only to the company's functioning but also to others beyond our company was as much for my benefit as for the men I was going to lead. People do not want their time wasted. They want to feel like

---

38 Title of a poem written by the Reverend Jesse Jackson, 1971.

what they do is important—that it matters, and that they matter. It is almost a platitude to say that people want to make a difference, but it is true. Making a difference is a deep need in each one of us. We are in a constant search for meaning, and leaders have to tap into people's aspirations and help them find that meaning. Leaders themselves must have a personal, positive purpose.

A few days after assuming my duties as the ambulance platoon sergeant, I approached First Sergeant Rogers and told him that I still had a desire to put my training as a medic to use. I knew that our company did MEDCAPS (Medical Civic Action Programs). If I could not attend to wounded in combat, I thought that I could use my training by participating in those programs. Wars are always fought on multiple fronts—on the battlefield as well as in the hearts and minds of the nation's people. MEDCAPS were aimed at the hearts and minds of the Vietnamese civilians. The first sergeant's response was, "You sure can, Beach. And I'll up you one. MACV (Military Assistance Command Vietnam) has no medics, and they are looking for someone to do some MEDCAPS for them, so you can get involved there as well."

In our case, MEDCAPS involved a small medical team going to a designated village or orphanage and holding sick call. When we went to a village, we would meet with the village head, and he would show us where to set up. There were generally three of us: a physician, a 91C (enlisted nurse), and me. The care provided was better than nothing, but not much. We had no equipment to take or test specimens, and for security reasons, there was virtually no follow-up. There was no routine to where we would go or when—at least none of which I was aware. We were armed with stethoscopes, antibacterial soap, antibiotics and syringes, antifungal medications, and analgesics. There was never a shortage of villagers—mostly women, children, and elderly men seeking attention. I suspect our greatest medical successes were in providing relief to, and prevention of, skin diseases.

In spite of the rudimentary medical care provided, the MEDCAPS were successful in furthering the American foreign policy objective of winning the hearts and minds of the Vietnamese. In hindsight, our contribution could have been greater if we had taken ARVN (Army of the Republic of Vietnam) soldiers along and trained them to do what we were doing. They, too, had to win the hearts and the minds of the civilian population. Given their familiarity with the language and culture, it is likely that the ARVN soldiers could have been more effective than the Americans, and more important, they could have continued to provide these services after the Americans left.

Our visits to orphanages were special for me. While others treated children in need of medical attention, I spent my time in the nursery picking up and holding each infant. The staffs running the orphanages were small and the number of orphans large. In the nursery, the infants spent most of their days lying in what amounted to wooden fruit crates with slats so that they did not lie in their own waste. It was not that the staff, mostly nuns, was neglectful; they were simply overwhelmed. I was familiar with the studies that showed the high mortality rate among infant orphans who are not held and cuddled. I did what I could to make each one feel precious for at least a few moments. Since we did make return visits to the orphanages, I hope the cumulative effect of my brief contact with the infants had some positive long-term impact.

At some point, I wrote my mother to send me several hundred Tootsie Pops, which I took to one of the orphanages. I gave all but one to the head nun to distribute to the children. The one pop that I kept I offered to an Amer-Asian girl who was standing nearby. She was probably about three years old. I unwrapped the lollipop and handed it to her. She had no idea what it was or what to do with it. I went through all kinds of antics to get her to lick it. After a minute or two, she took one tentative lick and then another, and then with widening eyes and a big smile, she put it in her mouth and skipped off. My lollipop diplomacy was a success. It was magical.

Leadership is about the human spirit. James Quinn, Philip Anderson, and Sydney Finkelstein[39] wrote an article in the *Harvard Business Review* in which they note that in the era of the knowledge worker, the capacity to manage human intellect and to convert it into useful

---

39 J. B. Quinn, P. Anderson, and S. Finkelstein, "Managing Professional Intellect: Making the Most of the Best," *Harvard Business Review* (March–April 1996), pp. 71–80.

products and services is the essential leadership task. They go on to state that professional intellect of an organization operates on four levels. First, and most basic, is cognitive knowledge, which means that a person knows *what* to do to master his or her discipline. Second is advanced skills, which means that people not only know what to do but also know *how* to do it. We need the ability to apply principles and execute effectively. Next, people have to move beyond the mere skillful execution of tasks to *know why* they do what they do. Knowing why we do what we do allows us to anticipate interactions and consequences— intended and unintended. It results in what the authors call a "highly trained intuition"—the person is now able to recognize a good idea at the right time, adapt, and work around any obstacles to achieving the intended objective. And finally, people need to *care why* they do what they do. Caring why spurs action and allows for self-motivated creativity.[40]

Intellect resides in our brain, but the first three levels—knowing what to do, how to do it, and why we do it—can also be placed in an organization's databases and operating procedures. Metaphorically, the "care why" level resides in our "heart." It cannot be put in an SOP or manual. Leaders who "care why" and nurture the "care why" in their people will not only thrive in today's marketplace but will renew their cognitive knowledge (know what), advanced skills (know how), and systems understanding (know why), which will allow them to compete in the rapidly changing marketplaces of the future. When we "care why," we do not get complacent; we are always looking to get better.

However, there is yet another level of engagement that Quinn, Anderson, and Finkelstein missed or at least did not deal with explicitly, and that is determining *why people care why*. People can "care why" for a number of reasons. Generally, companies operate on basic self-interest. Caring is based on a reciprocal exchange between the company and the worker. If we do well, we will get a higher end-of-year evaluation, a bigger bonus, a raise, and maybe even a promotion. However, the most intense motivation comes from tapping into and awaking people's aspirations. When we identify with the values and

---

40 In subsequent chapters, I convert these four levels of engagement into what I term "trust vital signs."

goals of the organization for which we work, the work itself becomes rewarding: The harder we work, the better we feel, and it deepens our commitment. Leaders need to enliven the human spirit.

If winning, beating the competition, or the price of stock is our main motivation, it does not matter which company we work for or what we do. And the best that someone will be able to say in our eulogy is that we lived a life of luxury and died rich. There is a difference between being a person of wealth and a person of value. Value is worth more than wealth.

The MEDCAPS in Vietnam nourished my aspiration to use my training as a medic to help the United States win the hearts and minds of the civilian population in the war zone and to help make the lives of those civilians easier. I understood not only what to do, how to do it, and why I was doing it, but I also cared about what I was doing, and I understood why I cared. I could make a difference in people's lives, and doing so would help me become the person I wanted to be.

Tapping into people's yearnings and aspirations focuses them on higher, more transcendent goals. They move beyond self-interest to interest in improving the planet. The work itself becomes intrinsically rewarding, as does our association with the organization that permits us to do the work. Awakening aspirations builds our pride by allowing us to affirm a desired identity. Sam Palmisano, IBM's current chairman and CEO, has stated that "IBM's most important innovation wasn't a technology or a management system. . . . IBM's most important invention was the IBMer."

Being an IBMer is not just about making money. Being a soldier in Vietnam was not just about following orders. Regardless of what our job is, the fundamental motivation for doing it and for doing it well is the possibility of making a positive difference. Leadership is not only about getting people to *do* something; it is about helping them *be* something.

8

It's All You

"Sir, could you come in and talk to this trainee? I've been talking to him for forty-five minutes, and frankly, I have no idea what is going on. He wants out, but he is not going to have any trouble with Basic Training. I can't figure out what is going on, and I'd like you to evaluate him before I send him back."

"Sure, Lance, let's have a look."[41a]

It was my first assignment in the Army following receipt of my Ph.D. in clinical psychology and completion of my internship. I was stationed at Fort Dix, New Jersey. It was one of the thirteen posts that conducted Basic Combat Training for new recruits. Six years before, I had been a draftee going through Basic Training here, and now I was an officer and chief of the psychology section at Walson Army Hospital. The clinic I worked in was called the Community Mental Health Clinic; our clients were predominately soldiers going through Basic Combat Training and the staff that ran that program. We also served Air Force personnel stationed at McGuire Air Force Base, which borders Fort Dix.

41a This is a fictitious name. I do not remember the name of the behavioral science specialist involved.

The Army had changed since I had been at Fort Dix the first time. I and many of the soldiers in Basic Training with me had been conscripts. At eighteen, by law, we reported to the local draft board and then waited to see if and when we would be called to serve. Notification came in the form of a letter from the President of the United States that stated, "GREETING: You are hereby ordered for induction into the Armed Forces of the United States. . . ." Like any other invitation, it gave you the date and place to show up for the party. It was for most an accepted patriotic duty—even Elvis went.

By 1973, the Peace Talks in Paris had resulted in a cease-fire that led to the withdrawal of American forces from Vietnam and the ending of one of the most unpopular wars in American history. The baby boom had produced many more eligible young men than the armed forces needed. Universal service had turned into universal eligibility—but service was far from universal. Some argued that various deferments and other means of avoiding military service created a system that tended to target the poor and disadvantaged. Others were philosophically opposed to any kind of involuntary military service. Still others blamed the draft for the widespread opposition to the war in Vietnam and the breakdown of discipline that had plagued the military during that war. All these considerations led President Nixon and Congress to end the draft and institute an all-volunteer force. So, the young man I was about to meet was in the Army because he had made a conscious decision to be there.

Specialist Lance Madden was a behavioral sciences specialist—a paraprofessional counselor. My role in the clinic, in addition to having my own case load, was to be available to sit in when any of the specialists had questions, and it was my guidance that the specialists brief me before any first-time client was released from the clinic and returned to his unit.

As we walked down the short hallway, Specialist Madden reemphasized, "Sir, this guy has more going for himself than I do, but there is something going on here."

I entered the room and found a good-looking, well-dressed young man; he was still in civilian clothes, which was extremely unusual. He apparently had requested to visit the Community Mental Health Clinic while he was still in the reception center. He had been on post only a day or two at most.

I introduced myself, and we talked for a while. I learned he was from a well-to-do and fairly prominent family in his home state of Virginia.[41b] He had been an A student in high school, involved in the civil rights movement, and active in the campaigns of some well-known political figures.

It was quickly apparent that, except for being in civilian clothes, which was very uncommon, he was not experiencing any cognitive or perceptual disturbance, nor were there any odd behavioral mannerisms. His affect was normal except for an earnest but unexplained insistence that he had made a mistake and could not stay in the Army. Essentially, in terms of his mental status, all signs were positive.

"What led you to come into the Army?" I inquired.

"I was in my first year at Hampton University and was having trouble adjusting, so I left and thought the Army might be a good thing to do while I tried to figure out what I wanted to do with my life," he responded.

"Seems like you have been moving away from some things rather than toward something," I said inquisitively.

"Well, I sure made a mistake this time."

"Wendell, you haven't even been here forty-eight hours. How do you know you've made a mistake?"

41b For privacy reasons, his name, provenance, the exact date of the meeting, and other possibly identifying information have been altered.

"I just know I'm not going to be able to take all this."

"Wendell, the rigors of Basic Training are not going to be difficult for you. You are intelligent and obviously physically fit." In an attempt to use a little "stress inoculation," I continued. "Let me tell you a little about what to expect. Your freedom will be limited. You will be told what to do, how to do it, when to do it, and it is likely the drill sergeant will find some error in your performance—at least for the first few weeks. He considers it his duty to point out that anything you learned prior to being in his care was either incorrect or not up to his standards.

"You will probably get yelled at—don't take it personally. Basic Training is done with the volume up. When the drill sergeant asks you a question, respond as if he is hard of hearing. If you don't, he will get very loud and direct you to 'sound off like you have a pair!' And, under no circumstance call the drill sergeant 'sir.' If you do that, he will get up real close and personal—and inform you in his loudest voice—'Boy, don't call me *sir*. I work for a living!' He is then likely to order you to assume the 'dying cockroach position.' That is, you will lie on your back with your hands and feet vertical. It will quickly get uncomfortable. So, it's 'Yes, Drill Sergeant!' And 'No, Drill Sergeant!' And 'boy' is not a racial slur. You will be 'boy' or 'trainee' until you graduate. Then you will be a 'soldier.'

"Your day will start early," I continued. "You will be rudely awakened at 0500 and cleaned up, bed made, and in formation by 0530. At that time, even though you just cleaned up, you will do some PT (physical training). It will consist of running, sit-ups, and push-ups—regardless of the weather. The sit-ups and push-ups will be '4-count.' That is, every two sit-ups or push-ups equals one 'count.' One, two, three, four, ONE. One, two, three, four, TWO. So, ten sit-ups or push-ups will be twenty. And, I should mention, because of the change in your normal schedule and the speed with which you need to get ready, it is not uncommon for people to be constipated for the first few days. You will do a lot of marching, standing in formation, and sitting in classes. But you get to do some fun stuff, too, like learn to fire an M-16—and remember, this is a *weapon*, not a gun—or you will find yourself doing some extra push-ups. You will be in bed by 2130 (9:30 P.M.), and for one hour during the night, you will have 'fire guard.' Now, the barracks are all brick and concrete; they are not going to burn. However, depending on what hour is yours, you will either spend the time on your knees with a little green scrub pad removing black scuff marks from the floor, or if you are on earlier in the morning, you will be putting wax down or using the buffer to shine the floor. So, what you are about to face is intentionally stressful, but if you look around at the several hundred other recruits you came in with, few will be as capable as you to handle this. I'm just not sure what your concern is."

My monologue was followed by silence. It was pretty clear I was missing the mark on what was troubling this young man.

"Wendell," I said. "Specialist Madden and I have been talking with you for quite a while, and our whole purpose in being here is to help. I sense what is bothering you is only tangentially related to Basic Training and is probably the same thing that compelled you to leave Hampton University. We are a mental health clinic, and we have seen just about any problem you can imagine. People come in here who are flat-out crazy—and you are not in that category by any stretch of the imagination. We have seen people who abuse others, abuse themselves, indecently expose themselves in public, and get excited by wearing women's underwear or at the sight of a high-heeled shoe. Our job is not to judge these people but to see that they get the attention they need to live normal happy lives. I sense your desperation but have no insight into it. So, I know there is more going on than you have told us, and I would like you to share that with us. Right now, all I can do is send you back as 'fit for duty'—and that clearly is not correct, but I have no justification to do otherwise."

Wendell's momentary silence was broken by him asking for a pencil and a piece of paper. After writing just a few words, he folded the paper *many times* and handed it to Specialist Madden who passed it to me. When I finally unfolded it, in the center of the sheet, in very small letters, it said, "I am gay."

"Wendell," I said, "it's okay—being gay is okay. But I can see you are having difficulty coming to terms with this—I suspect a lot of people do—but can you tell me why you had to write it down and could not just tell us?"

"If I said it, I would have to believe it; and if I believed it, I would have to kill myself," he said softly.

"That seems extreme, Wendell. Please help us understand that."

He went on to tell us that although he had never engaged in any homosexual behavior, he had been aware of these feelings for as long as he could remember. Then, soon after arriving at Hampton University, he was approached by some other gay students, and this caused him so much anxiety that he left school. In explaining to his parents why he had left school, he opened up to them that he was gay. Their response had been immediate, emphatic, and devastating. They had told him that he had grown up in a Christian home with all the advantages that anyone could have and that if he had a problem, they would get him the best psychiatrist available, but there was never to be any further mention of his being gay.

Not knowing what to do next, he had decided, with his parents' tacit support, to join the Army to provide a more masculine image and hopefully to reorient him. It quickly had become clear to him, however, that he was making matters worse rather than better.

"Wendell, we will get you out of the Army. So, take that off your mind. It will probably take a few days, but it will happen. But I am now concerned with what happens then. You have expressed suicidal thoughts, and in the last few minutes, you have revealed to us at least two impulsive and bad decisions—you left college and you joined the Army. Each of those decisions made matters worse, not better. Fortunately, both these decisions are reversible. I need to feel confident you are not going to make a third decision that is even more misguided and that is irreversible. Straight or gay, you have a lot to offer the world, so I have to tell you, suicide is not an option that we want you to seriously consider. It is not unusual for people making any major adjustment to the way they see themselves to have suicidal thoughts, but in time you will see that such thoughts are not part of a rational decision-making process."

Wendell now had tears in his eyes, "Sir, thank you. I'm not going to commit suicide. For the first time in a long time, I have hope."

"Good, but your feelings of discomfort over your homosexual feelings are deep and will not just vanish. So, when you leave the Army, you need to seek some help working all this through. I'm also uncomfortable with just getting you discharged without a plan. And, I'm not sure your home is the best environment just yet. Is there any place you think you could go?"

After some discussion, we decided that a possible immediate destination would be to live with a maiden aunt who lived in another part of Virginia. She owned a small general store. With his consent, I called her and explained the situation. She reacted as I had hoped. Without hesitation she stated, "I don't know much about homosexuality, but I know Wendell is a good and decent young man, and he is welcome here. I have a room in the back of the store, and I can put him to work while he is trying to sort all this out. He can stay as long as he needs to." Wendell was clearly moved when I told him of his aunt's reaction.

But there were still some things we had to address. I was now in "tell" mode.

"Wendell, before sending you back to the replacement center for transfer to the separation unit, I want to talk to you a bit more about your suicidal thoughts and getting some professional help. First, suicidal thoughts are usually a mixture of things. And in addition to your own feeling of the unacceptability of being gay, I suspect there is some anger toward your parents. I know it is hard, but give them time, too. No doubt they are struggling with this. They grew up in different times, and even the scientific community is just starting to modify its perspective on homosexuality and trying to figure out its exact nature. Don't expect miracles or an abrupt reversal of their attitudes. They are scared and confused, so at least give them time.

"More important, you are dealing with the same feelings they are. You have stated that you, as well as your family, are deeply religious, and so you will have to resolve being a Christian and being gay. I do not see these as incompatible, but you need to come to terms with all this, and it will take effort. There are a lot of issues that are far from resolved. So, I want to see to it right now that you get some qualified help. Would that be okay? My intent is to locate a mental health clinic near your aunt's place, get on the phone, give them a summary of our talk, and then put you on the phone and you actually make an appointment. Is that okay with you?"

"Yes, I would appreciate that. How long do you think it will be before I will be at my aunt's?"

"To be safe, make the appointment for about three weeks from now. Hopefully, you can be there sooner, but I want you to have an appointment on their books." With that, I took Wendell to my office while I located a clinic, and we made the arrangements for him to get continued treatment once he was separated from the service. We then got him transportation back to the replacement center and completed the paperwork necessary to get him into the system for discharge. I can only hope things turned out well for him.

The incident with Wendell took me back to Vietnam and my time as a platoon sergeant. One night several of us were playing cards, which was pretty routine. There was the usual banter. Ray Wiley and Rudy Garza[42] continued to joke about the fact they were playing cards with no money at stake, and Charlie Brown was at least thankful they did not have to share any of the beer with me. In response to I can no longer remember what, James Irwin—whom we called "Georgia Peach"—related that not too long ago his father had died of cancer. He had spent the afternoon of the day he died at his father's bedside. His father had asked him to come back that evening, and he had promised he would. However, he decided to go to the movies with his friends instead, and as fortune would have it, his father died that evening without the two ever seeing each other again. Understandably, he was still carrying some guilt about

---

42 Not his real name. I am concerned I may be passing on what is still private information.

the choice he had made. Frankly, he got more teasing than sympathy from us.

Several hours later, Rudy and I were outside the hooch just having walked to the latrine before turning in for the night. Leaning against the sandbags that formed a protective berm, Rudy got a bit quiet and then stated, "Young 'Georgia Peach' feels guilty—that ain't nothin'." He went on to relate an experience he had had about nine months into his tour. His former unit had been on search-and-destroy missions and had never made contact with the enemy. Since all the units around them were frequently getting into fire fights, they began to see themselves as "the golden eagles," so feared that the NVA (North Vietnamese Army) was afraid to tangle with them. Then early one morning on a fire base near the Laotian border, he was awakened when an RPG (rocket-propelled grenade) exploded in the tree trunk just above where he was sleeping. The base was under a sudden and fierce attack. Rudy, a combat medic, though wounded himself, started treating other wounded.

At one point, a fellow soldier was screaming, "Medic, medic, my buddy's been hit; please save my buddy." The two were up the hill from Rudy, but he made his way up, crawling as close to the ground as he could because the fire up the hill was intense. Upon reaching the wounded soldier and his distraught comrade, without getting up, Rudy reached his hand over a fallen tree to feel the wounded soldier's pulse, quickly pronounced, "I get no pulse; he's gone," and rolled back down the hill to the more protected area where he continued to treat the wounded.

As was common, Medevac helicopters were waiting to come in when it was clear enough to do so, and before Rudy could make a final check, the soldier that he had pronounced dead was in a body bag and taken away. "The problem," Rudy continued, "is I still think I did feel a faint pulse. But I was so scared, I just wanted to get off the hill. I don't know why it gets to me so. Before I was in the Army, I was in a gang in L.A. I shot at people. I never hit anyone, but I can't get this out of my mind. I didn't even know this guy. He was new to the unit."

I had to let this sink in a bit. My impulse, and I think it would be most people's reaction, was to focus Rudy on what he had done right. He had treated the wounded and received a Bronze Star for his actions there. He was a hero. But if I had taken that tack, I might have caused more harm than good. So, putting my hand on his shoulder, I replied, "Rudy, I suspect there is a little hero and a little coward in all of us. It's just some have the chance to find that out and some don't."

"Well, I guess one could say I got my chance." And with a bit of a smile, he added, "War is hell."

"Yeah, and here I am in the middle of one, and I'm depending on cowards and ingrates to get me through."

"Only the good die young. The rest of us will make it, Jack. I don't know about you!"

With another pat on his back and some understanding chuckles, we reentered the hooch and went to sleep.

But why resist the impulse to focus Rudy on his heroic actions? Understand, the issue here is not about evaluating performance; it is about self-acceptance. To reassure Rudy that he had not given into fear would make the fact that he had done so even more troubling to him. It would have intensified his guilt and reinforced his need to deny and hide what he had done. I would have been signaling that I could not accept him if he had shown weakness. And if others could not accept him, he would not be able to gain an appropriate perspective on his action, integrate it into who he was as a complete person, and move forward. Rather it would have reinforced his need to run from reality and to fragment his sense of self. If we cannot look honestly at ourselves and put our strengths and weaknesses in perspective, we will not be able to change what we can change or accept what we cannot change; we will never be whole persons. We will be like Humpty Dumpty; neither we nor anyone else will be able to "put all the pieces together again."

Often we identify with only part of ourselves. Wendell was going to kill his whole self to get rid of part of himself. He was not going to kill himself because he was an A student or because he was active in civil rights and the campaigns of several great public servants. He was looking only at his sexual orientation. When he revealed that part of himself, his family reinforced his feelings of unacceptability. Those feelings prevented him from looking at himself as a complete person and kept him from making sound, constructive decisions. How often do we say, "I was not myself today" or "That's not really me"? Who are we at those moments? What we generally mean is, "I was not behaving in a manner that I find praiseworthy or that I wish I had." Keep in mind you are talking about behavior—but it is *your* behavior.

Acceptance of who we are gives us the information we need to grow and to come closer to the person we would like to be and to achieve the goals we would like to achieve. People often define themselves and others by a few minutes of their lives, as though one act of heroism makes a person a hero or one act of cowardice makes a person a coward. Leadership is not binary—something you are or are not—nor is it a steady state. You need to earn it every day. Leaders must look at themselves completely and honestly and must help others to do the same.

9

Of Frogs and Leaders

My quick errand to the supermarket to get ice cream—it was on sale—morphed into a sentimental journey of sorts, with frogs leading the way as I jumped from one memory to another. The express line was anything but. However, my worries about the ice cream melting were quickly replaced by the glaring headline "FROG BABY BORN IN KANSAS!"[43] Yes, there was even an exclamation point.

"That's crazy!" I thought. "Why is that such big news? After all, frogs are born every day, everywhere." It was not until I was back in the car—and honest, Three Dog Night was blaring out about their good friend Jeremiah[44]—that the utter nonsense of the headline hit me. At first I laughed to myself, but then I found myself laughing out loud. The golden oldie had nothing to do with my reaction. This was science and my memories of catching tadpoles in the mountain streams near my boyhood home. "Frogs aren't born," I mused, "they are the result

---

43 *Weekly World News* (Sept. 8, 2001), p. 1.
44 Reference is to "Joy to the World," a song written by Hoyt Axton and made famous by the band Three Dog Night. The song's opening words are, "Jeremiah was a bullfrog. Was a good friend of mine."

of metamorphosis." Could that have been the big news? Somehow, I doubted it.

I consider myself somewhat of an expert on frogs. My offices, both at home and at work, are adorned with frogs: some big, some small, some serious, some whimsical, some hard—made of metal or porcelain— others soft and fluffy. But not all green. After all, "it's not that easy being green."[45] And none named Kermit or Jeremiah. No famous frogs here— just frogs. Actually, they were not *just* frogs: They were gifts, each one of them. And each one was precious—to me anyway. I had received my first frog in 1977 and the last in 2005. Almost three decades of frogs.

My relationship with frogs all started when I was caught off guard by a surprise farewell celebration. An Army officer, I was being transferred. I had to say something, but what? "Thank you." That was the easy part. Fortunately, at such times a pause is okay. I made good use of it.

"What a privilege it has been to work with each of you, and what a great honor it is to be able to serve this great nation and its people." It was getting tougher, both to control my emotions and to find the right words. The clichés, true as they were, were all used up. Now what? I did not want to be flippant. Surprisingly, even to me, the nearly ten years I had already spent in the service were having a deepening impact on me, and I wanted to share that with the folks who surrounded me. Most of the people who stood before me were sergeants and junior officers. They were tasked with developing other soldiers. At the same time, they were a behavioral sciences unit—not a very glamorous job.

"Each one of us in this room has an obligation to lead," I continued. "I know we spend most our time with the Army's biggest 'problem children.' But what we do every day is important." Another pause. "There is an old fable. Each of you knows it well, but I am going to recount it to you anyway. I really can't think of anything else to say.

---

45 Reference is to "Bein' Green," a song written by Joe Raposo in 1970 for the first season of the children's television program *Sesame Street*. It was originally performed by Kermit the Frog.

"There once was a frog. But it wasn't really a frog; it was a prince who had been bewitched. He had been turned into a frog, why or how I really don't know, but the only remedy was for a pretty maiden to kiss him." I was gaining some momentum. "Now, looking around this room, I know that does occur. Most of us men 'married up.' But you get the idea; this doesn't happen often—almost never, except in fables.

"As each of us floats on our particular lily pad down this river we call life, we all know what it's like to be a frog. Some days we get up and make croaking sounds instead of beautiful music—some of us more often than others. Too frequently our behaviors and tone tell the world what is wrong rather than what is right. We are full of problems and short on solutions.

"Well, one day (back to the fable) a fair young maiden was walking along the swampy moat around her father's castle. I guess swampy moats were often preferable to damp castles. Anyway, she saw this large brownish-green frog; maybe she was alerted to his presence by his solitary, plaintive croaking. And, for whatever reason, she leaned over and picked up this animal, which was unattractive to the point of ugliness, both in looks and sonorousness. She probably had to wipe some moat scum off his lumpy head, and then the most improbable thing happened: She kissed him!

"You all know the rest of the story. POOF! He turned into a prince. So, what's the point? What does this say to us as leaders? What is our mission and purpose? Well, to kiss frogs, of course!"

I got more hugs (if you are in uniform, hugging is a guy thing, too) than applause. When I returned to the office the next day to clear my desk, there sat a little green frog. Not being that creative, I have returned to this fable often, sometimes in humor, more often in earnest, and at times with as steely-eyed a glare and as firm a tone as I can muster. The steely-eyed glare and raised voice never resulted in hugs, or applause, but it did increase my collection of frogs.

Because of more than a lack of personal imagination, however, I frequently come back to this fable because it represents my signature life theme. A pivotal moment in my life occurred in 1974. I was having lunch with Howard Prince. We were both clinical psychology interns at Silas B. Hays Army Hospital, Fort Ord, California. I was a new lieutenant and he a major. Not too many years before, we had both returned from Vietnam. He had been a company commander, and I an enlisted draftee disgruntled by the experience and disillusioned by the leadership I had witnessed. I had reentered the military reluctantly and only out of economic necessity. My expectation was that it would be a temporary fix, and when I learned I would be working side by side with an airborne ranger who was a master parachutist with a silver star and two purple hearts, I was not favorably disposed. I could not have been more mistaken. The experience changed my life.

Howard, though only slightly older than I, had been an officer for eleven years longer. He had graduated as a distinguished cadet (top 5 percent) from West Point. Subsequently, he became an Olmstead Scholar and enrolled in the University of Bonn, Germany. Upon completion of his studies in Germany, he was assigned to the 1ˢᵗ Cavalry Division in Vietnam, where he served as an infantry company commander. During the Tet Offensive in early 1968, he sustained life-threatening wounds and was medically evacuated to the United States, where he was hospitalized for almost a year.

Although Howard survived the wounds, his injuries were so severe that he was unable to remain in the infantry. A medical board recommended that he be medically discharged from the Army. He fought that recommendation and won, but he had to change from infantry. The Army offered to send him to obtain a doctorate in clinical psychology, and he accepted.

Throughout that year together, Howard and I often talked about leadership. On this occasion, I was railing at him about the quality—or lack of it—of his fellow officers. They were full of clichés and treated those of lesser rank with little respect.[46] He listened quietly and with

---

46 In hindsight and with distance, my overly negative evaluation of the military leadership that I had experienced was an emotional response based on a few officers. Even at the time, I would have admitted that most of the officers whom I had encountered carried out their duties and led well. I suspect that my reaction was in part the displacement of a general anger that I felt at what I saw as the needless waste of lives by our government.

some amusement—he was getting used to my rants. When I finished, he said with an understanding smile, "Jack, that's the difference between the developers and 'weeder-outers.'" Though not among Howard's more eloquent statements on leadership, it hit me like a bolt of lightning. To Howard, leadership was a special trust. To him, the obligation of leaders was to help others become better people—better at what they do, how they do it, how they feel about themselves, and more able to function both independently and interdependently. Leadership was about developing others. I now had a renewed sense of purpose—to kiss frogs!

10

Talk

John,[47] an instructor on my staff at West Point, came into my office. John had already exhibited qualities of leadership and shown the potential to become a senior officer. However, like many bright people, he was not immune to losing his focus. He came to me frustrated over what *another* instructor was *not* doing. According to John, Phil had repeatedly not met his commitments to their project, and the project was in danger of not being completed within the deadline.

When people approach me about problems with colleagues, my initial inquiry is always the same, "John, what did Phil say when you talked to him?" John's answer was not atypical. His evasive words and fidgety body language made clear that he had not talked to Phil.

So, I continued. "If I go to Phil, I'm going to have to state my evidence and the source of the complaint. Then what's going to happen?"

---

47 All the names are fictitious. If they match the names of any people that served with me, it is coincidental.

"I'd prefer this just remain between you and me." Again, the common response. At that point, I came out from behind my desk and sat in the empty of the two chairs that I position in front of my desk for just such impromptu "coaching" sessions.

"John," I said, "can we switch roles for a minute? I want you to be me, and I'll be you."

"Okay," he said with a quizzical look on his face. I sensed he was beginning to question the wisdom of his dropping in for a chat.

"Now, John, I want you to get into my head. As me, who are you and what is your job?"

"Well, I'd be the head of this organization, and I'd be responsible for seeing that things run smoothly and effectively—and that we are able to meet or exceed our commitments to the department and to the Academy."

"What's that feel like?" I asked.

"Actually, a little scary," he replied with a nervous laugh.

"Yes, I know just how you feel," I laughed. "Now, let's roll the tape forward, and someone on your staff has just told you that something is eating at the very fabric of your organization, and then he requests that you keep it just between him and you. Now, what are you thinking?"

"I guess I'm thinking, 'What good will that do?'" John replied. After a few seconds of reflection, he continued, "In fact, it will probably do harm. Nothing will get better, it will only get worse."

"Now I want you to get into Phil's head," I continued. "If you were Phil, how would you feel if I came to you and started probing to see if anything was bothering you or why you weren't meeting your commitments? Assume for present purposes that I was subtle and skillful in my questioning of Phil and did everything possible to keep him from getting upset; it is still likely he is going to ask, or to at least wonder, what instigated this conversation. And I would have to tell him that you and I had talked."

A few moments passed, and, with a sigh, he became John again. "I guess I'm going to be talking to Phil about this. And, as difficult as that conversation might be, it will probably be easier for me to go to him than to have him coming to me after hearing from you." His gaze had gone to the floor, but with another sigh, he looked at me with a smile and said, "I'm not looking forward to this, but I'll figure it out."

As he got up to leave, I said, "Look, John, I know talking to Phil won't be easy. Truth be told, I didn't find this conversation with you very easy. But if someone with your talent and promise can't work this problem out with Phil, who can? You aren't the only person to come into my office with similar complaints about others. We can't have people emoting over every perceived failure of a coworker to do his or her part, but if you feel strongly that a colleague's performance is getting in the way of you doing your job, or you need something from Phil that you are not getting to achieve our mission, then you must talk to him. If that doesn't work, *then* come to me."

"Thanks. I'll give it a try," he said, and with a handshake and pat on the back, he left.

John did approach Phil. The world did not come to an end, and they apparently resolved the issue. At least Phil stopped me in the hall and told me that John and he had talked and that the project would be on schedule.

Any successful relationship requires trust and respect. Building and maintaining trust and respect requires members of the group to talk to each other honestly about concerns. Any parent or spouse knows how difficult some conversations are, and they also know that the most difficult are often the most necessary if the relationship is going to succeed and grow. Fortunately, conversations among colleagues at work are seldom as difficult as family discussions.

Not all problems have to be resolved. Some do not interfere with work, and others go away. Judging which problems we can live with, which ones will go away, and which ones need to be addressed takes experience. But chances are that during important long-term projects, some colleague-related problems will need to be addressed. Developing a culture of respect and trust before the problems arise will make addressing them easier. When problems do arise, we have to approach the discussions with colleagues honestly and with both the present and future in mind. Having coworkers hold others accountable may cause temporary strains, but dealing straightforwardly with these strains maintains and strengthens the trust essential to achieve the aggressive goals that we have the responsibility to meet.

I knew that John would probably be sitting in my office again, but I also anticipated that in the not-too-distant future, people would be coming into his office with issues that they would need to resolve with colleagues. I hoped that his discussion with Phil—and with me—would prepare him to assist those who sought his help.

In response to a question in a session with new IBM executives, Gregg Demar, at the time IBM's managing director for Verizon, passed on a remark that a senior executive had made to him when he was a new executive. Gregg inquired as to the most important responsibility he had as an executive. The senior executive did not give him the reply he had expected, which was to "make your numbers and grow IBM!" Rather, he simply said, "Build organizational capability. All businesses have upturns and downturns—but long-term survival depends on the increased capability of the employees." An organization cannot build long-term capability without colleagues who trust and respect each other and who can discuss and work out differences among themselves. Leaders must model and foster the behaviors necessary for this to occur.

11

It Pays to Treat People Unjustly

He deserved a lower rating. I had a lot of officers to rate, and all were excellent—actually outstanding. All were instructors at the U.S. Military Academy, and you do not get that position based on looks or luck—at least none of mine had. The selection process is rigorous. You need to be good. And, while his performance was still stellar, his attitude had become anything but. He had become sullen and less communicative. The behaviors were subtle. More than being overtly negative, Matt[48] was just less positive. If you did not know him, you might not have noticed, but I knew him and so did the rest of the team. He was upset and angry, and we knew it. And I knew why.

Matt was already overworked, and I had given him yet more to do. Others were just as busy, which is why I had reluctantly given the extra work to him. It was a burden. However, he was an instructor; we had sent him to school to get a degree specifically in social psychology, and when enrollments in that program increased to the point that we

---

48 This is not the individual's name. Any resemblance of this name to anyone I served with at West Point is strictly coincidental. Although I do not feel I am putting this fine officer in a negative light, I do not want to take the chance he would see it differently.

needed to add an extra psychology section, he was the one most able to handle it.

The extra section was not the course he was presently teaching, so it meant a good deal of course preparation in a short period of time. Moreover, in addition to the course he was currently teaching, I had placed him in a leadership position that involved significant administrative duties that the others did not share. But having placed him in a position of leadership, I had the right to expect more exemplary behavior from him than he had displayed over the past three months. I had to take his attitude into account as I completed his annual Officer Efficiency Report (OER).

As I wrestled with what to do, my thoughts slipped back a decade or so to my time as a draftee undergoing the Primary Leadership Development Course and Advanced Individual Training at Fort Sam Houston, Texas.

"Fort Sam" was and remains the largest and most important military medical training facility in the world—and "Home to the Combat Medic." It is one of the Army's oldest posts and has a rich history. In 1910, for example, military aviation got its start on what is now the parade field.

The first soldiers arrived at Fort Sam in 1845, and the post has been in operation ever since.[49] Construction began in earnest in the 1870s under the supervision of a West Point–trained engineer, Major General Edward Ord. Today, the post has more than 900 buildings of historical significance, and in 1975, it was designated a National Historic Landmark. And, it seems that careful preservation of these structures was a key developmental methodology of the Primary Leadership Development Course.

We were housed in a barracks not far from the Quadrangle, which was completed in 1876. It is a park-like area where deer, peacocks, and other animals roam freely. It is also where Geronimo, the Apache war leader,

---

49 Much of the historical data is taken from http://en.wikipedia.org/wiki/Fort_Sam_Houston.

and other Apaches captured with him were held while the federal government debated whether they were prisoners of war or common criminals. It is a serene and beautiful place shared by some of the world's gentlest animals and the headquarters of the Fifth Army, one of the world's most powerful armies. The centerpiece of the Quadrangle is the clock tower, which is San Antonio's second-most-visited historic site—exceeded only by the Alamo. After initial processing into Fort Sam and the Primary Leadership Development Course, the training sergeants gave us our first orders, which were to prepare for inspection at 0530 the next day. They pointed out that they were going to inspect not only our uniforms and sleeping area but the entire facility.

I assume that we were housed in one of those structures that had caught the eyes of the historical preservation folks. It consisted of two buildings: the sleeping quarters and the latrine. The latrine was a thing of beauty—if not a joy forever. In my memory it was a massive building, but I suspect more accurately a large one—at least for a latrine. And "latrine" does not quite do it justice. It had more than a dozen urinals and an equal number of toilets along with sinks, showers, and numerous drains in what looked like a marble floor. The fixtures on every urinal, toilet, and sink and the drains in the floor were all of solid brass. It was the type of place that some years later came to my mind when listening to Annie's first impression of Daddy Warbucks' home: "Leaping lizards! Just look at this joint." And the sergeants' orders were the forerunner of Miss Hannigan's threat to the weary orphans: "Clean up this mess! . . . [T]his room had better be regulation before breakfast . . . Or kill, kill, kill! . . . . And if this floor don't shine like the top of the Chrysler Building, your backsides will. Y'understand?"[50]

Those of you who have never served in the military might not understand that my fellow trainees and I spent all but the last hour or so before the inspection just getting ready. And what minutes of sleep we got were on the floor next to our beds, not in them. As the training sergeant made his rounds, he stopped and paid close attention to my bunk. He then called all the other trainees over and announced

---

50 From *Annie* (the musical), music by Charles Strouse, lyrics by Martin Charnin, 1982 (http:// en.wikiquote.org/wiki/Annie_%28musical%29).

that this was what a well-made bed should look like. As he turned to leave, he hesitated, leaned over the neatly and tightly drawn blanket covering the bed and with his index finger, picked up a piece of lint, which he examined closely and held for all to see. This was quickly followed by his ripping the covers from the bed and letting me and all assembled know that I was not as good a steward of the government's resources as he had initially thought and that bedding was to be CLEAN and not a receptacle for garbage and other waste products! With that, he moved on, leaving me standing at attention beside a blanket, two sheets, and a pillowcase in a heap.

Having just completed Basic Combat Training,[51] I was not overly surprised or distressed at serving as a conscripted supporting actor in the action comedy called Initial Entry Training. Every drill sergeant, training sergeant, and at times company commander seemed totally devoted to the mission of getting into the head of each new recruit and draftee that he was now in the Army and "not back on the block." At times it was personal and necessary, and at others, you were merely a target of opportunity—a serendipitous foil for some sergeant to use a well-rehearsed line. With years and hindsight, one lesson I gleaned from that incident was that even small lapses can have grave consequences in battle, but somehow, I am not sure that that lesson was foremost in the training sergeant's mind. The most immediate lesson for me at the time was that making a bed twice was a lot easier than trying to get it perfect or near perfect the first time. I never failed another bunk inspection, but I also never made a bed as well as I made it that first night. I am not sure anybody could.

Such incidents ranged from the comical to the stupid to the downright mean. Approximately seven weeks later, we were out at Camp Bullis. Camp Bullis takes up about 12,000 acres of Leon Springs Military Reservation, which is located twenty miles or so from Fort Sam. It is a tranquil area, lush by Texas standards, and in the early twentieth century, in addition to being a military training site, it had been a favorite Hollywood movie location. *Wings*, which won the Academy Award for Best Picture in 1927 and in which Gary Cooper played a

---

51 Today it is called "Basic Training" (BT) rather than "Basic Combat Training" (BCT).

small part, was filmed there. A slightly larger section of the reservation is known as Camp Stanley. Camp Stanley was used mostly for storage and testing of ordnance materials. All other military activities at the Leon Springs Military Reservation were conducted at Camp Bullis. Camp Bullis was and is still used for firing ranges, maneuver areas for Army, Air Force, and Marine combat units, and field training of the various medical units from Fort Sam, which is why we were there.

After spending the day marching the nearly twenty miles from Fort Sam to Camp Bullis, we bivouacked, and at about 2200, we were finally in our pup tents for some much wanted and badly needed sleep. Within minutes, the tent I was sharing with a fellow soldier came falling down. I scrambled out from beneath the fallen tent to see Captain Weed, the company commander, proceeding down the line of about ten tents, kicking the tent pegs out. Without thinking who he was or who I was, I ran up to him and incredulously inquired, "What the hell are you doing?"

"Look down there," he said angrily. And without giving me a chance to respond, "See that tent at the end? Does that look like it is in line with the others?"

Admittedly, it was noticeably out of line, but not by much. I said, "So what?" only to myself. "Yes, sir," I replied, "I can see it is out of line—but do you tear down ten tents to get one in line?" Trying unsuccessfully to gain a more respectful tone, I continued. "Do you realize we have been up since 0400, marched all day, set up camp, and will be up tomorrow at 0500—and it is now 2200?" And, without giving him a chance to respond—I was not interested in his answer—I concluded with, "Sir, we are out here to see if we can apply what we've learned in the classroom about saving lives on the battlefield, not to see if we can get tents in formation! Now, I will see that tent gets straightened out, but let's let people get their rest so they can be at their best tomorrow."

Glaring at me, but also hesitant as to his next move, he angrily ordered, "Get that tent in line!"

"Yes, sir," I responded in a less than enthusiastic manner, and rendering a far-short-of-stellar salute, I walked to the far end of the line of tents, roused the two very worn-out soldiers, and we quickly got the tent in line. Meanwhile, my tent-mate and the two soldiers in the tent next to ours had returned our tents to their standing positions. The captain had left the area, and the three of them just looked at me, shaking their heads and smiling. "What's he going to do?" I muttered. "Send me to Vietnam?"

That encounter was the last time that I can remember speaking with Captain Weed. I suspect that he was as motivated to avoid me as I was him. And, as noted in a previous chapter, the payback came upon graduation when I did not get the promotion I had earned. I assume that he did not inflict more drastic retaliation because he did not want to put himself in the position of having to justify his actions in front of his superiors, which he would have no doubt had to have done.

There are a number of takeaways here. First, if you find yourself purposely avoiding one or more of your employees or if your employees are avoiding you, there is a problem, and it ought to be addressed in a positive manner.

More important, "truth to power" is often not given in an effective manner, and not infrequently, it is rendered at the point of exasperation. Focusing on *how* truth is conveyed is a lot easier than on *what* is conveyed. Rich DeSerio, an insightful colleague and manager at IBM from whom I often seek counsel, once put it this way: "Too often when you hold a mirror up to people, it magically turns into one of those two-way mirrors. You think you are holding the mirror for them to see their reflection, but they are on the other side looking through it as though it were a piece of glass and only seeing you." This impulse to ignore the face in the mirror and to look at the person holding it is understandable. It is a defensive maneuver that we all tend to make if we are not vigilant. We say we *want* feedback, but we *need* affirmation. The desire for feedback is a value, something we feel we ought to want. The hunger for affirmation, however, is a deep need as old as the species itself, and it pushes for satisfaction. So, our impulse is to impeach the witness. Leaders must be mindful of this predisposition and not give in to it. Resistance is not easy.

Leaders must recognize that an ineloquent or rude truth is no less *the truth*. Communications are always a mixture of content and emotion. Poor phraseology or an inappropriate tone makes the message no less true; the inartful delivery just makes diverting our attention from the message to the messenger easier. Leaders must take stock of the truth first and deal later with the fact that it may have been ineptly or embarrassingly delivered. The truth is about *them*; the clumsy manner in which it is brought to their attention is about someone else. Making this separation is difficult. Not only do leaders have to overcome the natural inclination to defend themselves, but there is also what psychologists call a *figure-ground* phenomenon at work.

Our perceptual field, generally speaking, is divided into two parts: *figure* and *ground*. The figure is what we notice, the information of which we are most consciously aware; the ground is what is not the focus of our attention, the information of which we take little note. A glaring outburst, as in my case with Captain Weed, is more noticeable and becomes figure, especially to Captain Weed. The message and the motivation behind its delivery become mere background and do not enter our conscious awareness unless we shift our attention and change our frame of reference. Bear in mind that although figure and ground are fixed properties of any situation, what is figure and what is ground is not. They shift as we change our focus.

We are continually engaging in selective attention. For centuries, philosophers and psychologists have been aware that our perception is not an accurate re-creation of the environment around us. Perception is an active process. There is just too much going on out there for us to attend to it all. So, our brain selectively attends to those things that it ascertains are most relevant to our current circumstances. For example, if we are at a large gathering and in conversation with the person next to us, we can follow that conversation because we screen out, or at least dampen down, the many other sounds, such as the other conversations, music, and laughter going on around us and entering our auditory sensory channel. However, should our name come up in a conversation some distance from us, we may start to attend to that conversation and not to what the person right next to us is saying. Much like when we are listening to a colleague on a conference call and we get an instant message, we are likely to respond to the instant message; although we have not lowered the volume on our speaker phone, we will inevitably lose track of the conversation. But if the person speaking refers to us by name, our attention is likely to revert quickly to the conversation on the phone.

Another undeniable fact is that truth spoken is truth heard—at least at some level. We cannot be unmoved by the truth. Our response may be to suppress, mask, or employ other means of distortion in an effort to keep truth in the shadowy ground of our conscious awareness—much like the din surrounding our personal conversation with a friend at a party—or our response may be to bring truth into the open, as figure, and use it as a means of self- and organizational improvement. That Captain Weed did not overtly discipline me for my outburst when many in his position would have done so attests to the fact that, at some level, he grasped the truth of what I said. Remarkably, he entertained this information long enough to hesitate and change course; many others would have employed sterner retribution to defend themselves and to highlight my egregious behavior. We can deny truth, but we cannot escape it.

So, what has all this to do with Captain Matt Marshall[52] and his rating? Remember him? Well, several things. First, at the end of the year when we are writing employee evaluations and determining bonuses and raises (if any), too often we hear, "The ratings are too high. We need more of a spread." We then must engage in activities that have us looking for the lint on the well-made bed and the one out of ten tents out of line as a means to justify lower ratings. In team-based decision-making sessions, common to most organizations, we start by making ordinal lists grouping people in the top, middle, and bottom third. Then we have to justify our list: "If Jack is in the middle third, how can he have the same rating as Jill in the top third?" And when that exercise does not result in the desired spread, we do lifeboat exercises: If you had to throw one of your people out, who would it be?

---

52 Matt Marshall is a fictitious name.

Not for a minute do I mean to undermine the key and necessary role managers play in performance differentiation. Rating performance and ranking employees requires consistency across the organization and must be done fairly. But almost always the concern is more about overrating people than underrating them. The end product of all this effort is that a majority of the people are demoralized. Moreover, contrived ratings make ongoing feedback throughout the year difficult. For example, if a manager's perception is that a person is exceeding his or her commitments and the manager continues to provide feedback in line with that appraisal, but then at the end of the year provides a rating that neither the employee nor manager would have predicted based on those interim feedback sessions, the result not only hurts morale but also makes performance management difficult.

Among other laudatory comments I made on Captain Marshall's efficiency report was, "Captain Marshall leads in such a manner that he creates a climate of high performance and high morale," and I noted him as a top performer. In providing that evaluation to him, he did not say much. However, three days later he came into my cubicle, sat down, and said, "Jack, I have not been the officer you described on my efficiency report."

"No, Matt," I replied, "but you will be."

And, truth be told, he always had been that officer—just not for three months. We discussed all that had taken place, and I had another opportunity to thank him for the extra load he had been carrying. Not only was Captain Marshall the officer I described for the rest of his tour, but he was among the very top officers I have ever known and that have ever served in the Army. Leadership often requires a leap of faith in others. Leaders have to believe in people before they perform, and when they do, people will strive to live up to the high expectations set.

My relationship with Captain Marshall and his performance could have gotten either better or worse. I believe if I had focused on Matt's deficiencies and set up a development plan, things would have gone perceptively downhill quickly. Focusing on what, truthfully, was an understandable reaction on his part, even if not the most desired, would have increased his sense that I had treated him unfairly, which would have made him more rankled and would have called for even more of my attention. The downward spiral would have been almost inevitable and because of my own actions. And now we are back to human perceptual processes.

A few years ago, I went to my second-line manager in an effort to get one of my people, Michael, promoted. He was a relatively new employee who had been an intern with us before we hired him. He had his Ph.D. from one of the world's most highly respected and academically rigorous programs. Yet, he also had a good measure of modesty and did not present himself as the authority on anything—though he was—at least when compared to the others sitting around the table. It was not uncommon for him in meetings to undersell his capability to achieve a goal, and he tended to look for confirmation and direction before acting. He did not lack ability, he lacked confidence—perhaps an admirable quality in a newly minted Ph.D. (something yet to be discovered in a new MBA). After making my case, my second-line manager responded, "You are telling me what Michael knows and can do, but I know what he can't do!" And he did not support going forward with the promotion.

A year later I approached my new first-line manager about Michael's promotion. He was supportive and made it happen. Within a year, the second-line manager was stating that Michael was the organization's most important asset and saw to it that the company invested extra financial incentives as a means to retain him. This type of incentive is a rare occurrence for a nonexecutive employee. Michael deserved it. He is still modest but more confident, and when there is a priority project important to the organization's mission, Michael is involved as either the lead or a key player, and his input is always sound and respected. Had we focused on what he did not know, he likely would have been stripped of what little confidence he had and at best become an obedient and compliant employee exemplifying best practices, but not a leader. We do not build confidence by focusing on the lack of it and on weakness. We build confidence by recognizing talent, giving responsibility, and enabling success—and having high expectations.

Remember, our perception is an active process involving selection, inference, and interpretation. What we perceive is interplay between our experiences and our expectations. Our brains form a readiness or a bias for us to perceive certain available data and to ignore others. That brain function helps us predict our environment, which not only increases our safety but also keeps us from having to understand every new experience from scratch. Therefore, if we expect something to occur, we are more likely to recognize it than if we do not expect the occurrence. This predisposition is called *perceptual set*. For example, if you are reading a *Bugs Bunny* comic and then are shown the picture above, you will likely see a rabbit. However, if you were reading a *Donald Duck* comic, you would most likely see the figure as a bird.[53]

As interesting as perceptual set may be, one consequence of this phenomenon that is vital for leaders to understand is *self-fulfilling prophecy*. Self-fulfilling prophecy refers to the scientific finding that our expectations about events *and people* will affect our behavior in such a way that we unknowingly create the expected outcome. In the classic study by Robert Rosenthal,[54] he gave elementary school children a test at the beginning of the year. He then informed the teachers that certain of the students had been discovered to be "late bloomers" and would show great academic gains as the year progressed, when in fact they were selected at random and were no different than those not so identified. Any differences between these children and the rest

---

53 http://mathworld.wolfram.com/Rabbit-DuckIllusion.html.
54 Robert Rosenthal, *Experimental Effects in Behavioral Research* (New York: Appleton-Century-Crofts, 1966). Also, Robert Rosenthal and Lenore Jacobson, *Pygmalion in the Classroom* (New York: Holt, Rinehart & Winston, 1968).

of the class existed only in the heads of the teachers. Several months later, the teachers rated the so-called late bloomers as more inquisitive and interested in their work than their classmates. They were even perceived as happier. Most dramatic and important was that all the students were given IQ tests both at the beginning and end of the year. The data indicated that those singled out as late bloomers had significantly greater increases in IQ compared to their classmates.

Rosenthal concluded that a self-fulfilling prophecy was at work. The teachers had subtly and unknowingly encouraged the performance they expected to see. They spent more time with these students; they were also more enthusiastic about teaching them and unintentionally showed more warmth to them than to the other students. What is essential to understand is that the expectation not only affected the behavior of the person holding those expectations but the students' behavior and performance as well, even though the students had no idea of what was going on. This experiment has been replicated many times in many different settings with similar results.

Even before the concept of a self-fulfilling prophesy was scientifically demonstrated, it was vividly and entertainingly brought to life in the 1960s musical *My Fair Lady* by Alan Jay Lerner and Frederick Lowe and in the subsequent movie (1964), both based on the George Bernard Shaw play *Pygmalion* (1912). The story centers on Professor Henry Higgins' declaration to his friend Colonel Hugh Pickering that he could make a lady out of a flower girl. Or as he put it: "I'll make a duchess of this draggle-tailed guttersnipe."[55] The draggle-tailed guttersnipe was Eliza Doolittle. Professor Higgins sets about to achieve his goal by teaching Eliza proper grammar and enunciation and by instructing her in etiquette and proper dress.

In the end, Eliza produces this insight to Professor Higgins' mother: "You see, Mrs. Higgins, apart from the things one can pick up, *the difference between a lady and a flower girl is not how she behaves, but how she is treated* [italics added]." She continues, "I shall always be a flower girl to Professor Higgins, because he always treats me as a flower

---

55 http://www.allmusicals.com/lyrics/myfairladyscript/myfairladyscript.htm.

girl, and always will. But I know that I shall always be a lady to Colonel Pickering, because he always treats me as a lady, and always will."

Later Professor Higgins takes exception to what Eliza had said. He retorts, "My manners are exactly the same as Colonel Pickering."

Eliza pushes back, "That's not true; he treats a flower girl as if she were a duchess."

To which Professor Higgins replies, "Well, I treat a duchess as if she was a flower girl."

Good leaders forge positive self-fulfilling prophecies! They make duchesses out of flower girls—not flower girls out of duchesses.

12

Just Names

"Why do you want to stop here? It's just a bunch of f__ing names!" The question and self-supplied answer ring in my head, if not my ears, these thirty-five years later. Stopping and turning my head, I came nearly face-to-face with a handsome young man. He looked as though he were auditioning to be a model for Brooks Brothers. It was a clear, warm August day in the nation's capital; he had a tennis sweater neatly tied around his neck, a patterned blue shirt, and a better-than-department-store set of khakis. I could imagine he had a girlfriend equally attractive, from a well-to-do family, and in the best sorority on campus.

He was stunning. But more stunning was his behavior. He was calling to a friend who had gotten ahead of him. But why so foul? Why so loud? And why here?

Brad Scott, a close friend and colleague, and I were in Washington to attend the American Psychological Association's annual convention. At the time, we were Army officers teaching at the U.S. Military Academy at West Point. We had taken a break from the sessions and decided to visit the Vietnam Veterans Memorial. Brad, a younger officer, had continued to walk as I stopped at the entrance. Intuitively, he knew I would appreciate some time alone here. I had stopped to look at the guide to find the location of Brent Law's name. In the fall of 1969, Brent and I had trained together as combat medics at Fort Sam Houston in San Antonio, Texas. Upon graduation, as was the case with most of the other soldiers in our training battalion, we received orders to Vietnam. The government was charitable enough to allow us a Christmas leave before reporting.

By happenstance, Brent and I had run into each other when we arrived at the airport in Oakland, California, and along with Harold Kellogg, another medic we bumped into at the airport, we hung out together that night before we had to sign in at the debarkation point at Travis AFB the next day. Once at the debarkation point, we joined hundreds of other soldiers who were now restricted to a large hanger, where we spent another two days or so playing cards and just milling around waiting for a manifest with our names on it. Again, as chance would have it, Brent and I flew over to Vietnam together. We landed at Bien Hoa on January 7, 1970, and ended up at the sprawling logistics and replacement center at Long Binh.

At Long Binh, we waited around again for a few days. The Army is known for "hurry up and wait," but there was no hurry-up at Long Binh—just wait. Finally, we were told to assemble, and we stood in a long line with a sergeant at the other end with a list of destinations. When I reached him and reported "PFC Beach," looking at his list he said, "Phu Bai."

"Where is that?" I asked.

He replied, "Up north, Hue, 101st Airborne Division."

"I don't have wings," I murmured (i.e., I'm not airborne qualified). "Are you sure that is correct?"

"You're a medic. The puking buzzard needs medics. Make peace with your god, son. Now, get out of my line."

I moved to the area where I was to get the plane for the seven-hundred-mile flight north—and there again was Brent. He too was headed to the 101st. To tell the truth, I was pretty psyched to know I would be serving with the 101st Airborne Division—the famed Screaming Eagles. And, I have to admit, I was also excited that I would get to see Hue, which had been the capital and imperial city when Vietnam was ruled by emperors. It was well known for the battles that took place there during the Tet Offensive in 1968. At the time, my excitement far outweighed any apprehensions I might have had.

The several-hour flight to Phu Bai made clear that the Army was making no effort to interest passengers in joining its frequent flyer program. I was not an experienced flier. Until I was in the Army, I had never been on a plane. But even an inexperienced flier could tell that this was not a flight bound by FAA flight-safety regulations. We boarded a C-130, which is a four-engine turboprop aircraft most often used for cargo. There were no seats. We sat on the floor. When the plane took off, we slid to the back, and when it landed, we slid forward. No "secure all carry-ons" or "fasten your safety belts" or "we know you have a choice in airlines, and we appreciate your business" on this ride. In flight, the fuselage of the plane made creaking sounds, and vapors hissed from tubing along the ceiling. Nothing about this experience encouraged a feeling that the country that had invited me to Vietnam cared about my comfort—or safety.

We landed about midnight at a small airfield just outside of Camp Campbell, where dinner consisted of the C-rations that those who had eaten earlier in the evening had not chosen—no spaghetti and meatballs or beans and franks, just ham and lima beans. They were not my favorites when served separately, but mixed together in a can, I just was not that hungry. We spent the night there, and the next day we went through some initial processing. The clerk looked at my file and then at me and declared, "You don't want to be a medic." I must have looked surprised—which I was. "You have six years of college; we can use you other places."

"I've been trained to be a medic, and that is what I want to be," I replied.

"Look, this is the 101st—the f__ing puking buzzard. There are no hospitals here. You are not going to be wearing whites and emptying bedpans."

I knew he was trying to help me, but I reaffirmed my desire to do what I had been trained to do—to be a combat medic. With one last look at me, he made a few marks in the file and sent me on my way.

We soon boarded trucks and drove north on Highway 1, the same stretch that the French troops who had fought in the first Indochina war called La Rue Sans Joie (Street Without Joy) and which Bernard Fall chronicled in a book by the same name. Many lives had been lost along this highway. At the head of the convoy was a truck armed with a 50-caliber machine gun and emblazoned with "Grim Reaper" and a hooded figure with a scythe on the side. At the rear was an equally equipped truck: "The Devil's Agent." Except for the two guns and the war paint, we were exposed to whatever might happen.

While I still had a fair amount of a youthful sense of adventure, the apprehension that had begun to creep in during the flight to Phu Bai was increasingly present. "Highway" was a bit of an overstatement. The road was barely two lanes wide; there were no lane lines or shoulders, and we shared it with other vehicles—mostly motor scooters, some small cars, and other military trucks, in addition to people walking and young boys prodding water buffalos. I kept thinking that the convoy drivers were not showing adequate concern for the size of the trucks and the width of the road. Since we were by far the largest vehicles on the road, I am sure our drivers were delegating that concern to those who shared the road with us.

Alongside the road were mostly rice paddies with an occasional cluster of tiny huts and houses made of cement blocks, wood, and corrugated tin. Some of the roofs were thatched. And at every bridge, no matter how small, were ARVN (Army of the Republic of Vietnam) soldiers living in pup tents and guarding the bridges from attack. After a few hours, we ended up at Camp Evans for the normal in-country training before being sent to our units. Officially, the in-country training was called SERTS (Screaming Eagle Replacement Training School). We learned how to set up claymore mines, fire an M-60 machine gun, and set up ambushes, and we went on patrols.

I was also adjusting to the weather. I had expected it to be wet, which it was. The Hue-Phu Bai area is one of the wettest in Vietnam, and January is still under the influence of the northwestern monsoon, which is the rainy season. What I had not expected was it to be cold—relatively speaking. January is the coldest month, with the average temperature in the sixties, but at night it often was in the low fifties or forties. Although mild compared to the temperatures in New York where I was raised and in Maine where we had lived for the past two years, when you are wet and with no source of heat, it was uncomfortably chilly at night. We had been told to leave our field jackets in bins at Travis AFB before we got on the planes. So, we were not well equipped for the cooler temperatures. I began to wonder if the folks who had told us to leave our field jackets in the States had ever been to Vietnam. Admittedly, we would not have needed them much of the time—but it would have been nice to have had them in January.

With the six days of training completed, both Brent and I and a third comrade from our medic training at Fort Sam Houston, Chris Christopherson, ended up with the 326th Medical Battalion at Camp Eagle, the base camp for the 101st Airborne Division. It was in what was called I Corps. Vietnam was divided into four military regions from North to South (I Corps Tactical Zone, II Corps Tactical Zone, III Corps Tactical Zone, and IV Corps Tactical Zone). I Corps was the northern-most military region. The base was situated in a narrow coastal strip in Thua Thien-Hue Tri Province about forty-five miles from the DMZ. The South China Sea was ten miles to the east, the Annamite Mountains were about thirty miles to the west, and Hue was about four miles to the north. Given the topography of the general area and the proximity to the remains of the ancient Citadel in Hue, I could not help but think to myself, "This will be a great tourist spot—someday."

My assignment to the 326th Medical Battalion was not the result of careful consideration of my skills and the nation's needs by anyone in the Pentagon or anywhere else. For whatever reason, they did not have a set of orders for me, and so the sergeant, after a minimal search for my orders and without seeking any guidance from a superior, took a piece of paper from the trash can next to his desk, wrote a note assigning me, and without expending the energy of looking up, directed us to leave with a flick of his finger. Though disconcerted that the Army apparently had sent me to Vietnam without knowing where I was going or what I was going to do when I got there and that my fate was going to be determined by a less than deliberative sergeant's notes scribbled on a piece of wastepaper, I was in no position to question this act of creative administration. Brent, ever cheerful, snickered, "Was that guy awake?"

Brent and I had trained together, flown over to Vietnam together, served together, but we did not return together. On July 21, 1970, Brent was killed when the Medevac helicopter he was riding in came under fire while making a desperate attempt to extract wounded fellow soldiers on Fire Support Base (FSB) Ripcord. I had seen Brent just hours earlier. He had shown me a hole in his flight suit where a bullet had passed through, just missing his shin. I had jokingly said, "Come work with me. You've had enough fun."

And with his ever-present smile and ever-ready happy quip, he confirmed, "I'm having too much fun."

"Take care," I replied, patted him on the back, and left—having no inkling that this would be our last conversation and that, for Brent, just how little time remained. I envied him. He was doing what I wanted to do.

Ripcord was a FSB on the eastern perimeter of the A Shau Valley near the Laotian border—often referred to by the marines and soldiers who fought there as the "Ah Sh_t Valley" because of the tough terrain, very limited vision due to the incredibly dense forest growth, and the infestation of poisonous snakes and insects—not to mention large numbers of very effectively concealed enemy soldiers. It was not a good place to be.

The idea had been to secretly set up a fire base to support and provide artillery protection for a planned offensive against enemy supply bases in the area. Unfortunately, this activity had not gone unnoticed by the

North Vietnamese. Their reconnaissance teams had been observing the rebuilding of this firebase, and enemy troops had massed for an attack. Eight battalions, approximately twenty-five thousand enemy soldiers, were in the area, and on the night of July 1, 1970, about four thousand of them launched a surprise attack. Firing small arms, mortars, and artillery, they assaulted the base, which was defended by about four hundred soldiers from the 101st Airborne Division.

Outnumbered ten to one, the soldiers on the firebase had fought under constant fire for twenty-one days. Three days before, on July 18, the enemy had shot down a CH 47 (Chinook) aircraft. The aircraft and the sling of 105 mm ammunition it was carrying crashed into an ammunition storage area on the base and burst into flames. The resulting fire and explosions of munitions went on for eight hours. The mishap destroyed all but one of the 105 mm howitzers on the firebase, and the gun that remained was badly damaged. Needless to say, the defensive capabilities of the firebase were greatly diminished. Under heavy enemy fire, Brent and the other members of the helicopter crew willingly and selflessly flew to evacuate the wounded from the crippled firebase. Their Medevac chopper was unarmed except for the personal weapons that the crew carried for their protection should they end up on the ground. During two and a half hours, the five-man crew made five runs to Ripcord. When they landed at Ripcord for the fifth time, North Vietnamese were overrunning the base. The crew piled wounded onto the floor of the helicopter and struggled to lift off, but before they could clear the area, a North Vietnamese soldier sprayed the helicopter with his AK-47. The enemy fire punctured the helicopter's Plexiglas windshield. One round blew off the co-pilot's arm, fragmented, and struck Brent just below his protective vest. The fragment pierced Brent's liver. He bled to death on the chopper floor. For this action, Brent was posthumously awarded the Purple Heart and Silver Star— and his name was etched in granite on "The Wall."

I learned of Brent's death from the company's first sergeant. After a moment of silence to soak it in, I asked what the division's next move was, and he informed me that the order had been given to extract all the remaining personnel, abandon the firebase, and carpet bomb the surrounding area. "Why?" I asked. And with some hesitation, he replied,

"I guess it was determined they had accomplished their mission." So, on July 23, two days after Brent's death, the beleaguered firebase was evacuated.

The cost in American lives during those twenty-three days of fighting was sixty-eight dead and four hundred and forty-eight wounded. Counting from the initial reopening of the firebase in April, the number of American soldiers killed in the battle for Firebase Ripcord was two hundred and forty-eight. It was the last major confrontation of the war between American soldiers and the North Vietnamese, and it was difficult for many of us to see it as anything but a crushing American defeat. I could not help thinking, "Why had they not just carpet bombed the area in the first place?" Carpet bombing areas in Vietnam was a controversial tactic because it risked killing civilians and destroying crops—or killing nothing but trees. However, this was not a populated area where such a tactic would have risked civilian casualties or damage to crops.

The official After Action Report confirmed some of the cynicism I felt. It mentioned as factors critical in the decision to close FSB Ripcord the domestic and foreign political concerns and adverse publicity that might arise if another U.S. firebase underwent a siege like that which the Americans had suffered at Khe Sanh or the French at Dien Bien Phu. Not mentioned, but believed by many, was that continued losses at Ripcord would have brought into question the strategic value of the area and the wisdom of the initial decision to man Ripcord so lightly. Such a discussion might have raised another Hamburger Hill controversy. In fact, later reports indicated that the senior military leaders tried to play down the entire event. They discouraged the press from visiting Ripcord, and until they could no longer hide the facts, they insisted that the casualties were "light."

Just a year before, not far from FSB Ripcord, U.S. commanders had ordered a direct assault on Hill 937, which the press and the troops later dubbed "Hamburger Hill" because the soldiers who took that hill compared the assault to being put through a meat grinder. The direct assault, a controversial tactic to begin with, resulted in massive U.S. casualties. To make matters worse, soon after the hill was taken, it was abandoned because it was considered of little strategic value. The parallels between FSB Ripcord and Hamburger Hill turned my initial sadness at learning of Brent's death into a mix of anger and bitterness. Questionable decisions by the military leadership that showed such lack of concern for those under their command were the source of the nihilism that so many troops expressed by the oft-repeated phrase, "It don't mean nothin'!" And now a man about Brent's age at the time of his death was dismissing the list on the Vietnam Memorial as "just f__ing names!"

Fighting my emotions, I continued to walk the pathway beside the one hundred and forty-four panels of the gabbro wall. For many the wall is a tourist attraction, but for others it is a compelling pilgrimage. It is a place where burly men hug, mothers bring children to see the name of the father they never got to know, and parents come to assure themselves that the nation has not forgotten and will never forget their son's or daughter's sacrifice—and that their children's lives mattered not just to them but to others. I do not know whether it was the disrespectful and profane youth or the symbolism of the tapering walls signifying the deepening wounds as one walks toward the apex of the monument, but emotion was taking hold. Yet I did not want to open the wound. I wanted to close it. This is not a place for confrontation. It is a place for quiet reflection.

For me, the simplicity of the monument is inspiring. This dark coarse rock when smoothed has a luster that reflects the image of the onlooker as well as highlights the engraved names. Yes, they are *just names*—no ranks, no awards, just the honored dead. All having made an equal sacrifice. All equally deserving of their nation's gratitude. The names are listed in the chronological order in which the men and women died, starting on panel 01E and going to panel 70W. They are *just names*, but repeated in solemn and caring whispers. It is not a meaningless list of *just names*, for whom time spent acknowledging their sacrifice, not for self-gain but for others, is time wasted. And it certainly is not the dismissive "*just a bunch of f__ing names.*" I arrived at panel 08W, and there on line 38 was Brent Law—just his name. But I could no longer hold back my tears—nor did I care to. His death and those of the 58,266 others deserve our respect and our grateful appreciation.

Perhaps in a flight of self-absorption as I turned to rejoin my colleague, Brad, my thoughts were not just of Brent and all those who had not returned but of those of us who had. My mind went back to another day: November 29, 1970. It was the day to which I had been counting down for almost a year. It was the day I left Vietnam and "returned to the world." Time zones being what they are, we left Vietnam and arrived in the States at about the same time. Our flight had left about 0400 on November 29, the Sunday after Thanksgiving. We went from Vietnam to Japan and were supposed to land at Seattle-Tacoma Airport in the state of Washington. As we made our descent, the pilot suddenly and precipitously aborted the landing. He eventually came on the speaker and announced that there was too much ground fog and that since we did not have enough fuel to circle, we were heading to Vancouver, British Columbia, Canada.

Once safely on the ground in Vancouver, the civilian crew had flown their requisite hours, so they deplaned. Not making matters any better, we were foreign troops on foreign soil, and the Canadian authorities would not let us off the plane. As I recall, we just sat there most of the day—no food, no information. Surprising to me, as I remember it, we all just rested and quietly sat. There was no protest. Finally, after many hours, buses drove up to the plane, customs agents got on and cleared us, and we got off the plane directly onto the buses for the four-hour ride to Fort Lewis, Washington. There we got measured for new uniforms so we would look our best when we arrived at our final destinations. As luck would have it, however, the truck bringing us our new uniforms broke down, so we had another two hours of waiting around. At least this time we had food. The Army had constructed a steakhouse on base specifically for those returning from Vietnam. The idea was that while we were waiting for our uniforms to be tailored, we could enjoy a free steak dinner. The free dinner made the waiting durable. The steakhouse was not elaborate, but it was evidence that someone in the Army bureaucracy cared.

Late in the evening, I finally got to the Seattle-Tacoma Airport. Given that it was the last day of the Thanksgiving vacation and there was an airline strike, the lines for the available flights were very long. I was confident, however, because I already had a ticket. Standing in line was one large and very loud woman saying, "Look at all these mother-f__ing GIs. They're going to get preference for seats over us." She was talking to those around her but with an amplification that was not intended for a private conversation. There were hundreds of GIs because several planes of returning soldiers arrived each day, and the bad weather and the strike had disrupted the normal flow. Minutes later, I heard another quieter voice from a young woman standing right behind me saying, "Watch out. Be careful." I looked around at a very 60s-looking couple. The man was holding a cute toddler in his arms. The cigarette he was also holding had touched the sleeve of my uniform and singed it. His response was, "It don't matter. He's just a GI."

The dark brown mark on my new uniform was probably accidental; the lack of regard for me and my service was intentional and burned much more deeply. Exhausted and not looking for a confrontation, I did not respond other than to brush off my sleeve. When I got to the counter, I was told that the ticket I had was not good on a holiday weekend and that I would have to fly standby. I protested that I had specifically asked about restrictions when I purchased the discount ticket in Vietnam and was told there were no blackout dates—but to no avail. I had to fly standby, which was going to take a while. Things were not going well. The USO had a room with bunks. They also had a list of departing planes and would wake you in time to get to the gate. I went to sleep— but at the airport, not at home with my wife, which had been my hope and expectation.

I got a flight the next day, but it was not a direct flight to my final destination. I settled for getting to New York City. Albany airport, which was much closer to my home, was my desired final destination. I landed at LaGuardia on Long Island. However, because of the airline strike, there were no flights from LaGuardia to Albany. So I had to get to Kennedy, which I did by bus. Once there, the attendant at the ticket counter told me that there were no available seats. He was very reluctant to sell me a ticket that would at least get me on the standby list. At this point, I lost patience. I leaned across the counter and got in his face, literally and figuratively. He sold me the ticket. It seemed everyone from New York was at the gate. It was packed, and I was still sitting there when all the passengers were on. Now, sitting alone, I resolved to get a bus. As I got up to leave, I asked the attendant at the gate if she knew how to get to the Port Authority where I could get a bus to my hometown of Catskill, New York. She informed me a bus would be the cheapest, but she also informed me there was seating available on the plane and I could get on if I wanted. If I wanted?! Would anyone have told me if I had not approached the gate attendant?

I finally did get home. When I entered the apartment, Brandon, our firstborn and my yet unseen nine-month-old son, was dressed in tan overalls and a yellow mock turtleneck shirt, standing in his playpen. With his big brown eyes, he looked quizzically at me and then back at his mother. I stood and gazed awhile before slowly approaching and picking him up. He permitted me to do so, but he kept his eyes fixed on Maureen for reassurance. He was all his mother: dark hair, dark brown eyes, and beautiful. It was great to be home.

After having been home a week, Maureen and I decided to go to Maine to see some friends and check to see that everything was set for my return to graduate school at the University of Maine that fall. When we arrived, I discovered that the University had a record of my graduating with my master's degree but no longer had me enrolled in the Ph.D. program. Fortunately, the head of the psychology department remembered me, and I was able to reenroll.

We were staying with friends, Jim and Margaret Greenough. Jim was a fellow graduate student. The next day when we got up to leave, our car was gone. Frustrated, I called the police to report a stolen car. They said to check to see if by chance it had been towed. Since I had parked outside my friend's house, on a residential street, right next to his and other cars, and they were all there, I did not think towing was a reasonable explanation.

Reasonable or not, my car had been towed, and it was going to cost me sixty dollars to get it back. I was a mixture of totally bewildered and really ticked. So I went to the local police station to inquire about why my car had been towed. I was told that every day during the first week of November a notice had been printed in the local paper to let people know that, for snow removal purposes, cars could not be parked within fifty feet of a corner. I protested that I was from out of state, there was no sign to let nonresidents know of the regulation, it had not snowed, and besides, during the first week of November, I was in Vietnam. The police officer's response was, "Don't think you'll get any special consideration just because you were in Vietnam. I was in Korea."

"I'm not looking for special consideration," I retorted, "just common sense and common decency." I asked if there were someone else I could speak to and was taken to the town manager or some sort of civilian official, I am not really sure who, but his response was identical: "Don't expect any special treatment because you served in Vietnam." Realizing my continued protests would be to no avail, I paid the sixty dollars, which, considering that my monthly pay was only a little over two hundred dollars, was a lot of money.

It was now close to noon, and my wife and I, already feeling as if we had had a very long day, decided to go into the diner at the University Motor Inn in Orono, Maine, to get a quick bite to eat. We sat at the counter and an older woman—probably younger than I am today—was waiting on us. She said the perfunctory "How are you today?" and I, still upset, told her the events of the day. When I was done, she put down the coffeepot she had in her hand, looked me in the eye, and said, "I'm not a very educated person, and I don't know much about foreign affairs. And I don't know if we should be over there in Vietnam or not. But I want to thank you for your service." I broke down and cried. I still do.

This has been the longest of my stories and heavier in tone than the others. There are numerous messages here, but I want to highlight just one. And that is a seemingly obvious one: Care for your people. Be ever mindful of their welfare, and show appreciation for their work *and* their effort. People are an organization's most valuable resource. And their well-being and commitment are crucial to its long-term success. Demonstrating concern and showing appreciation are among the simplest and most powerful leadership behaviors. But in a results-only world, we too often view showing concern or expressing appreciation as unnecessary and inconsistent with "no-nonsense leadership."

A short while ago, I was talking with one of the nation's most successful and talented business leaders. We were talking about leadership and performance. She stated, "I'm tired of people telling me, 'I'm giving 110 percent' or 'I'm minus 25 percent; I'm below empty.' People need to do what needs to be done!" I held my tongue, an unusual behavior on my part. Unquestionably, she is a decent, well-intended, capable executive and deserves the success she has earned, but I wondered if she fully grasped what she was saying. I could not help but think of names etched in a wall to honor people who had given "their last full measure of devotion" but who had ultimately failed in their mission. Outcomes frequently are not solely the result of effort and motivation; admittedly effort and motivation give a competitive advantage, but great effort, ingenuity, and courage on the part of people executing a mission do not always determine the outcome. We need to honor effort as well as specific outcomes. Committed effort is one of the best guarantors of long-term success.

In our performance-oriented world, with its laser focus on short-term results, we too often assume lack of success is solely the result of lack of motivation and failure on the part of those tasked to execute. How often do senior people explain lack of performance on "a failure to execute"? The message is, "You folks below us are at fault." True as this may at times be, it is not always the case, and in almost all instances, the lack of successful execution of a strategy or failure to accomplish the given missions is not solely the fault of those on the front lines. Few would argue the American defeat at Ripcord or the outcome of the war in Southeast Asia was solely the fault of those on the ground who were tasked to execute the strategy.

I am not suggesting that all papers students turn in deserve praise and a good grade or that every soccer player should get a trophy at the end of the season or that employees who put in time but little competent effort deserve bonuses. However, in today's interconnected global marketplace, with the relentless innovation cycle and merciless competition, where maximum return on investment is paramount and technology has not only made us more efficient but has also made us available anytime and anywhere, and vacations often amount to work from home (or wherever you happen to be), people are working almost constantly and making significant sacrifices in their efforts to do well and help their companies succeed. While leaders need to acknowledge maximum effort, leaders also have a duty to ensure that employees understand that they are entitled to reasonable limits on access and availability and that setting such boundaries is not seen as lack of commitment.

Finding fault is not difficult, and sometimes people in leadership positions seem to justify their status by showing others how what they have done could have been even better. Moreover, sometimes people in leadership positions feel a need to demonstrate their idea of "toughness" and to be "no-nonsense leaders." There is nothing wrong with a no-nonsense approach. But toughness does not justify a lack of care and concern for employees' welfare. All too often, bosses—and I say "bosses," not "leaders"—send people away feeling deflated, less confident, and sapped of their energy. People should always leave feeling more capable of contributing—even if mistakes need to be corrected.

Leaders care. Brigadier General (ret) Howard Prince, a decorated war hero and the first Professor and Head of the Department of Behavioral Sciences and Leadership at the United States Military Academy at West Point, is a man who sets extremely high standards for himself, those who work with him, and the students in his classes. In spite of his toughness, he also fully understands the importance of showing care and consideration for those from whom he demands so much. While at the Academy, he endured gibes from some of his colleagues for being too "touchy-feely." His response was straightforward, "I'm not sure what 'touchy-feely' means, but if it means we develop leaders who care for their troops, I embrace it." All leaders should.

13

On Leadership and Kite Flying

It was Memorial Day. We were starting what has become our annual family vacation at Nags Head, North Carolina. It is a tradition my son, Brandon, and his wife, Julia, started. In 2001, they had married on the beach at Nags Head at sunrise! I have to tell you, with no canopy or Plan B for bad weather—and the thought of guests having to be dressed and ready for a formal wedding, except for bare feet, at about 6:00 A.M.—the plan did not inspire a lot of confidence in their judgment. However, the result was spectacular. The weather and sunrise could not have been more beautiful if we had been able to select them from a catalogue. Since then, we have all—our families as well as Julia's parents, siblings, and their families—gathered at Nags Head.

Walking into the beach cottage having completed my morning run, I was greeted by joyful shouts of "Pop-Pop" from our two grandsons, Pierce, almost five, and Jacky, three and a half. They were eating their breakfast at the long table that stretched the width of the house. Such exuberant greetings from one's grandchildren make all the trials of raising their parents worthwhile!

Mimicking their enthusiasm, I replied, "Good morning," and with some hesitancy, "Do you know what day this is?" Jacky ignored the question and continued to devour his cereal, but after a momentary quizzical look, Pierce with his eyes closed and a clinched-teeth smile, chirped, "Vacation day!" Clearly my question was one I knew would not be answered, at least not correctly, and one Pierce felt no need to take seriously. And I have to admit some disquiet with the asking, but frankly, I felt compelled to do so.

"It's Memorial Day." Maybe it was because I had spent a career in the Army, served in combat, and lost a friend and several acquaintances in battle, or maybe it was because just the Friday before a colleague at work had, with all good intentions, wished me a "Happy Memorial Day." "Thanks," I said, but it did not sit well with me. When I was Pierce's and Jacky's age, it was called Decoration Day, and it came on May 30th. We would decorate our bikes with red, white, and blue crepe paper and follow the parade through the village to the cemetery, where someone would recite "In Flanders Fields" and the Gettysburg Address. A bugler would sound "Taps" with an echo in the distance, followed by a 21-gun salute. In the late 1960s, the name was officially changed to Memorial Day. And it ceased to be a day and became *a weekend*—the commercial start of summer—"Vacation Day!"

A few years ago, my wife and I took a cruise on the Queen Mary 2 during November. November is when the British and their former commonwealth nations mark what they call Remembrance Day. The ship's captain led a Remembrance Day service. The grand hall was filled. Everyone was dressed up. It was a dignified, poignant, and uplifting event. The losses, though painful, were in service of great causes, not in pursuit of personal gain, so that we and others could have the freedoms we enjoy. All left feeling inspired by the sacrifices others had made on our behalf and aware of the obligations we each had to live the values for which they had died. I wanted our grandsons to know that such service is vital to any country's survival and should be celebrated as a day, or at least part of a day, of solemn remembrance and deep gratitude for all those who died so others could be having a good day—in fact, 365 of them each year.

"Memorial Day," I continued, "is a very special day when all of us—grown-ups, anyway—take some time to remember soldiers who went to war but didn't come back." Jacky continued to eat, but the bewildered look had returned to Pierce's face, and with a bit more seriousness to his tone, he said, "Pop-Pop, Maimy [their name for their Aunt Amy] said she was going to get us kites to fly."

Okay, I had done my job. It was as much of a civics lesson as a three-and-a-half- and an almost-five-year-old could handle. And, on my run, I had stopped to right a small flag that had blown over. Now it was time to, well, have fun. I sensed that the honored dead got all they needed and that they felt good that we could have some fun. It probably made their sacrifice worthwhile. And if Pierce remembered it was a special day, maybe not a conceptual understanding but a feeling of seriousness, even if momentary, to the day he had not before felt, I had achieved my purpose for this year.

I proceeded through the house, out the back door, and into the ocean to cool down—which happens immediately in the temperature of the Atlantic off the coast of North Carolina in May. When I came out, my daughter Amy was assembling one of the two kites she had bought while Pierce stood by being as patient as a soon-to-be-five-year-old can be when filled with the expectation of flying his first kite. Down the beach a short distance, he could see a dragon-shaped kite with many tails soaring above the gulls, which swooped up and then landed again to clean the beach of any edible pieces of debris they could find. It was a near-perfect day to fly a kite, clear with a moderate breeze.

"Can I fly it now, Maimy?" Pierce eagerly inquired, as Amy, with the kite now assembled, headed down the beach.

"Just a minute, Piercey," Amy replied. "Let me get it started, and then you can fly it." Having completed the kite assembly, Amy started running into the wind along the beach, but to her disappointment, as she let the string out, the kite failed to take flight and would fall immediately to the ground as soon as she stopped running. Making matters worse, while running she stepped on a broken shell, which added physical pain to her emotional frustration.

Doing what dads and grandfathers do, I reflexively intervened. "What seems to be the problem, Amy?"

"These cheapo kites don't fly." Her voice and expression, though calm, manifested a mixture of annoyance, frustration, and disappointment. Helping Pierce and Jacky fly their first kites was something she had looked forward to every bit as much as her nephews had, and she had promised them they would go kite flying. She knew she had to deliver.

Pierce stood by, a bit bewildered by what could possibly be the problem. He was confident that Aunt Maimy could do anything. Moreover, he could see that dragon kite hundreds of feet in the air. "What's the matter, Maimy? I want to fly the kite."

"Piercey, I think Aunt Maimy is going to have to buy another kite. This one won't fly. We'll go get another one."

"Let me see," I said. I tended to believe Amy was correct, that the kite probably was a piece of junk, much like the useless toy tennis rackets and play guitars we buy kids that no one can really do anything with. Adding to my assumption was the fact that Amy, already a commander in the U.S. Coast Guard, was far more technologically and mechanically capable than I. But as a dad and grandfather, the impulse to get involved was irresistible.

She handed me the kite. It was very colorful and in the shape of an osprey. By a stroke of luck, after a pretty quick look, the problem seemed obvious, though I have to admit that I, too, had doubts about how well the cheapo thing would fly. The struts, which spanned the expanse of the wings, ended with slight u-shaped indentations, and at the end of each of the plastic wings were little openings where the string, which went through the outer border, appeared. What was needed was to simply bend the struts just a bit and hook the string, which now gave tension to the wings.

"Look," I said to Amy and Pierce. "See these indentations and this string? You need to hook the string in there." I then slipped the string into each end. "See, now the wings will hold firm and not just flap in the wind; that will allow it to fly." I handed the kite to Amy and asked her to walk down the beach in the direction of the wind for about fifty feet or so.

"Piercey, you stay by Pop-Pop, and when the kite gets in the air, I'll give you the string."

"Okay, Amy," I said. She had gotten what seemed like the right distance. "Now turn around and throw the kite into the air." As she threw it into the air, I pulled the line in, which gave the kite lift, and then started to let the string out slowly, and to the delight of all, the colorful plastic osprey continued to climb higher and higher.

With hands outstretched toward the ball of string, Pierce eagerly pleaded, "Let me hold it, Pop-Pop."

"Okay, here you go," I said handing it to him—but still holding onto the line to ensure it would hold steady if caught in the inevitable gusts that would destabilize it and possibly put it into a tailspin.

"Let me do it!" Pierce insisted. He could tell that as long as I had my hand on the string, I was still pretty much in control. All he was doing was holding the ball of string. At almost five, he was not that easy to fool.

"Okay, but you can't control the wind, and you can't see it. So, you have to keep your eye on the kite, and if it starts to go into a tailspin, you have to tug on it a bit. See?" I said as I demonstrated. "You'll also be able to feel it in the string if the wind gets too strong or if the kite starts to fall."

"Okay!" he said in exasperation. "Let go!"

"Okay, here you go. Also," I continued, "you can let more string out after you tug on it, and it will go even higher—but don't let too much out all at once." Frankly, I am not sure even an attentive child could process all the information I was trying to cram into his head in such a short time, but by this time Pierce was more excited about showing me what he could do than listening to my tutorial on kite flying.

Now on his own and in full control, Pierce's face was a mixture of excitement and determination. However, within a minute the kite had become unstable, causing Pierce to freeze. He just stood there holding the ball of string until the kite tumbled onto the sand—at which point, string in hand, he raced to pick it up.

Having retrieved it, we now had a kite and kite string in what would technically be called "a tangled mess," which Pierce started yanking on in an effort to straighten it out.

"No, no, Pierce," I stated in a calm but urgent voice. "Don't pull so hard on the string; you'll only make it worse. Let me see it."

Handing me the ball of string, much of which was now a mass of tangles and knots, I gently pulled on it until I encountered a knot. "Piercey," I said. "See this?" pointing to a knot. "If I pull on this, I will only tighten the knot and make it so I can't get it untangled. So, I need to loosen it by gently pulling on the other end of the knot. See?" I continued my painstaking work and was able fairly quickly to get it all straightened out and wrapped neatly back into the ball, and once again with Amy's help, the kite was back in the air.

Continuing my program of instruction, before giving the control of the kite back to Pierce, I showed him how tugging a little on the string and then letting some string out gave lift to the kite and allowed it to soar even higher. I then had him hold the string, and I did it a few more times so he could get the feel of it, and then with me just loosening my grip on the line, I had him do it a few times before relinquishing full control— though I stood nearby, reaching out for the string every time the kite swayed to the left or right and giving it a bit of a tug.

The osprey was now flying with the gulls. After a few minutes, however, it started into a tailspin, and as I reached out to grab the string, I realized that Pierce had quietly moved to the side and back so the string was out of my reach—and as I looked back, I could see a determined but utterly gleeful look on his face as he repeatedly tugged on the line, and the kite once again stabilized. I got the feeling that there were many old soldiers looking down on this scene and smiling, too—families being able to spend peaceful days together in the sun.

Having accomplished his first experience of flying, only a few miles from Kitty Hawk where the Wright brothers had given birth to manned flight, the attention of this soon-to-be-five-year-old turned to other things. Handing the ball of string to Amy, he suggested, "Amy, let's run races."

"Okay, Piercey, but you are awfully fast. I don't think Aunt Maimy has a chance. Let me get the kite down, and then we can run races. Maybe Pop-Pop will time us."

"Pop-Pop, will you time us?" Pierce asked.

"I sure will," I replied, "but you have to wait until I say ready, set, go. Then go all the way down to the pier and come back here to the finish line."

With the kite down and the string again wrapped neatly in a ball, I made a line that would be both their start and finish. "All runners take your places at the starting line," I announced, and once the runners were in position, I continued, "Ready! Set! Go!" And with just a bit of a false start on Pierce's part, they were racing down the beach—Pierce sprinting and continually looking back at Amy who was trotting behind praising and encouraging every step Pierce took until he finally, after some stops along the way, came laughing across the finishing line announcing his own victory: "I beat you, Maimy. I beat you, Maimy."

"You sure did, Piercey," replied Amy in a feigned breathless voice. "You are a really fast runner."

Meanwhile, the man who had been flying the dragon kite, the one that seemed effortlessly to rule the wind and sky, had decided to anchor the string to a stick, which he stuck in the sand next to his blanket. He then lay down to enjoy the sun's warmth, the sea's breeze, and the sound of the surf. Not too long afterwards, however, I heard Pierce calling, "Mister, Mister, your kite fell." Apparently, although the unattended kite did continue to fly for several minutes, seeming to self-adjust to the erratic gusts, a bit of turbulence finally brought it tumbling to the ground as if Saint George himself had put his lance in it. Pierce, noticing the rapid decent and crash landing, ran to the water's edge, picked up the now-soaked dragon kite, took and handed it to the now-awakened sunbather, informing him, "Mister, your kite fell. You need to watch and pull on the string so it won't fall."

So, what does all this have to do with leadership? Well, a lot! How often have you heard people in positions of leadership pat themselves on the back by saying "I just turn the work over to the smart folks and let them go"? Admittedly, that is not always a bad thing, but all too often we envision simple delegation as empowerment. And all too often, if the people delegated the responsibility are not successful, we blame it on their lack of capability when it may be we have not adequately prepared and enabled them.

Amy is one of the finest young leaders I know, yet her first reaction to the kite not flying was to blame the kite. Her assumption was that it was just a "cheapo kite" that could not fly. The real problem was she had not prepared it to fly. All the necessary parts were there, but they had not been fully assembled. There was no way that it could fly, no matter the quality of the kite or the conditions.

True empowerment is not just delegation but ensuring that people can be successful when given responsibility. Good leaders continually prepare their people to take on increased responsibilities. And when things are not going smoothly, leaders first assess what *they* need to do to enable success. Too often leaders simply declare "the problem is a failure to execute" and assume they have done their job, and to fix the situation, they need simply, or not so simply, to get the right person in there. The problem is seen as one of proper selection rather than careful development.

Second, leadership is ultimately a group activity. Increasingly, good leadership must be defined by how well people work together, discover, and create rather than solely on the ability of an individual to provide a grand vision or innovative answers and solutions. Admittedly, once the kite was correctly assembled, one person could have gotten it in the air. But to do so, the person would have to move forward—rapidly, I might add—while spending most of the time looking backward. This maneuver can end up painfully as in Amy's case when she did not see the broken shell in front of her (what if it had been a sunbather!). Collaboration and careful coordination and cooperation between Amy and me, with her taking the kite, moving down the beach, and throwing it up in the air while I held the line and was able to focus solely on getting it stably airborne, were clearly more effective. Even people who are not in positions of leadership need to engage in acts of leadership if organizations are going to be successful. Leaders need to create the environment in which that will happen.

Third, leaders need to create the conditions for success. For Pierce to fly the kite, we had to see that he had the necessary equipment, in this case a properly assembled kite and ball of string. We also had to ensure that he had a place reasonably free of obstacles. An open beach has no power lines or trees for the kite to get snagged in, and in this case, it also did not have many other kites to compete with for air space. Nor were there any buildings or other structures to interfere with the normal flow of the air currents, which even under open conditions can be problematic. Of course, we also did not suggest that Pierce try to fly his kite when there was no wind, too much wind, or in the pouring rain. The wind on this day was a moderate breeze—just right for an almost-five-year-old's first attempt to fly a kite. Just like having the right tension on the kite was necessary for it to soar, we too have to be at the optimal level of stress, which science has determined to be a moderate level, to perform at our best. Being too relaxed or too anxious does not yield the best results. Leadership is about high standards and stretch goals, not about achieving the impossible—or just having fun.

Conditions for success also involve creating a learning environment, an environment in which there is necessary instruction, guided practice, role models, and on-the-job coaching, an environment in which when mistakes occur, people are helped to sort out what happened and why and then continue to own the work and become more capable. So, we explained to Pierce what to do, how to do it, and why. We then showed him how to do it and let him put his fingers on the kite string and actually see and feel what it was like to deal with a kite turned dive-bomber before giving full control of the kite back to him.

Next, leaders have to give people full responsibility and autonomy to make the decisions they have to make to do their jobs. Pierce needed to have more than the ball of string in his hand; he needed me to let go of the line. It is also important to note that he needed a lot of string. You cannot fly a kite with a short string. We need to give people all the authority they need to be successful with the responsibilities they have been given.

Leaders need to stay involved. It is not just about "turning things over to the smart folks and letting them run with it." Leaders must continue to monitor the situation—but to do so positively, and not to micromanage. I stood close by so I could observe what Pierce was able to do and not able to do, so that I could continue to help by giving a quick tug on the line when it was needed. Moreover, I was able to keep informed of any changes in the operating environment. If the wind had gotten stronger, I would have noticed and been able to intervene to provide more information and other resources. For example, if the wind had become stronger, I could have told Pierce that we probably would have to put a tail on the kite to keep it stable. If I had just left Pierce alone and the conditions had suddenly changed, it is likely that he was still too inexperienced to adapt and the kite might have fallen into the ocean. Pierce could have become so frustrated that he would have quit trying to fly the kite. Even after Pierce confidently stepped out on his own, I maintained a watchful eye on him and the kite. Remember the man who had the kite that seemingly flew itself? Soon after he stopped attending to it, even this expensive and sophisticatedly engineered kite stopped performing and fell to the ground. Leaders' ultimate obligation is to ensure their people have the necessary abilities, resources, and motivation to accomplish what they ask them to do. This responsibility is an ongoing activity.

Keeping the string in mind, remember the tangled mess? Well, there is a message there, too. Leaders need to think systemically and then act with a systemic perspective. Pierce's immediate reaction was to yank at one end of the string. And although the initial effect was the string seemed to be unraveling, had he continued to pull on the string, he would eventually have not only made the knot tighter but also created others.

To untangle the kite line, it was necessary to pull gently until we could see where a knot was forming, which often signals a necessity to pull another part of the line in the opposite direction. Leaders have to strive to detect the underlying patterns and relationships that allow them, in the face of complexity and ambiguity, to take the right actions and not to continue to engage in behaviors that are not only no longer productive but which may make matters worse. Another thing to note, although it did not occur on this outing: If your kite collides with another and the lines become entangled, you must move toward the other person, not away, if you want to get the lines untangled. Too often when leaders tangle with one another, they move apart and become more entrenched rather than being open to another's perspective. Leaders do not just influence; they have to be open to influence from others.

A kite, of course, is a system, and the string line is an essential component—which reveals yet another important point. Just as leaders, kites soar against the wind. They can only do that, however, if they are anchored to the ground. Leaders, too, although they challenge the status quo and meet resistance, must be anchored and grounded by a set of values and a vision of the future. These values and sense of purpose provide stability and focus in the swirl of events around them.

If we were to let go completely of the kite string, the kite would momentarily pitch forward but would soon plummet and become just another piece of litter flitting haphazardly across the sand. The string acts as an effective anchor, however, only when in the hands of a person who knows when to give it a tug and rein it in or to loosen his or her grip and let it out. Remember the man who just fastened the kite string to a stick and stuck it in the sand? With no give and take to allow the kite to adapt and adjust to the ever-changing conditions, it fell from its heights to the ground. I am not suggesting compromising values, but values change—and some may need to be added as the world continues to change. Moreover, strategies must be "intent-centric," not a rigid plan. In the face of change, people need to be able to change tactics and move forward. And one final note: The inelastic anchor held the elegant dragon kite in place. The best it could do was maintain its position; it could not rise to new heights. How often is it that as individuals ascend the corporate ladder, less and less attention is given to their development and nourishment of their great potential. We assume they can now do it on their own—and they stagnate. Like kites, people can only continue to reach new heights if someone is there to tug on the string to add tension and then release it to add lift.

So, what does this all boil down to? No kite can fly by itself, but even a kite that is not made of the best materials or cut to precise specifications can soar if in the right hands. And so can the less than perfect people we lead. And, of course, even an almost-five-year-old can do it—if in the right hands. Be the right hands.

Leaders in Search of Leadership

14

Leader in Search of Leadership[56]

A hesitant knock on my door interrupted my thinking. The door was open, but my back was to it, as I have placed my desk so I can look out the window while I am thinking.

"Come in," I said before getting fully turned around to see who was there. "Oh hi, Bob, come in. What can I do for you?" I did not know Bob well; he had been a participant in one of our programs for high-potential mid-level executives. Very few executives get to attend this class. It is an invitation-only event. You have to be good—very good—and, in IBM's view, headed for even bigger things.

"Sorry to bother you, Jack, but if you have a few minutes, I'd like to talk to you about some of the things you said in the course the other day."

---

56 The next four chapters are packaged more neatly than they occurred. They are, however, an accurate summary of conversations and emails between Bob Hoey, currently GM for general business in IBM's Global Technology Services, and me over an extended period of time.

"Absolutely, please sit down," I said as I removed papers stacked in the spare chair in my office, doubling the height of another stack already on the floor. "Tell me more, Bob."

"First, when you ended the session, what you said caught me by surprise. It really got me thinking. You made the point that although we were seen as a select few, IBM had sent us here for one specific purpose, and that was to be *different*. That caught me by surprise. I suppose it's true, but I had not thought about it that way. Frankly, I found myself spending much of the time trying to convince the others, and myself, that I deserved to be there! But you are right; IBM is investing in me and the others. As you put it, to IBM, we are still 'a promise, a possibility,' and I now feel an obligation to develop what potential I may have. That was not the attitude I had just three days ago. You helped me realize that leadership is a special trust and confidence that IBM has placed in me, and I want to live up to that."

I have to confess to a rush of euphoria. First, Bob was telling me that I had had a positive impact on him. I constantly try to convince myself that my "words of wisdom" have an impact. I suspect others in the leadership development business do the same. I envy people like architects, who can take their grandkids by the hand and show them the outcome of their labors and can know that long after they are gone, these children will be able to do the same with their children. One of my great-grandfathers was a civil engineer, and more than one-hundred-and-fifty years ago, his company built the abutments for a railroad trestle that spans the creek in my hometown. To this day, I remind my children and their children of that fact every time we pass under the trestle when we go back to visit my wife's and my hometown. I envy all who have tangible legacies of their time on this earth—assuming those legacies are of a positive nature. So, Bob had tapped into my desire to have an impact—and, I confess, my need for recognition and appreciation.

Secondly, here was a person who had demonstrated the potential to be a great leader and, rather than being self-satisfied, wanted to explore what he had to do to realize his full potential, and he was asking me to help. While Bob's seeking my input was exhilarating, I was experiencing a tinge of self-doubt. Did I have anything to offer this already-successful leader? I shared Bob's sense of obligation and did not want to disappoint him or fail my company. Standing in front of others and pontificating on what *they* should do, especially when I do not have the financial and business commitments to the company that they have, is a lot easier than being face-to-face with someone asking for help. Bob's polite and trusting request alchemized in my head to, "Okay, buddy, come out of your ivory tower and enter my world. Show me this stuff works!"

Just as my words had caught Bob by surprise, Bob's request for me to explain and back up what I had said made me a bit uncomfortable. I was aware that my own misgivings were the catalyst for the alchemy taking place in my head—but what was the basis for my misgivings? I was confident in the validity of the ideas. Perhaps it was not my doubts in the ideas but doubts in my ability to help translate those ideas into action. So, sitting in my office were two people feeling a bit anxious—yet expectant. "This is good," I reassuringly told myself. "The perfect circumstances for growth to occur!" I remembered from my days as a clinical psychologist that an anxious client was much easier to treat than one who was not. The latter is not aware there is something wrong; the former, on the other hand, knows he has a problem and therefore is much more open to help. No personal growth or development will occur without disequilibrium.

"It's funny," Bob said. "In my nearly eighteen years in this corporation, I have known many successful leaders, but none of them have led the way you are suggesting."

"Bob," I replied, "I've been in the leader and leadership development business for over forty years, and I admit, I have very few examples to draw on either. Maybe exploring why that might be would be a good start. Look, I know your time is valuable, but if we are going to work together, it will take some time. Are you willing to set aside time on a regular basis for us to talk?"

"You bet," he said. "How much time will it take?

"How about an hour a week for the next month for a start?"

"Great, you're on. Let me check my calendar and get back to you. Thanks a lot, Jack."

"I'm looking forward to it, Bob—and if possible, make it the first thing in the morning so I can stop off at your office on my way into work. I pass your office on my way in. Any time after 6:30 is fine with me. I'd like to meet face-to-face when possible. If that is not convenient, just see what's best for you."

"Great," replied Bob. "Given your availability that early, we should have no problem. I normally don't get to the office quite that early, so it is not likely to conflict with any other meeting. Let me see what day will be best and get back to you."

We shook hands, and he and I headed toward our respective homes. As I let the conversation sift through my mind on my drive home, it hit me. What seemed at first like a lack of self-confidence was anything but. Bob was not lacking confidence, quite the contrary. He was manifesting humility and sharing his sense of vulnerability. This willingness to open up takes a great deal of confidence. Humility is an all too rare but essential leadership characteristic. I say this for two reasons. First, without it, leaders would at best be complacent and at worst arrogant. Neither complacency nor arrogance is a positive characteristic in leaders, and both inhibit learning and change. Second, by any definition of leadership, a leader's success is determined by *others'* success. Humility allows leader to give others the credit. The exhilaration was racing back. "This is going to be good," I said to myself. In the weeks ahead, I was going to learn a lot from working with Bob.

15

Packing Parachutes—Leadership Isn't What It Used to Be

By the time I had gotten home, Bob had already sent me an invitation via his smartphone for 7:00 on Tuesday. That was four days away, but the time went quickly. As I got in my car Tuesday morning, I wondered what to expect. Too often these sessions ended up with the executives I had offered to coach passively expecting me to tell them what to do rather than getting on the mat and wrestling with ideas. In those cases, the executives are inevitably disappointed, and I wallow in self-doubt and have to fight to pick myself up again. "Jack, stop! You are focusing on yourself. If you listen to Bob, all will go well."

I often hear great entertainers confess to butterflies before every show. I can empathize with them. I had to get myself ready, and that involved tuning into myself and replacing my negative self-statements with more positive ones. I reminded myself that Bob had shared his sense of vulnerability with me and that his openness would only continue if I, too, were willing to show that I was vulnerable. My task was not to impress Bob but to help him. My twin brother, a corporate lawyer, likes to remind me that what I do is not "rocket science." He is right—it is not that easy! Together, Newton and Einstein laid out principles that explain with some certainty the behavior of the universe. Following those principles got us to the moon and back. Admittedly, for engineers to create the systems to get us to the moon and back was an incredibly complicated task, but they at least had calculations that would give predicable outcomes. The world of human behavior has no Newton or Einstein, no mathematically demonstrable rules.

I pulled into the parking lot about 6:50. From the looks of it, it seemed the food service folks were there, along with the maintenance people, and I guessed the sweet silver BMW roadster meant Bob was there, too. I proceeded to his office. He rose to greet me.

"Thanks again, Jack, for agreeing to meet with me. Can I get you a cup of coffee?"

"No, no thanks," I said. "But if you have some hot water around here, I brought my own cup and a packet of hot chocolate. For some reason, I never could tolerate the taste of coffee—so, it's tea or hot chocolate."

"I can do that," he replied, directing me to follow him. "Poland Springs brings us cold water, room-temperature water, and hot water all in one machine. Will wonders never cease?"

As we walked back into Bob's office, he continued, "Talk about changes. When I started out, we were still selling copiers and scanners, and we all wore blue suits, red ties, and white shirts—Big Blue was red, white, and blue! We didn't even have voicemail. And now we have petaflops—and are on our way to exaflops. I used to know the people who worked with me, and now I'm responsible for billions of dollars of revenue, and I lead a worldwide matrix organization of about a thousand people from across the globe. Leadership isn't what it used to be!"

"Things certainly have changed," I concurred. "What makes leadership different for you?"

"Where do I start? The operating environment is more complex—more abstract, volatile, and uncertain. I interact with increased organizational levels, vertically and horizontally. The need for me to lead virtually is much greater. And, the stakes are really high. I'm depending on a lot of folks to get things done—many of whom I don't know or don't know well, and they are depending on me."

"What are they depending on you to do?" I asked.

With a bit of a hesitation, Bob responded, "Well, that's probably the biggest change. It used to be that people depended on me to tell them what to do and to see that they had the resources to do it, and they were accountable for execution. It's not that easy anymore. It's impossible for me to know all that is going on, and certainly not in time to respond quickly enough to achieve our goals. The CEO has said we need to shift the control of decision-making to the IBMer, and he is right. There is just too much going on too fast for the people at the top to make all the decisions—or even to know what decisions to make. So, the people in my organization are depending on me to shape organizational climate. I need to set the tone of this large organization to one that encourages subordinate leaders to take initiative and that enables them to foster high-performing and deeply engaged units and teams. But I have to admit, I get mixed signals. It seems there are still a fair number of people who are waiting for me to tell them what to do before they act."

It was easy to see why Bob had risen so far and so quickly. "So, whether they are asking for it or not—and it seems some are and some aren't—people are depending on you to create an organizational climate that inspires and enables them to take responsibility and to act?"

"Yes, but it can't be chaos, either."

"They need to be able to use their judgment, make decisions, take actions, and do so within corporate intent?"

"Yes, exactly."

"So, let's make sure we are both clear on what successful leadership would look like to you. To be most effective as a leader . . ." and I motioned to him to finish the sentence.

"Ah, I would be able to motivate and enable my globally diverse and dispersed set of people to take responsibility to self-organize, collaborate, and to be proactive problem identifiers and solvers in their efforts to leverage IBM's enterprise-wide capabilities to deliver value to our clients. And they would do that in line with IBM's strategy and values—and," he added with a laugh, "I'd feel confident they could *and* would do that."

"Well, I think that the confidence that you just mentioned is important. Forgive me for passing on a conversation I had just a few days ago, but I think it is apropos and will help put a perspective on what we're aiming for."

"Please do," Bob responded.

"Just the other day, I was chatting with a friend and colleague of mine—a guy by the name of Bob Goett. Bob is a West Point graduate and spent some time in the Army before coming to IBM. He was talking about his airborne training. What is relevant here is that to be jump qualified, you have to make five jumps. On his first jump, he recalled thinking, 'I wonder who packed this piece of cloth? Did he graduate near the top of his parachute riggers class or just squeak through? What had he been doing the night before? How focused was he when he inspected and packed the chute?'"

"So, you are jumping out of a perfectly good plane with a parachute *someone else* packed!" interjected Bob with a "gee whiz" grin on his face. "I imagine these folks take keeping each other accountable to a whole different level!"

"And a sense of personal responsibility," I added. "My friend also noted that as part of their training, the riggers not only pack their own parachutes but, at times, jump with chutes randomly picked from a pile packed by their fellow riggers."

"Well, I'm a Coast Guard Academy graduate. We didn't worry too much about parachutes, but there are certainly enough life-and-death situations Coasties encounter that call for that kind of trust. Your friend's story really does drive home this idea of 360 degrees of trust you referred to in class. The parachute riggers had to be confident in their own and in each other's ability to do their jobs since sometimes they were jumping with parachutes packed by themselves, and sometimes they were jumping with parachutes packed by others."

"Yes, exactly; they are acutely aware that until people sprout wings, they will depend on their parachutes. There is no such thing as 'good enough' in their work ethic."[57]

"Well, I hope the riggers at least put a slip of paper in the parachute that says, 'This parachute was packed by. . . .'" But then his wry smile altered, and with more earnestness in his voice, he continued. "This really is why I wanted to meet with you. I wouldn't have put it just that way, but I need to trust that any one of my people can pack a parachute. And I want an organization where everyone feels that level of confidence in each other. Let me be more specific. In your session last week, you talked about principle-based leadership, and that really resonated with me. I think it resonated with the others, too. In fact, I wrote it down."

Reading from some notes he had, he stated: "You said, 'Principle-based leadership is how leaders communicate and embed not only values but also conceptual controls that guide and enable individuals, at all levels throughout the organization, to make decisions that the individual employee and those in positions of authority are confident will be within the corporate intent. Moreover, the employee experience and the culture created encourage individuals and teams to assume personal responsibility and ownership while directing their actions toward achieving organizational purposes.' I'd like you to help me lead like that. I mean, we have been talking about leading by values for some time, and as far as I can see, that means being a person of integrity, modeling IBM's values, and embedding them in my organization. I think I am doing that—but there's got to be more."

---

57 http://www.qmfound.com/riggers_pledge.htm. These sentiments are part of the "Rigger's Pledge."

"Great! Let's see if we can figure that out."

We continued to discuss the concept of principle-based leadership and the evolving nature of work in a large organization. Bob noted that the marketplace has changed. Information technology and telecommunications have created a truly global marketplace, with intense competition and the need for quicker response. As Thomas Friedman and others have noted, the world has indeed become "flat." Moreover, inside corporations, more and more low-skilled jobs are being replaced by highly skilled knowledge workers who have access to information that enables, and at times requires, decentralized decision-making. I shared my point of view that the rigid systems and processes that once disencumbered work and increased productivity have now become obstacles. And, we both agreed that nowhere is all that more true than within IBM.

I ended this discussion by offering a summary to the effect that the pressure to move away from organizations run by rigid rules and detailed objectives is not a question of becoming more ethical; rather, it is a question of learning to deal effectively with ambiguity and the resulting uncertainty experienced by employees. Leaders can no longer rely just on providing clarity. The subordinate employee's role had shifted from passive compliance to proactive self-organizing and self-management. Principle-based leadership is a shift from leadership focused on strict rules and specific objectives to one based on conceptual controls; leadership that relies on employees' judgment, not their compliance; leadership that helps employees deal with uncertainty, not avoid it. Leaders now have to help their people deal with the ambiguity and uncertainty they encounter. While principled-based leadership involves leading by values, it also includes using non–value-based principles that provide guidance to people's decisions and actions.

Now we were at the point where we have to start to transform principle-based leadership from a catchy phrase into reality. "Bob," I said, "we both agree that employees now have to take responsibility for handling much of the ambiguity they encounter, but we need to deal with your uncertainty first. A few minutes ago, you said that you needed to feel confident that any one of your people could pack a parachute. I think building your confidence is where it all begins.

"The foundation of a climate characterized by principle-based leadership is trust. Leading by principles requires organizational climates characterized by 360 degrees of trust. Employees must trust their leaders and colleagues, but most important, leaders must trust their employees. Simply stated, and you have essentially said this yourself, you cannot rely on employees' judgment if you don't have well-grounded trust and confidence in their judgment. I want to share with you a heuristic that I find helpful. I call it The 5 Trust Vital Signs. Leaders must have confidence that employees (1) Know *what* to do; (2) Know *how* to do it; (3) Know *why* they do it; (4) *Care why* they do it; and (5) *Are enabled* to do it.[58]

"Looking for these vital signs not only helps diagnose why 360 degrees of trust may not exist but also indicates what has to be done to get there. Gaining confidence in these five areas, however, is no small feat. Bob, do you think it would be helpful for us to look at what it would take to gain the confidence that these vital signs are healthy in your organization?"

"Absolutely. I love it. This is very helpful."

"Great," and shaking hands, "see you next week, Bob."

---

58 J.B. Quinn, P. Anderson, and S. Finkelstein, "Managing Professional Intellect: Making the Most of the Best," *Harvard Business Review* (March–April 1996), pp. 71–80. This is a modification of Quinn, Anderson, and Finkelstein. Several of the questions are the same, but Quinn, Anderson, and Finkelstein were not using them in reference to trust. I see these as an organization's trust vital signs.

16

Leading Kindergarten Recess

When I arrived for our second session, Bob was standing outside his office door waiting for me.

"Hi, Jack, great to see you. You know where the hot water is; do you want some? If you didn't bring your hot chocolate or a cup, I have that, too."

"Yes, thanks, Bob. I'd like the hot water. I have my cup, and I brought some hot chocolate right here in this handy little packet. Not exactly what Mom used to make, but as you said last time, 'Things have changed.' Making hot cocoa has become easier; unfortunately, developing leadership, a bit more difficult. I'm not sure we will ever come up with the formula for 'instant leadership,' but we may be able to make developing leadership more understandable, which could at least help accelerate the process. Let me fill my cup and we can get started."

"Great. I have got something I want to show you." Bob disappeared into his office, and I proceeded to get my hot water—instantaneously dispensed by Poland Springs.

"Back in the day, they used to call those contraptions 'water coolers'; I'm not sure what they call them today," I chuckled, as much to myself as to Bob, as I returned with my freshly stirred cup of instant hot chocolate.

"Hadn't really thought about that. Water dispenser? Water cooler plus heat? Water contraption works for me. I'm sure there are some clever marketing people who have figured it out. But come over here. I have something I want to show you," he said with an air of excitement. "I plan to have meetings with all of my direct reports. My intention is for them to do the same and to have these meetings cascade throughout our entire organization. I want to get your thoughts on this chart I've made to guide our discussion."

"Let's take a look."

"It's really quite simple. I've listed The 5 Trust Vital Signs in the left-hand column, and then in the first set of columns to the right, I'll have people rate their perceptions of themselves and others' view of them on a scale from 1 to 5. In the next set of columns, they'll rate their perceptions of others [see Table 1]. Those ratings should give us an assessment of the trust within my immediate team, and with that information, we can create both an organizational action plan and various individual action plans to identify gaps that we need to close and to increase doing those things that we are already doing well. By cascading this process, we can eventually get data on the entire organization and specific action plans can be put in place. I know it won't be easy, but what do you think?"

Table 1: What are our Trust Vital Signs?						
Trust Vital Signs	**Perception of Me**			**My Perception of Others**		
Confidence in	Self	Leaders	Colleagues	Colleagues	Leaders	My People
Know *what* to do						
Know *how* to do it						
Know *why* to do it						
Care why to do it						
Feel *enabled* to do it						

Rating scale: 1–5, 1 = To a great extent, 5 = Not at all

"Bob, I'm not only impressed with what you have done, but I really appreciate that you have taken our conversation to heart, thought about things you could do, and have taken action."

"Well, Jack, the ideas about The 5 Trust Vital Signs and 360 degrees of trust really made sense to me and helped me conceptualize how to assess the trust within our organization. They took trust from a general issue to one where we can get specific information and take specific actions. It made 'trust' tangible to me."

"Great, I'm glad to hear that. It's good feedback for me. Now, Bob, what will you do with the information once you get it?" I asked.

"Well, I'm hoping you can just tell me what to do." His buoyant expression quickly morphed to one of resolve. "I think I know how to handle any problems that we may have in the areas of 'know what to do' and 'know how to do it.' You HR folks have already helped us create success profiles for our critical gap roles, which articulate the various competencies, skills, and capabilities that people need to be effective in those roles, and there are also learning activities attached to those profiles. I think we make full use of those profiles and create more for any other areas where we determine people feel deficient. So, we just reinvigorate our attention to, and use of, these profiles along with a reenergized focus on coaching and mentoring. I'll work with our communications people to create and implement a communications plan. I think just using phrases such as 360 degrees of trust and The 5 Trust Vital Signs—maybe even something having to do with 'parachute packing'—will infuse new energy throughout the organization. Marketing is not my area of expertise, but I think having a few catchphrases and memorable images will help get the message out, understood, and embedded. My intent is to explain not only the importance of creating 360 degrees of trust but also the obligation we have as the organizational leaders to do so. And I think this is where your principle-based leadership really comes into play."

"Okay, let's talk about that."

"I need to get a better handle on what it means to lead by conceptual controls. Could we talk a little about that?"

"Okay, let me share an example—one I think you may appreciate since it came from my days teaching at the Military Academy at West Point. I had a colleague there by the name of Scott Snook; he used to teach a course in advanced leadership theory. One of the exercises that he would give cadets was to prepare to lead kindergarten recess."

"Is it public knowledge that the American taxpayers are spending their money on a bunch of folks learning to lead kindergarten recess? Wouldn't it be cheaper just to send all those cadets to a state teachers' college? And did you say it was one of your *advanced* leadership courses?" Bob asked with a mischievous smile.

"Well, I guess I should have checked your security clearance before sharing such sensitive information! But let me ask you, if you were given this assignment, what would you do?" My inquiry was both to ensure that I had Bob's attention and to try to turn this story into more of a teachable moment than merely a transfer of information.

"Well, kindergarten recess was not one of my courses at the Coast Guard Academy," he replied with his smile turning to a more pensive look. "But I guess I'd figure out what the kids like to do. I'd see if we had the necessary resources to do it. If it took teams or instruction, I'd see that they were clear on what they were going to be doing and what the teams were."

"Okay, that is one approach—and that's about what the cadets came up with. Typically, the cadets would set about creating a plan that would include doing a needs assessment. They would determine the purpose of recess. They would assess the students' recreational interests and current capabilities. They would then select the activities, identify the resources needed, and sort the students into groups that they determined to be most appropriate. They'd make detailed plans and include backup measures to take into account any unexpected eventuality, like bad weather.

"Before executing their plans, however, Scott would take the students over to observe what actually takes place. The cadets would sit on the bleachers and watch. What they would see is the school doors open, the kindergartners pour out, and for a while, things would seem pretty chaotic. Some kids would run around, some would just stand around, some would talk hurriedly in small groups, but eventually, everyone would be engaged in some activity. Periodically, the teacher could be heard saying things like 'Jack!' in a cautionary tone or 'Thank you, Michael' in an appreciative voice, but other than that, she seemed merely to stand there and keep track of the time. At the end of recess, Scott would ask the cadets what they observed. The almost universal response was, 'It was chaotic. The teacher didn't lead at all. All she did was stand there!'

"Scott would then call the teacher over and ask her how she led recess. The teacher would generally say something to the effect, 'I don't really lead recess. At the beginning of the year, we come up with some rules—actually, I give them the rules and ensure they understand them and get their agreement. They are just five-year-olds, so the rules aren't complicated. We really have just three rules: (1) No fighting; (2) Everyone has to be included; and (3) You have to stay on the grass; you can't go in the woods or into the parking lot. Before recess each day, I have the class repeat the rules.'"

"That's actually very insightful—and helpful," Bob replied in a tone that indicated an 'aha moment' had just occurred. "Sometimes it seems like we have too many rules around here."

"Indulge me a bit, Bob; let me tell you a personal story and see if it helps further your thinking about what leading by concepts is all about. In the late 1970s, I was teaching at the Army's Academy of Health Sciences at Fort Sam Houston in San Antonio, Texas. Now, you were a bit young, so you may not remember that in the 1970s, the United States suffered a number of oil crises. In 1973, OPEC embargoed Western countries in an attempt to punish them for their support of Israel during the Yom Kippur War and in hopes of weakening their resolve. Again, in 1979, as a result of the Iranian Revolution, there was an interruption in the normal supply of oil. In response, President Jimmy Carter imposed price controls on gasoline and heating fuel and directed that the temperature at all federal facilities be kept at no higher than 65 degrees during the months of October through March—give or take a month. One pleasant day in February, which is not uncommon in San Antonio, I walked into one of our classrooms to find the air conditioning on. When I inquired as to why, I was told, 'Sir, federal buildings cannot be above 65 degrees. It was 72!'"

"Why am I tempted to say something about 'military intelligence'?" Bob's smile was back. "I'm glad they weren't Coasties! But I get the point. The kindergarten teacher left a lot of room for creativity—in fact, her principles demanded it. The government's directive on the temperature left no room for judgment."

"Uh-huh. One set of principles authorized decision-making and action, and the other restricted and limited judgment and discretion. What impact do you think that the different approaches might have?" I asked.

"Well, in the case you just described, the impact was clear; the restriction required behavior that defeated the purpose of the rule. The concept was to conserve energy, but following the rule ended up wasting energy and making people feel more uncomfortable. That was a 'lose-lose' outcome all the way around. But I'm also willing to bet that the people who turned on the air conditioning knew that what they were doing was defeating the purpose of the rule. They were just a bit ticked off by a rule that prohibited them from using judgment and making their own decision, and they were demonstrating the stupidity of the government's approach. I don't think we are that bad around here, but I fear we come close to it at times."

"I think that is a good insight. So, let me summarize. The boundaries set by the kindergarten teacher allowed, and in fact required, creativity and choice, whereas the edict set by the Carter administration that stated that buildings could not be above a specific temperature was restrictive. It was seen as arbitrary, and it did not communicate the underlying concept, which was the conservation of energy. Perhaps as important yet more subtle, such restrictive rules and directives fail to take into account human nature. People don't like their options restricted, and when they feel they are being denied the power to make choices, they will rebel against the rule either openly or by passive-aggressive behavior. It is likely that the maintenance personnel, by following the 'letter of the law,' were saying, 'If these people don't think we have any common sense, we will show them how stupid they are!' Does that sum it up, Bob?"

"Yes, probably better than I could say it—but yes, exactly. I think I am seeing why one of The 5 Trust Vital Signs you spoke about is 'people have to *know why*.'"

"Talk to me more about that, Bob," I urged.

"Well, to make reasoned judgments, people have to know *why* they are doing things. They not only have to *know what* to do and *how to do it*, but the intent behind the activity. So as leaders we must communicate the *why*. That seems to me to be one of the main things, if not the main thing, we are talking about when we speak about conceptual controls. To a degree, it is the *nature of information* leaders communicate that is the defining component of principle-based leadership and leading by concepts." It was clear that Bob was gaining a new understanding of the leadership he was seeking to demonstrate in his own organization.

"I like the way you put that, Bob. What you said makes a lot of sense to me."

"This is amazing," Bob said with some added excitement. "You know as a former Coast Guard officer, I have been taking some real pride in how well the Coast Guard performed during this Hurricane Katrina[59] mess along the Gulf Coast. And I have been stumped a bit by why FEMA[60] just didn't seem up to the task.

"For example, I've been reading about Air Station New Orleans. It was devastated. Many personnel lost or had heavily damaged homes. Hangars, maintenance shops, and barracks were uninhabitable. People slept on cots and floors of an administration building. For much of the time the operations center was without power, running water, and air

---

59 Hurricane Katrina, which wreaked havoc along the Gulf Coast of America in August of 2005, was one of the costliest and most deadly natural disasters in U.S. history.
60 Federal Emergency Management Agency.

conditioning. The Coast Guard's IT was knocked out along the entire Gulf Coast, and they had lost their radio towers all the way to New Mexico. In New Orleans, they had only one working cell phone. These folks were operating with little or no contact with central command.

"Now, they had dispersed their people, planes, and as much equipment as they could before the storm's arrival. But within hours of the storm's impact, the Coast Guard dispatched personnel and equipment from every unit in the country—we're talking pilots, maintenance specialists, and logistics folks from all over. Many crews were made up of people who did not know each other. And yet aircraft maintenance crews and logistical support personnel throughout the region were able to self-organize and keep the aircraft in the air and the necessary resources flowing. The result was that by around-the-clock flight operations over a period of seven days, the Coast Guard flew 723 sorties, logged 1,507 flight hours, and saved 6,470 lives. They also saved or assisted thousands of others by delivering tons of food and water to those who could not be moved immediately. They did all this without losing a single aircraft, Coast Guard member, or rescued resident. FEMA, on the other hand, literally could not get a truck full of needed food and bottled water unloaded![61] And I've been trying to figure that out. I mean, both the Coast Guard and FEMA are part of the Department of Homeland Security, and as biased as I might be, my guess is that, individually, FEMA has as good folks as does the Coast Guard."

"So, what do you think made the difference?" I asked.

"Principle-based leadership and conceptual controls!" He replied emphatically. "All Coasties are indoctrinated with the same set of operational principles: *clear objective, effective presence, unity of force, on-scene initiative, flexibility, managed risk,* and *restraint.*"

"You sound like a swab[62] reporting to an upperclassman," I said with a smile. And, truth be told, as the father of a soon-to-be commander in the Coast Guard, I felt a bit of Bob's passion and pride myself.

---

61 Trucks with needed food and water were made to sit for days before unloading because they didn't have a *tasker number*.

62 A freshman or 4th class cadet at the Coast Guard Academy is called a "swab."

"It's been more years than I want to think since I was in uniform, but those principles became part of who you were, and they guided our every behavior. *On-scene initiative* for example, involves Coast Guard personnel having the latitude to act quickly and decisively within the scope of their authority, without waiting for direction from a higher level in the chain of command. In fact, it obligates Coasties to do so. Similarly, the principle of *flexibility* basically says that when you are pursuing multiple missions with the same people and assets, which is not infrequent, you do so by adjusting to the variety of tasks and circumstances."

"And, how did that differ from FEMA?" I asked.

"Well, Michael Brown[63] in his testimony before Congress said that everyone at FEMA, including him, had to follow the chain of command and that everything had to go up to Director Chertoff[64] of DHS. The lack of initiative bogged everything down. FEMA instituted rigid controls in an effort to ensure that nothing could go wrong, but in a situation that was so chaotic, the controls did not permit the latitude needed to do the right things in the face of the changing environment. It's similar to the kindergarten teacher leading recess compared to the Carter administration's directive to keep all federal buildings at 65 degrees. I guess I did learn to lead kindergarten recess at the Coast Guard Academy. Now, I have to teach it here! I'll have to see if I can still fit in my uniform. It would be a great way to get folks' attention around all this at my next staff meeting."

"Please invite me if you do," I said with a smile as I got up to leave.

"Again, Jack, I can't tell you how helpful these sessions are for me," he said with an extended hand. "I really appreciate your help."

"Bob, I'm glad you are finding value in these talks. I'm learning a lot, too, and I certainly enjoyed our time together today. See you next week."

---

63 FEMA's director at the time.
64 Michael Chertoff, the director of the Department of Homeland Security.

17

On Their Knees at 2 A.M. in the Drugstore

Bob and I pulled into the parking lot together. It had started to rain, and I had not thought to bring an umbrella.

"Here, Jack, this is almost big enough for both of us," Bob said as he offered to share his umbrella. "We'll at least get no more than half-soaked."

"*Semper Paratus*,"[65] I remarked with a smile as we quick-stepped to the door.

"Yes, sir, I still try to live by that," Bob replied as he shook off his umbrella and we headed for the elevators.

We had our routine down. I got my hot chocolate and he his coffee, and we proceeded to his office.

---

65 *Semper Paratus* is the motto of the United States Coast Guard. It is Latin for "Always Prepared" or "Always Ready."

"Jack, again, I can't tell you how helpful this has all been. I have several of my folks tasked to determine what kind of guidelines we can provide that will enable our folks to make decisions and act. But I was wondering if you could just talk to me about the enablement and inspiration part of principle-based leadership. I'm looking for some education here."

"Okay, that might actually be the best use of our time today—and the good news is that with the efforts to create 360 degrees of trust and to provide conceptual controls, which you have already begun, the inspiration and enablement should naturally follow. So, it will be more an explanation than an education. I think you have already discovered the keys to creating the organization you said you wanted to create."

"Thanks, Jack."

"First of all, when people are confident that they know what to do, how to do it, why they do it, and are motivated to do it, the groundwork is set for good things to happen—yet more is needed. People have to feel they have permission to act. So, it's about how they see themselves and the environment in which they are operating.

"I think your analysis of the performance of the Coast Guard and that of FEMA during Hurricane Katrina was dead on—and it suggests how this sense of enablement occurs. As you indicated, Coast Guard personnel, regardless of their rank or position, know that they have a duty to take charge of an incident that they are sent to handle—and their leaders prepare them to do so. In addition to their seven principles of operation,[66] the Coast Guard has other conceptual guides such as their credo, their values,[67] clarity of their overall mission, and understanding of their relationship and obligation to the nation. These concepts—values, principles—are not only frequently affirmed in oral and written communications, but they are also instilled by positively reinforcing people when they demonstrate them and holding people accountable when they do not. These various concepts, and the culture they create,

---

66 For the list of the Coast Guard's seven principles, go to Appendix II.
67 For the list of the Coast Guard values, go to Appendix III.

help Coast Guard members to know *what to do*, *how to do it*, *why they do it*, *care why they do it*, and *enable them to do it*. They provide counsel as one weighs possibilities, and much the same as the invisible pull of gravity, these concepts keep Coast Guard members grounded in the volatile swirl of ambiguity and uncertainty."

"Well put, Jack."

"Let me recount some of what we discussed last week. As you noted, it is likely that most of the FEMA personnel were potentially as capable and motivated as the folks in the Coast Guard, but they were paralyzed by constraints that kept them from acting. Regardless of how well-intentioned FEMA's leaders were in their attempt to respond effectively to the chaos, they instituted rigid procedures. These procedures were intended to shield their personnel from uncertainty and confusion, but instead they created learned helplessness, which led to a breakdown of initiative and critical thinking. And herein lies another important aspect of principle-based leadership—*learning*. And, Bob, this relates to enablement."

"Okay, I'm all ears, Jack."

"Rather than learned helplessness, leaders who lead by principles or concepts create organizational climates in which complex learning occurs. New information emerges, people feel more confident, and they are more willing to act and better able to achieve. Learning not only helps people deal with uncertainty, it is an outcome of doing so. For example, if you are pursuing a particular goal, you need to monitor your progress. If you are not making progress, you can alter your activities to achieve your desired outcome. Monitoring requires both determining how well you are performing the intended behaviors and to what degree these behaviors, if being performed well, are ultimately helpful in achieving the intended outcome. So, we monitor for performance *and* progress.

"As you monitor, the feedback will either be positive or negative. When you get positive feedback, it tells you that you are performing competently and that the chosen activities are, as expected, moving you toward your goals. Positive feedback reinforces your behaviors and confirms your assumptions.

"The real value of today's employees *and* principle-based leadership, however, occurs when things do not go as expected. When things don't work, we try to figure out why. We not only question *what* we are doing and *how* well, but also the underlying assumptions of *why*. In doing so, we come to a new and often more complex understanding of what is required to achieve our purpose. The new understanding leads to new activities.[68] Such reassessment of performance and adjustment of behavior will continue until we are successful or eventually quit and move on—perhaps disappointed but having learned. This feedback increases learning and creates a more responsive and adaptive employee, which, in turn, enhances the value of the company's human resources."

"That makes a lot of sense," Bob said with a thoughtful nod.

"Good, but let me drill down into this a bit more. Learning informs judgment. Keep in mind that we are talking about exercising judgment, not license—remember in our second meeting you raised a concern that lack of control would lead to chaos. Leaders are not giving up control, only shifting the way it is achieved and adjusting the degree of constraint. We saw that FEMA exerted control by creating hierarchies with well-defined roles and by imposing rigid rules, regulations, and procedures that allocated authority and assigned responsibility for achieving specific objectives. The hierarchy created the rules and closely monitored adherence to them. Order and compliance were applied to chaos—and it didn't work! Why?

"Both FEMA's and the Coast Guard's chain of command exerted control. FEMA did so through strict rules and restrictive procedures; the Coast Guard did so through general principles and shared values. The former fostered compliance but stymied the creativity and initiative that the organization might have gotten from its people. The latter empowered,

---

68 Kenneth W. Thompson, *Intrinsic Motivation at Work: Building Energy and Commitment* (San Francisco: Berrett-Koehler, Inc., 2000), p. 34.

and in the midst of chaos, not only allowed people to perform effectively but also let them learn and get better! Rather than enforcing inflexible predetermined plans and procedures, the Coast Guard's senior leaders operate on the conditions surrounding the learning and development of their personnel. These differences provoke different group dynamics. In the former, people look above, wait for orders, and *do things the right way*. In the latter, people benefit from a culture that, over the years, has provided them the conceptual tools needed to exercise judgment, learn, and *do the right things*."

"So FEMA wanted to be a 'well-oiled-machine,' but even when working perfectly, all a machine can do is spit out what it did yesterday; it doesn't respond well to changes and the need to adapt—and there was a clear need to adapt when responding to Katrina," Bob mused.

"I like the analogy, Bob, and yes, I believe you are correct. As you well know, the Coast Guard also has a clear chain of command. However, the focus of their leadership efforts from the day a person enters the organization is to enable that person to take the initiative and lead. They do that by ensuring their people are technically and tactically proficient, and they instill ideological concepts that equip their personnel to use judgment in the face of volatility, uncertainty, and ambiguity. Control is exercised through shared beliefs in the mission, a common set of values, and a deep sense of community. Repeated experience of having their personnel perform under these conditions builds a cycle of trust. The entire chain of command gains confidence in one another, and each service member gains trust in himself/herself. This self-confidence allowed them to manifest courageous, informed judgment when proactively responding to the complex and chaotic environment of Hurricane Katrina. Empowered workers are self-empowered workers—but it takes the right leadership to create a culture of empowerment. The members of the Coast Guard feel confident that they know what to do, how to do it, and why they do it. They also feel they have permission to do it—and so they act. That is what enablement is all about."

"Funny," said Bob pensively. "When you are in such an environment all that happens so naturally. You are not even aware things could be different. You are not thinking about the environment or how it is shaping behavior. When I was in the Coast Guard, I experienced everything that you have mentioned, but I never had a perspective on it—it was just the way things were. I want that to be the way my organization runs now."

"Bob, I have a very dear friend, a retired one star[69] by the name of Howard Prince, who made the same observation. As he put it, 'At the Academy, leadership is in the air you breathe. It's not until you leave that you realize it is not that way in other organizations.' But, Bob, I think you are now doing things that will create that organizational climate. It's not only the Coast Guard that has or can create a culture of empowerment."

"You know," Bob continued, "I worry that too often I and many of my colleagues still see the 'well-oiled machine' as the desired metaphor of our organizational functioning. Yet my folks don't make *things*. Although they sell things, their main job is to consult and collaborate with others. My organization is *human*, and we work with other humans; there is very little machinery involved. IBM is IBMers. Machines don't know why, or need to know why, they do what they do. A thermostat automatically keeps the building at 65 degrees, but it doesn't necessarily conserve energy. The well-oiled-machine analogy just doesn't work anymore. We need people to use their judgment and adapt."

"Precisely, Bob. Knowing why or the purpose allows us to modify our behaviors to achieve that purpose. And as you said, such modifications require judgment. The need for judgment brings up another important aspect of principle-based leadership—the enlivening of the human spirit. It relates to *caring why*, enablement, and inspiration."

"Tell me more about that, Jack. Much of our data indicate IBMers as a whole are not as inspired or engaged as we would like, and I want my folks fully engaged—we need their engagement to achieve our goals, and equally important, I want them to find their work invigorating and uplifting." Bob had not missed a word.

---

69 Brigadier General.

"Well, there are many reasons why we care why we do something. In fact, generally there are multiple motivational forces working simultaneously. Some are extrinsic and some are intrinsic. *Purpose* or understanding why we need to do things is informational, but it can also be inspirational. In its simplest and most obvious form, inspiration comes from being part of a noble cause. Economic considerations, even when personally enriching, do not engender as deep a commitment as participating in a personally meaningful cause. The Coast Guard personnel engaging in heroics in the face of hardship and personal peril during Hurricane Katrina were not seeking economic gain. Their pay is modest. There were no promotions or special bonuses waiting to be handed out—and they knew it."

"No question about that," Bob interjected, "but you know they were all pumped and eager to be there. It will be the story that many will tell for the rest of their lives. I'm personally inspired by just knowing I was a part of an organization like that."

"Yes, it is not just about what they did or are doing but about *who they are*. So, an awareness of purpose gives people the information they need to make intelligent and informed decisions, but it can also provide an intrinsically rewarding sense of meaningfulness for their work and galvanize engagement."

"Don't tell anyone," Bob said wistfully, "but at times like Katrina I wish I were back in uniform—just to be a part of it. I suspect there are many future Coast Guard legends as a result of the heroic operations during the storm."

"I have no doubt, Bob. I have no doubts about that at all. But there is an important point I want to make about people using their judgment and making informed decisions. Inspiration and engagement don't necessarily have to be linked to a lofty undertaking. More subtle and perhaps even more powerful is the fact that when people use their judgment, they have to make choices. And choice ignites a very potent and solely human phenomenon: *ownership*. When a person makes a choice, at some intra-psychic level, there is a declaration, silent but felt: 'This is mine!' Choice involves freedom of thought and action, and exercising that freedom transfers responsibility. This sense of ownership deepens commitment and intensifies our engagement and resolve to succeed."[70]

"That's so true, Jack," Bob said with a flash of insight. "The importance of ownership is so obvious, and yet we too often don't take that into consideration—at least I don't. What this also suggests, which is really good news, is that people's engagement and sense of being a valuable member of an organization do not require involving them in feats of legendary proportions but just ensuring that they understand they matter and that the success of the undertaking is theirs."

"Can you think of anything that inspires us more than that, Bob?"

"No, nothing even comes close."

"And you can see, Bob, that with repeated instances of people using their judgment, not only will trust build between the employees and the manager, but the employees will also start to feel freer to use their capabilities and to realize the possibilities they hold. Let me give you a very simple example.

"My youngest daughter, Emily, on one of her several breaks from college was working in a CVS drugstore. She worked the night shift, which involved the not-so-glamorous task of restacking the shelves. About 2 A.M. one morning, as my daughter and one of her co-workers were on their knees diligently, if not enthusiastically, stacking the shelves, the young manager came walking down the aisle and declared with great exuberance and animation, 'You are my golden stackers! Just look at this aisle. This is why customers come into our store, because they can see we are a quality store. Everything is neat, orderly, and easy to find. You set the example for all the others to emulate!' He then proceeded to point to items and say things such as, 'Look at this. This looks really nice! Ah, this is great! CVS is so lucky to have you.'

---

70 Robert J. Thomas, *How Do You Find What Matters in Experience?: Becoming a More Effective Leader* (Boston: Harvard Business, 2008), p. 65.

"Now, admittedly my daughter was not engaged in a complex task—and as a result of this event, she did not strive to be a career product stacker; however, two things did occur. First, she felt good about what she was doing, and she became more energized to do her job. There was an added sense of meaning to an otherwise arduous and boring task. Secondly, she and her co-worker started to think of new ways to make the aisles even more inviting to the customers. These employees' acts of self-organizing—and I am not talking about their organizing products on the shelves—are of great importance. Having employees take initiative to do their jobs better is the ultimate desired outcome of principle-based leadership and conceptual controls.

"In this instance, my daughter and her co-worker knew what to do and how to do it, they knew why they were doing it, they knew that their manager had confidence in them to do it, and because of the manager, they did the job well. They began to care more about how and why they were doing their job. Once they felt that they had the manager's confidence, they had an added measure of confidence in themselves. The end result was that they felt that they had permission to act—and they acted.

"It is also critical to note that the manager did not say, 'Why don't you two figure out even more creative ways to display our products?' My daughter and her co-worker said that to themselves. So more than being empowered in the typical way—that is, the boss delegates responsibility to employees—they were *self-empowering*. And it happened without their conscious awareness. They didn't sit down and say to each other, 'Why don't we find even better ways to attract customers?' Rather, one of them would do something a bit different and say, 'What do you think?' The other would respond by saying, 'Yeah, and how about this?' Learning was taking place. New ideas were emerging. And, their assumption of control of their actions did not result in anarchy because they were bound by their understanding of the intent and the need to get others' support.

"So what had happened here? The manager, either wittingly or unwittingly, had connected my daughter and her co-worker to the identity of the organization. *Our* store took on new meaning, and *they* took on new responsibilities. And they now engaged more positively with their tasks *and* their co-workers. The excitement of what they were doing spread to the other workers in a noncompetitive way. It was their store, and they were making a difference. The change had not been imposed from the top down—but the conditions for it to occur had been shaped from the top."

"I've got it!" Bob said with semi-mocked enthusiasm. And rocking back in his chair and thrusting both hands into the air, he exclaimed, "I'm feeling inspired and enabled!" With his chair once again upright, he joked and continued with a more determined tone, "If it works on kindergarteners and minimum-wage employees, it sure should work for IBM!" Then getting up, and once more with his hand extended, he said, "Jack, these talks have been invaluable to me. I really think I can do this."

"I know you can, Bob, and I'm confident you will." Realizing our mission together had now been accomplished, I concluded, "Bob, I think I've learned as much as you, and I can tell you, I've really enjoyed the time we have spent together. Keep me up-to-date as things progress."

"Will do, Jack. And again, thanks."

18

"I Can't Get No Satisfaction"[71]

"If a__holes could fly, this place would be an airport! It's ridiculous. You pick up *Fortune* magazine, and it tells us we are financially stronger than ever. Over the past few years, our earnings have quadrupled and the stock has soared. And the CEO tells us we have record profits and free cash flow, and the dividends and the earnings per share have gone up every year for almost a decade—yet my bonus is a joke and my raise near undetectable. When the company does well, it is important that the rewards make it to the employee, and that's not happening. There is always an excuse, but there need to be incentives for the top performers!!!!" He did not need the four explanation points to let his boss know he was upset.

"Okay, Jack, you're our leadership guy. What do I do with this? This guy is not alone; he's just the one who put it in writing."

---

71 Although the quotations that start this chapter are real, all persons (e.g., Jim Slice, Mary, Dr. Simmons) and any suggested background information on these people are strictly the creation of the author. This chapter is in large part a contrived conversation.

Mary was troubled. The email she had handed me was from Jim Slice, one of her direct reports who was one of her best people. But she sensed that in addition to the dissatisfaction that he was so pointedly expressing, there was a pervasive malaise throughout her organization, and she wanted to figure out what she could do to improve the climate within her group.

"If you would like, Mary, I would be glad to share some ideas. It just so happens I've been thinking about that very problem recently because I know that Jim is not alone in his feelings, nor is your situation as a leader unique. We are in a very competitive environment, and these feelings of dissatisfaction are widespread."

"Enlighten me," she said with her arms spread wide, her humor tinged with frustration, and then more seriously, "I really would be interested in any thoughts you may have."

"Well, even though there are likely logical explanations for people's bonuses and raises, I don't think Jim and the others would be convinced. And frankly, in the end, money is a 'dissatisfier'; it is not what deeply motivates most people."

"I agree. And decisions about bonuses and raises are made above my pay grade anyway."

"Right, so leaders need to focus on what they can control and things that motivate and enliven the human spirit. I think you are familiar with our Leadership Framework that focuses on Employee Engagement."

"Yes, I probably need to go back and freshen up on it, but in general, I am aware of the concept."

"Okay, to refresh your memory, when we talk about employee engagement, we are referring to a *state of mind* in which employees are intellectually and emotionally involved in their work and are positively connected with both their co-workers and the larger organization. This state of mind fosters a sense of pride and a willingness to exert discretionary effort, and most importantly, it generates energy that would not otherwise exist. A paycheck does not create this environment, but I believe leaders can create organizational climates that increase the probability that employee engagement will occur."

"Jack, you have my attention."

"Good. Let me share with you what I am calling The Engaging Leader's Dozen."

"Catchy. I like that."

"Mary, in this business you spend a lot of time trying to figure out things that people will remember!"

"I think you've succeeded. Ask me next week to be sure," she said with a smile.

"You're on. Be prepared for a pop-quiz. Now, just as the 'Daily Dozen' is a set of arduous military exercises, I see these as twelve difficult journeys. There are no quick, easy fixes.

"First, *do a 'gut check.'* Do you have a fire in your belly? You need fire to ignite others. Identify your passions—instances when you refuse to lose. I'm not talking about the competitive urge to beat the other guy; I'm talking about seeing that something you deem important gets done. You possess ideas, but what ideas possess you? Passion will fuel the emotional resolve and provide the physical stamina to persevere when things get tough.

"Reflect on why that passion exists. Knowing why and how it came about will provide insights to igniting passion in others. Get your 'juices' flowing. Identify what impact you are having. Approach your organization with an appreciative eye. Identify what's working, and determine what else needs to work. Reflect on a time when the group really performed well. Reflect on a time when you were really proud to be the leader of this group. Learn from your successes, not just your mistakes. Too often we get very focused on what is wrong and put all our energies into filling gaps. We all but ignore what is going well and fail to put our effort into repeating what we do right. Just doing less of what we do wrong may not be as beneficial as doing more of what we do right."[72]

"Jack, there really is so much that is going right. My people are engaged in very exciting research that will lead to innovative products—some really neat things are on the horizon, things that will not only grow the business but will also make the world a better place—more efficient and cleaner."

"I am confident that is the case. Try to focus folks' minds on the impact of their work. That principle is in line with a second journey, *instill meaning*. Communicate the impact achieved, not just the work done. Mary, you can look at work as a series of activities or as a set of purposeful outcomes. For example, in my line of work, I could have people do a needs analysis and then design and implement a leadership program, or I could ask my group to design and implement a program to increase the leadership capability of the enterprise. At the end of the year, we could look back and say, 'We developed a leadership development program for new executives' or 'There are now seven hundred leaders better able to lead and grow the enterprise.' I think the latter is more powerful."

"I couldn't agree more, Jack, but wouldn't I then have Jim and the others saying, 'Look at all the impact I am having; now show me the money!'?"

"Mary, I don't think money will ever be a nonissue, but you will have roused a competing and more powerful source of motivation and satisfaction. Humans are *meaning-seeking* and *meaning-making* beings. We are in a constant search for meaning, and leaders can tap into people's aspirations and help them find that meaning. So, leverage human nature. Engagement is about intangible, intrinsic motivation."

"Ah," and with a wry smile and a bit of rhythmic swaying back and forth, "so 'I don't care too much for money, money can't buy me love.'"[73]

---

72 Sue Annis Hammond, *The Thin Book of Appreciative Inquiry* (Bend, OR: Thin Book Publishing Co., 1998).
73 John Lennon and Paul McCartney, "Can't Buy Me Love," 1964.

"Exactly. Focus on the significance of what people do individually and as a group. Doing work we see as worthwhile and helping a greater good are innately pleasurable. So, continually remind yourself and your people why you—as a group—exist. Reinvigorate yourselves about what is important to you individually and as a group—what you do, why you do it—and maybe even what would happen if you didn't do it.[74] Elevate your people's aspirations. The end result is that the work itself becomes rewarding. If our focus is money, then the answer to 'Why do I do this?' becomes indistinguishable from any other task— efforts cease to be *causes* and become 'just work.' And it certainly does not create the 'IBMer.'"

"I can do that, and I really need to do that for myself and my people." Mary's reflective tone suggested that, like too many managers, she had gotten so focused on the day-to-day tasks that she had lost sight of what *they* were all about and realized that it was very likely her people had also lost their sense of purpose as well.

"I heard a story once," Mary continued. "I'm sure it's apocryphal, but it makes the point. It was about the construction of Saint Paul's Cathedral in London. The cathedral was built from 1675 to 1710. Christopher Wren was the architect, and one day he went out to the building site to see how things were progressing. As he mingled unrecognized among the laborers, he chatted with several and asked them what they were doing. In response, one of the workers stated, 'I'm cutting stones'; another, 'I'm earning a day's wages'; and a third declared, 'I'm helping Sir Christopher build a magnificent cathedral.'[75] I think too many of us are cutting stones or earning a day's wages and not seeing the grand cathedral. We are making the world a smarter, better place. I have to make that real to my people without making it a cliché."

"I think reminding Jim and the others of the difference they are making will improve their attitude, Mary. It is often the unmentioned and even unperceived intangibles of our work that are the source of our greatest

---

74 Robert Kegan and Lisa Laskow Lahey, *How the Way We Talk Can Change the Way We Work* (San Francisco: Jossey-Bass, 2001), p. 189.
75 This story has many versions and has been told by others: http://www.the-happy-manager.com/leadership-quality.html.

joys and our greatest dissatisfactions. When an unrecognized intangible need goes unfulfilled, it can cause a general sense of malaise, which may manifest itself in complaints about less significant but more easily identified irritants, such as the size of bonuses or raises.

"A third, related journey is to **give authority, not just work.** We need to feed responsibility. Give tough, challenging, stretch assignments. Set and enforce high standards—and create the conditions for success. Supply resources. Remove obstacles. Provide instruction when necessary. Coach. Help people think through *their* problems by *themselves*. It is important to clarify choices and to require decision-making. Choices and decisions inspirit the uniquely human phenomenon of *ownership*, which strengthens commitment and emboldens empowerment. Empowering people is a forceful statement of trust and the best way to develop leaders and deepen engagement."

"This is great, Jack, but help me get a better handle on the 'clarify choices' part of that."

"Mary, that is closely linked to a fourth difficult journey—**lead by concepts.**[76] Leading by concepts requires imparting clear purpose and intent and being explicit about values. These concepts, in turn, provide guidelines that help our people deal with the inevitable ambiguities and detours they will encounter. They assist us in determining the parameters and boundaries within which decisions can be made. Guidelines enable judgment.

"Guidelines should authorize rather than restrict. They should be broad enough to allow flexibility and initiative and encourage innovation. Guidelines that authorize help employees who willingly do what they are directed to do to become people who take initiative to do what needs to be done *without* being directed."

"Okay, got it. Leading by concepts gets people out of the compliance mode of responding. They can become more self-directed—makes them feel like it was important for them to have brought their brains to

---

76 For a fuller discussion of leading by concepts, see Chapter 16, "Leading Kindergarten Recess."

work. No question that feeling is more energizing, and we need what is between their right and left ears—that's why we hired them. But I have to admit, too often my people don't feel that way."

"I think it's an all-too-common circumstance, Mary, and a fifth aspect of becoming an engaging leader is very much related to making employees think that their brains are important—**add value sparingly; deepen ownership.**"

"Well, I think I have the 'adding little' value down; I'm not sure about the deepening ownership! But once again, Jack, you have my attention. I thought my purpose was to add value. Isn't that how I got to where I am? Seriously, Jack, are you saying that when you handed in your evaluation of your achievements for the year to Steve, you said, 'My biggest achievement was I didn't add much value this year'? That is a unique approach."

"First, Mary, I did not say 'do not add value.' But I am suggesting you might add value by adding value sparingly!" (I couldn't resist.)

"You're on a roll, Jack; don't stop now. I want to hear the end of this story!"

"The point is to validate your people, not yourself. Leaders often feel a need to validate *their* worth by finding what could be 'even better' in the work their people have done. Frequently, the improved result in the product is not worth the loss of ownership and confidence in the people involved. Consider this when reviewing work. Work that is never 'good enough' does not foster initiative—it breeds dependency."

"Jack, that is a great point. I think I'm actually pretty good about letting my people know that they can do things better than I can, but I'll redouble my vigilance to see that is the case. Trust me; I'm more concerned when I think I know a better answer than these folks!"

"Mary, that trust is essential. In fact, a sixth difficult journey is to **build 360 degrees of trust.** Check The 5 Trust Vital Signs: You need to be confident that your people (1) know what to do; (2) know how to do it;

(3) know why they do it; (4) care why they do it; and (5) feel enabled to do it.[77] If your people are not exhibiting strong vital signs, you will not be able to provide them the space they need. Assess your team, and take actions to increase your confidence that each of these vital sign is strong. And encourage your people to do the same. Keep in mind, 360 degrees of trust includes individuals trusting that *they themselves* can use their judgment, make decisions, and act within corporate intent. Check it out. Do they? Also, convey your trust. Your people have to know and feel your trust—without it, they are less likely to act. People who feel trusted experience deepened engagement and a stronger determination to succeed. Furthermore, it is vital to embed the norm that all team members hold themselves and each other accountable and take actions to address shortcomings."

"I really like the trust vital signs idea, Jack—another pithy, sententious quip by Dr. Beach!"

"Oooh, 'sententious,' now I'm impressed!"

"Mom and Dad didn't send me to Barnard just for the view! But these are excellent questions to ask. Again, I feel confident I can answer yes to these when it comes to my people, but it will be interesting for me to get their view. And I also need to embed the norm that each of us take responsibility to remedy the situation if we see trust eroding."

"Good—and speaking of Barnard College, a seventh journey that engaging leaders must take is to **create a learning environment**. Just like the need to find a sense of meaning and purpose, the desire to develop, to become increasingly capable, and to realize our potential starts at the instant of conception—and it never stops. Leverage it; don't stand in its way. Becoming more capable at what we do is innately pleasurable. So, work itself can become compelling. People do what they love, but they can also *love what they do*. Loving what you do is the result of seeing yourself getting better at it. Some of our best work experiences were ones we went into 'kicking and screaming.'

---

77 For a fuller discussion of 360 degrees of trust, read Chapters 6 and 15, "Trusting the Untrustworthy" and "Packing Parachutes—Leadership Isn't What It Used to Be," respectively.

So, support people seeking developmental projects and assignments. Encourage trying new approaches. Let people fail. Accept that people who are inexperienced or who are trying new things will make mistakes. No one will get everything right all the time. You want people who can survive mistakes. Allow people the space to experiment within the bounds of corporate intent. Distinguish between mistakes that are the result of a genuine and well-considered exploration of new ideas and ways of doing things and irresponsible and reckless behaviors. When mistakes occur, help people sort out what happened and why. They will continue to own the work, become more capable, and deepen their engagement.

"In addition, set the expectation that all organizational members will engage in self-development and foster mutual development. Create opportunities for people to share knowledge and expertise. Allow time for self-development, reflection, and personal growth. Promote dialogue throughout the team that provokes deeper thinking and the reframing of issues. Seize 'teachable moments.'"

"We could, and definitely should, do more individual and group self-development." I sensed Mary was feeling more optimistic than when she first came in.

"An eighth engaging leader journey is to *inquire into assumptions; do not give constructive feedback.*"[78]

"Did I get that correct, Jack? 'Do not give constructive criticism'?"

"Yes, Mary, you heard that right."

"I've always considered that a key leadership responsibility. I'm not saying I am good at it, but you have definitely piqued my interest."

"First of all, note that you substituted the word 'criticism' for 'feedback.' We do consider these terms synonymous; my asking you not to give 'constructive feedback' will become clearer as we go on.

---

78 For a fuller discussion of these ideas, see Kegan and Lahey.

Now, I am not saying constructive feedback is never appropriate, but I am taking this idea from the work of Robert Kegan and Lisa Laskow Lahey from Harvard. I can't take credit for the logic, but I find it very insightful, and I think the impact is one that fosters both learning and engagement.

"Mary, think about a time when you received what might be called constructive criticism."

Mary's response was without hesitation, "I was eighteen. My grandmother invited me to a picnic on the lawn outside her and my grandfather's home, and I showed up in jeans with a ripped knee and a missing back pocket. I thought I looked pretty cool, but Mother and Grandmama were not pleased."

"I take it 'cool' was not the theme of the day."

"Ah no, classy and elegant would be a better description. This turned out to be a catered picnic with linen napkins, nice china, the works— and a guest that was to be a surprise. Fortunately, my cousin and I were the same size and she lived nearby, so I was able to borrow more-appropriate attire."

"Well, since this event was some time ago and it still comes to mind, it's probably a good example—though, I confess, not exactly what I expected."

"A few years have gone by since then," Mary said with a smile, "but talking about my college days quickly brought it back. I was mortified, and they were, I don't know, aghast—maybe disappointed in me would be a better word."

"Tell me a little more," I inquired.

"Well, the mention of Barnard is what brought this all back. My grandmother went to Barnard, my mother went to Barnard, and I was going to be entering in the fall. Unbeknownst to me, my grandmother, who was thrilled that I was carrying on the family tradition, had invited her former roommate to this picnic. Her roommate had gone on to have an academic career and was the associate dean of students at Barnard when my mother was there. I did not have all those details before I arrived. It was supposed to be a surprise. My mother and grandmother had mentioned this person in conversations over the years, but I had never met her. Well, SURPRISE! Admittedly, I was a bit more casual than I would normally have been. My grandparents' home was more a small estate with a lawn that rolled down to the Hudson River. It was a nice place. But it was summer. It was my day off from work. It was a picnic."

"Specifically, what was their reaction?"

"My mother greeted me with, 'Did you bring a change of clothes? You can't spend the day looking like that.' My grandmother's remark was, 'Dear, I've invited Dr. Simmons. I would like you to look nice for her.'"

"So, in this instance, as in all constructive feedback, there was an attempt on the part of one person, or in your case two people, to provide you information in an effort to change your behavior. So, when providing constructive feedback, the focus is on the actions or inactions of the other person, and those actions or inactions are seen as inappropriate or ineffective. The assumption is that the information provider is correct, that is, knows what is true and right, and that the receiver either lacks awareness or is missing, overlooking, or ignorant of that something that the provider knows. Now, undeniably, at times this may well be true. But the goal, even in the gentlest and most positive way, is to set this person straight—and perhaps in those less positive instances to teach this person a thing or two!

"Now, let's look at another way of handling this situation. They could have inquired into your assumptions."

"Well, Jack, I had the clear impression they were saying, 'What were you thinking!!!'"

"It sounds so, but with the explanation points, I don't get the feeling, and I sense you didn't either, that your mother and grandmother were attempting to begin an investigative conversation. They, in fact, told you the correct answer to the situation without even allowing you the opportunity to explain. So, they either presupposed what you were thinking or weren't interested in what you were thinking—or quite possibly assumed that you weren't thinking."

"Ah, probably the last option. And I now know why I said constructive 'criticism'—though I am not sure 'constructive' fits."

"Mary, inquiring into someone's assumptions, if done as genuine inquiry as opposed to 'What the heck were you thinking!' creates the context for mutual discovery and mutual respect. The assumption is not one of right or wrong, but the sharing of an observation of behavior that is puzzling to you and asking the performer of those behaviors what ideas and theories he or she was operating on that led to those behaviors. You would also have the opportunity to suggest other behaviors and discuss the assumptions behind them that lead you to think those behaviors might be more appropriate or effective. The situation certainly does not preclude that the other person has faulty assumptions or even may have acted 'without thinking' and that you have a wiser course of action in mind, but regardless, it is one in which both parties can rethink their assumptions and learn. And, I think, especially in the workplace, a mutual probing of each other's assumptions and ideas conveys the feeling that we are all worthy co-collaborators. This feeling in turn infuses the organization with intellectual energy and creates an engaging organizational climate."

"I really like that, Jack. I certainly would have felt better if there had been a sharing of assumptions. My immediate feeling was that I was being scolded because I was not using mature judgment and had done something wrong. My assumption was I was attending a *family* picnic—a fun day with my parents, grandparents, aunt, uncle, and cousins. And I was also upset that I had not been given a bit more information. After all, I could have been told ahead of time, 'Some of your grandparents' friends will be there, so do not dress too casually.' That information would have been enough to allow me to make an informed decision and little enough to still be surprised by who the special guest was.

"I really, really do like this," Mary continued. "In fact, had we discussed each other's assumptions, all of us might have altered our behavior a bit. What were my mother's and grandmother's assumptions about Dr. Simmons' expectations? They were looking at this through their own eyes and assuming what she would enjoy. They were not really thinking about her. Keep in mind, she was a college professor and dean. She was used to being around grubby college kids. And I have to tell you, she was no slave to fashion and clearly did not spend money on hairstylists. She showed up nicely dressed but not outfitted to the level of my mother and grandmother. I think she may have felt uncomfortable that she was not appropriately dressed. In fact, when I was showing her my grandmother's gardens, she commented to me, 'This is quite an affair, not like the picnics I went on as a girl.' That may well have been her way of saying that she thought she had not dressed properly for the occasion. However, we all had a great time. It was a wonderful day. In the end, we all just enjoyed each other's company. And for a kid about to enter college, it was great to be able to listen to all of them talk about their college years."

"That's great. I'm sure Dr. Simmons was comfortable enough in her own skin that she just appreciated your grandmother's hospitality, and I sense that your grandmother did not care what Dr. Simmons wore and that she felt good that she had gone all out for her friend.

"The ninth difficult journey is about appreciation—*communicate personal appreciation, not just praise.*[79, 80, 81] Much of what I am going to say also comes from the work of Robert Kegan and Lisa Laskow Lahey.

---

79 Many of the insights expressed and some of the terms used in this item are to a great extent those of Robert Kegan and Lisa Laskow Lahey and not this author's.

80 It may help to define personal appreciation. In their book, Kegan and Lahey use the phrase "the language of ongoing regard." As stated by Kegan and Lahey, "Ongoing regard is not about praising, stroking, or positively defining the person to herself/himself or others . . . it is about enhancing the quality of a precious kind of information. It is about informing *the person* about *our* experience of him or her" [italics added]. p. 101. I have substituted the term personal appreciation for ongoing regard.

81 It is very important to note that here we are talking about going from *very good to even better*—not bad to good. However, subtle changes in the way we speak can add exponential power to our words and the impact on those to whom they are directed.

"They point out that how we communicate affects our individual and social energy. They specifically talk about moving from being 'indirect, nonspecific, and attributive' (conferring of attributions or traits) to personal appreciation. Being 'direct, specific, and nonattributive' will add energy to the work environment—or any relationship. They state that 'we do better at work if we regularly have the experience that what we do matters, that it is valuable, and *our* presence makes a difference to others.'[82] However, we tend to under-communicate our genuinely positive, appreciative, and admiring experience of our co-workers."

"I suspect all that is true," Mary stated intently.

"Little things mean a lot. Something as simple as using people's names makes a noticeable difference. 'Thanks, Mary' has more impact than just 'Thanks.' Also, speak for yourself—make it personal: '*I* really appreciate that, Mary' has more impact than '*We* really appreciate that, Mary.' Now, let me make two statements, and you tell me which one feels better to you. I could say, 'I'd like to acknowledge Mary. *She* has, without a doubt, been the driving and most creative force behind this effort.' Or I could say, 'I'd just like to acknowledge Mary. *Mary, you* have been, without a doubt, the driving and most creative force behind this effort.'"

"The latter one is a stronger statement. It makes me feel more appreciated. It's funny; changing one word made a difference."

"Yes, and when Kegan and Lahey talk about being *direct*, not *indirect*, they are saying 'talk *to* people, not *about* people.' In the first example, I converted you to an impersonal third person, and the communication was directed to the audience about you. That was an indirect communication. You became a bystander listening in on my conversation with others. I am talking about you to others. In the second example, I am always talking directly to you, and the audience is given the opportunity to eavesdrop on that personal conversation."

"Interesting. Such subtle differences have such noticeable impact. After having flashbacks to my mother's criticism, I like hearing nice things about Mary. Don't stop now!"

---

82 Kegan and Lahey, p. 92.

"Okay, there is more. Similarly, it makes a difference if you are *specific* as opposed to *nonspecific*. Again, let me give you two examples, and you tell me which is more powerful in terms of you feeling personally appreciated."

"You're on—more nice things about Mary."

"Okay, first, 'Mary, I can't tell you how great it was to have you at the meeting with Software the other day. I honestly don't know what we would have done without you.' Second, 'Mary, I can't tell you how great it was to have you at that meeting with Software the other day. Your analysis of the data was not only insightful, but you also delivered it overnight. And you showed real leadership by holding your ground and getting the participants to really interrogate what some of the data were telling them, which many did not want to hear.'"

"Again, the second statement, without a doubt." Mary was clearly enjoying this part of the conversation but also proving the point.

"And what made the difference, Mary?"

"The second one was definitely more specific than the first. Both were nice, but the second one also gave me more information."

"Precisely. Nonspecific information leaves the individual feeling good but not really knowing why. Specific information not only leaves the individual feeling good, but the individual also gets concrete data on what he or she did that was seen as adding value. Furthermore, to be specific, the person showing appreciation has to think through the experience with Mary and Software, and in doing so, gains more knowledge of what skills and behaviors are important to the team and what it means to have Mary on the team. So, the speaker is also more informed of what is important about the person being addressed and about what the team should do. Now, let's look at the difference between being *nonattributive* and *attributive*.

"Again, let me give you two examples. The first will be an attributive statement. 'Mary, you are a gifted speaker.' The second is a nonattributive statement. 'Mary, I was really touched and inspired by your talk. I'm really glad I came tonight."

"The nonattributive statement is more powerful. Now, don't get me wrong, I'd love to be a gifted speaker—but I'm not. Again, it gave me more information and, Jack, as you mentioned earlier, it provides me feedback on my impact."

"Good. So Mary, let's look at what you said. First, as much as you wished it were true, you do not see yourself as a gifted speaker. So in a way, being attributive is also being a bit presumptuous. You are telling the person who and what he or she is. If the person disagrees or out of modesty plays down what you said, the compliment is drained of some its power. On the other hand, if the person agrees, you have told that person nothing new. Also, as you pointed out, the nonattributive communication gives the recipient new information in terms of the impact he or she had—and that information is unassailable. It is the speaker's experience, not yours. It is hard to argue that you did not inspire the person or that he or she wasn't really glad to have attended your talk. Ironically, the speaker is actually talking about himself or herself, not you. But it does tell the recipient that what he or she did made a difference, which also conveys that he or she is the difference. That pumps oxygen into any person or organization that nourishes engagement so it can thrive.

"Being attributive may even have negative consequences. For example, saying 'Mary, you are really brilliant' not only does not provide much information, it may also provide inaccurate information. More important, it may set up a need or desire on your part to defend that attribute. So you may feel that you must say something brilliant in every meeting that you are in. This need may keep you from fully listening to others and may make you more insistent on your point of view—or you may not participate at all because you do not feel confident in that particular conversation and you don't want to reveal your lack of knowledge. On the other hand, telling you, 'Mary, I can tell you really worked hard on this. It really is a good piece of work,' reinforces working hard—which by the way is what often differentiates one brilliant person from another. Finally, being attributive is also more subject to formulaic insincerity."

"It's amazing; just your made-up examples made me feel good. And, it's intriguing how subtle nuances in the way we communicate can have such different impact. But it also tells me that I need to be conscious with my messaging."

"Yes, and though these things don't cost a cent, they yield great returns.

"A tenth leadership imperative to becoming an engaging leader is to **build bonds**. I've said it before, and I'll say it again: Leverage human nature. Humans are social beings. We are hard wired to co-exist in groups. We have a compelling need to associate with others and to form social bonds. It is innately pleasurable for us to be a valued contributing member of a group—but not just any group! We choose groups based on the frequency of the opportunity we have to interact. So, find opportunities for non–task-related gatherings in addition to work-related meetings, for example, having lunch together or even virtual lunches, virtual birthdays, team picnics—but probably not at your grandparents'. Become familiar with the obstacles and solutions to leading virtually.

"We also want to interact with others who share our values and common goals. Make your values and the values and norms you expect to govern the team's behavior known. Make them particularly salient to new members of the team. Instill and reinforce a common sense of mission. Collective passion is a unifying force. Very much related to instilling meaning, we are attracted to groups who are involved in activities that we find inherently rewarding, so it is important to ensure that members know how they are contributing to the overall goal. Help new members get to know the team and its people. Have a planned, consistent, and effective on-boarding process. For example, assign a team member to assist the new arrival in learning the ropes, and make sure that they have all the equipment they need to settle in and do their jobs—immediately.

"Just as you mentioned with your grandmother's picnic, there was a need to appreciate the guest's expectations. Put yourself in the frame of mind of the new member, and see that his or her needs and concerns are met. For example, did this require relocation? Is this a first job? Is the person a seasoned professional? All new members will want to be accepted and to prove themselves—give them opportunities to make noticeable contributions. Make sure new members know why they have been given particular responsibilities, what strengths they bring and what they are expected to learn. Have an updated but standard presentation that describes the organization, mission, major accomplishments, priority projects, and the like. Help the new members to know why the team exists. Share any 'classic stories' and unit bios, provide a list of people important to his or her and the unit's success, and help them to set up interviews with these people.

"Our bonds to a group deepen as it has collective success at assigned tasks. So, build individual and team capabilities. Assign challenging missions that require interdependencies. Remove obstacles and supply resources. Note progress toward goal achievement. Celebrate success. Collective success creates an infectious 'can do' attitude that elevates pride and draws organization members emotionally closer. Members will go to great lengths not to let their colleagues down. Building bonds obviously relates to the building of 360 degrees of trust that we talked about earlier. Bonds strengthen when people have a well-grounded confidence in their leaders, their peers, and themselves. In the end, engagement is about the emotional bonds people have to their co-workers, their mission, and the greater organization. So a primary task of leadership is to build bonds."

"Yes, I agree, and that has been my concern with the malaise that seems to be setting in. But you have given me some really good ideas to think about, Jack."

"Let's talk about money for a minute. After all, that is what got us talking about all this to begin with. There is no getting around it. Money is a troublesome issue. It is an essential part of our reward system, but it has dangerous side effects. The next journey for the engaging leader is to use money so that it achieves the intended purpose of reward without experiencing the harmful side effects. In terms of employee engagement, and ultimately their performance, an eleventh leadership journey is to **reward performance, not relative contribution**. It is a dilemma to reward the right things in the right ways."

"Why is it I think I just woke up in a Greek myth? Like all oracles, you give inscrutable advice. Reward performance, not relative contribution? They sort of sound the same to me. Continue to enlighten me, Jack."

"It can be confusing, Mary, but let me try to explain. There are three ideas that must be understood. One is the difference between norm-referenced evaluation and criterion-based evaluation. A second is that performance and contribution are not necessarily synonymous. And third, not all rewards are monetary.

"Norm-referenced evaluations are intended to rank-order people from best to worst or vice versa. For example, when I was in college, grades were often norm-referenced. The grade I received depended on how well I did in comparison to the other students in the class, and grade distributions were roughly a normal distribution, more commonly known as a bell-shaped curve. You probably have heard the term 'ride the curve.'"

"Yes, I have heard it, but fortunately, we were not graded that way."

"Right, Mary. Eventually, many, if not most, colleges went to a criterion-referenced mode of evaluation. The professors determined ahead of time what the expectations should be for the students at their college and in their classes and graded accordingly. You knew ahead of time what the criteria were for getting an A, a B, a C, etc. And it was possible for everyone in the class to get an A or an F. The difference in evaluation methods is probably one reason why some old-timers assume grade inflation and younger folks think kids are just smarter today."

"Jack, I think I get where you are going, and I get this part of it. We rate people at the end of the year on a 1-to-4 rating scale,[83] and we really don't know what's a 1, 2+, or 2 until the end of the year. Generally, 3s and 4s are a bit easier to determine. But I know when I am giving midterm evaluations, I often get asked, 'Am I on track to get a 1?' and I feel sort of like the guy who gives kids the tests for a driver's license and the kid asks what he has to do to pass and I tell him, 'Well, these are expectations, but I really won't know until the other testers and I get together and see how all the other kids do today before I know if you have done well enough to get your license.' The kid would think I was nuts."

"Yes, exactly, Mary. The reason people want to know if they are on track to get a 1 is that the high numerical rating in and of itself is rewarding. The number grade is a nonmonetary reward that gives them positive feedback on their performance and capabilities. Remember, we've already discussed that it is intrinsically pleasurable and rewarding when we get more capable and are acknowledged for that achievement. It is essential that the performance criteria require true differences in excellence, but if the criteria are met, the achievement should be acknowledged even if the high achiever does not receive a bonus or a significant raise."

"You're right, Jack; regardless of the money, it feels good to be told you did well and not so good to be told you are just average. I've experienced that myself."

"Mary, let's say you magically had a team of Albert Einstein, Sir Isaac Newton, Leonardo da Vinci, Galileo Galilei, and Stephen Hawking."

"That *would* be magic!"

"Yes, but extreme examples sometimes help. And now, in another stroke of magic, in a norm-referenced world in which most people are *mathematically* determined to be average, we would turn most of these

---

83 Corporations have different scales, but at IBM there are four ratings: 1, 2+, 3, and 4. 1 is the highest and 4 the lowest.

outstanding folks into just 'average.' Measuring them against a set of criteria, however, rather than against each other, would affirm each individual's true excellence. The perniciousness of the norm-referenced evaluation, which mathematically transforms a group of outstanding individuals into a group of mostly average folks, is that it risks deadening each individual's sense of engagement and will likely lower the team's overall performance. As W. Edward Deming points out, 'No one can enjoy his work if he will be ranked with others.'[84] Comparisons create winners and losers. And as I think you can understand, rendering high performers as 'losers' or even 'average' or 'mediocre' sucks out the oxygen needed to sustain engagement."

"Jack, I can see that. That makes sense. We say evaluate based on performance *and* relative contribution, but by the time it's all through, the performance rating is determined by the relative contribution. So, we are really evaluating on just relative contribution."

"Yes, and the consequences of rewarding relative contribution are opposite to its intent. Rewarding relative contribution maximizes the risk of money's harmful side effects. It creates negative competition among workers, which decreases overall organizational performance, and lowers employee satisfaction. It also diminishes the level of engagement even in the top performers or the people who would be considered 'winners' under this policy."

"Well, that's what brought me in here. Jim is among my best folks and a top performer, and yet he is not a happy camper."

"Mary, once we make money, bonuses, and raises the main focus, as you see in Jim's email, we change people's perception of the purpose behind *why they work*. As is typical under such systems, Jim has lost sight of what it's all about. And he is thinking *me*, not *we*. Again, that is the natural outcome of that type of reward system. It worked fairly well in a manufacturing culture but not well with knowledge workers

---

84 W. Edward Deming, *The New Economics for Industry, Government, Education* (Cambridge, MA: MIT Center for Advanced Engineering Study, 1993), p. 112. Quoted from Kenneth W. Thomas, *Intrinsic Motivation at Work: Building Energy and Commitment* (San Francisco: Berrett-Koehler Press, 2002), p. 80.

who have to collaborate and where contributions to ultimate outcomes are often very difficult to determine. Also, understand that not only can we separate the level of performance and the level of contribution, rewarding work and rewarding engagement is also often not the same."

"Help me understand the last statement about rewarding work and rewarding engagement not being the same."

"We can buy compliance. People will *work* harder and expend more physical energy doing what they are told to do for more money or other extrinsic rewards. *Engagement*, however, results from investments of emotion and intellect. Such investments are the outcomes of intrinsic motivators—money really 'can't buy you love'! And I believe these intrinsic motivators create energy that extrinsic rewards do not."

"I like it, Jack, but I'm not sure I fully understand it. Explain how we can rate employees the same and give one a greater monetary reward."

"Mary, remember I said that performance and contribution are not always synonymous? Performance is about meeting and achieving standards, and contribution is about the value we add. Employees are not always given the same tasks to achieve, and it may be all the tasks have to be done for us to achieve our goals, but not all are of equal difficulty or value. If we reward just based on the comparative value a person adds, then there are times that no matter how well some people do their work, they cannot be a top performer. They are doomed from the start. So, there can be varying levels of contribution within performance levels, and financial incentive can be tied to the level of contribution. However, as you noted, too often performance ratings are solely determined by the financial incentive we think the employee should receive and not the excellence exhibited by the employee's performance. High performers can feel proud of themselves and their work and still understand that raises, bonuses, and promotions are in limited supply."

"So, what would the system look like?"

"Set goals and standards and confer rewards to the degree they are achieved. And award the right rewards in the right ways. For example, give visibility and credit. These nonmonetary rewards validate competence, and remember that knowing we are getting more capable and are deemed worthy and valued contributors to the groups of which we are part is intrinsically rewarding. All these also build trust, strengthen bonds, and set into motion a spiral of escalating engagement. And again, these rewards are free, yet they pay dividends.

"Let me add, also reward the right things. For example, effort counts. Not all good ideas and good efforts yield good results, but reward the engagement. Idea sharing is good. Not all ideas shared are good, but sharing them is, so reward sharing. Increased sharing of ideas and deepened engagement are much more likely to produce a winning idea and profitable results in the long run than decreased sharing and diminished engagement. Moreover, organizations need annoying people. Too often we see the person who keeps coming to us with ideas (not just dissatisfactions) as an irritant, and we give more favorable evaluations to those whose point of view and thinking fit the status quo. Unfortunately, although the less annoying people may perform 'best practices' with great skill, they may be less inclined to produce 'next practices.' Bad ideas often trigger good ideas in others; bad ideas are good, if really listened to."

"Intriguing. So we've gone through eleven of your difficult leadership journeys; what's the twelfth?" I think Mary was looking at her watch.

"The twelfth is *immerse yourself in IBM's Leadership Framework*.[85] We have repeatedly noted that you can't extrinsically incentivize engagement. Engagement is the unfolding of human nature and uplifting of the human spirit, but you can become a leader who creates the conditions that align and ally with that unfolding and ignite and enliven that spirit. To do so, check to understand fully what it takes to realize each of the nine IBM Competencies, how to prevent the various Derailment Factors, and how to nurture the seven dimensions of the

---

85 For a fuller discussion of IBM's Leadership Framework, go to Appendix I. Even if you are not an IBMer, the principles behind it should apply to any company.

Organizational Climate that enable high performance and foster deep engagement.[86] I realize that you are probably familiar with these competencies, but too often people mistake familiarity with them with being good at achieving them.[87] Keep searching for new understanding of them. We don't need new concepts; we need to get better at the ones we have already articulated. I often heard a former company chairman and CEO tell executives, 'I know people who spend a lot of money to improve their golf swing or to become gourmet cooks, but they never see the need to practice leadership.' He would go on to say even after his long career and having held significant leadership positions, he still felt the need to consciously practice leadership and get better."

"Whew, Jack, you have given me a lot to think about, and I can tell you that you have already increased *my* engagement. I feel much more confident than I did when I came in."

"That's great to hear, Mary. It's experiences and feedback like that that keep me going, and I can assure you they are worth more to me than money. Let me caution you, however, that The Engaging Leader's Dozen are not only difficult journeys but journeys without end. Even after remarkable progress, they will require vigilant attention. The very undertaking of them, however, has the potential of establishing an organizational ethos that 'we do good things that matter—and we do them well. I know *I* am making a difference and that *we* are making a difference. I can't think of work I'd rather be doing or people I'd rather be doing it with.'[88] Pretty engaging!"

---

86 For a discussion of the IBM Competencies, Derailment Factors, and Organizational Climate, go to Appendix I.

87 This comment can apply to more than just IBMers. When non-IBMers look at the competencies, derailment factors, and employee experience, they may see concepts similar to ones they know.

88 Kegan and Lahey, p. 92.

19

Turbulence Creates Leaders / Leaders Create Turbulence

Leadership is about turbulence. Turbulence creates leaders and leaders create turbulence. It may well be more difficult to lead in good times than in times of disquiet.

In 1986, Lieutenant General Dave Palmer was installed as the fifty-third superintendent of the United States Military Academy at West Point. At the time, I was teaching in the Department of Behavioral Sciences and Leadership.

Shortly after his arrival, General Palmer noted that he was in the fortunate circumstances of arriving at West Point at a time when there were no crises and with no mission to straighten things out—even the football team was winning—and so we could take advantage of this quiet time to reexamine ourselves as an institution and look to the future.

Over the next five years, General Palmer made changes and set others in motion that went to the core of what the Academy was about. He articulated a clear purpose statement and had it chiseled in stone. He clarified the Academy's mission and made major revisions to the "Fourth Class System,"[89] changing it from a rite of passage focused only on plebes (freshmen) to a "Four" Class System known as the Cadet Leadership Development System (CLDS).[90] CLDS provided the guidance for developing all four classes from entry to graduation. In addition, he instituted an innovative graduate program for tactical officers to ensure a consistent and better-informed approach to cadet development. He even uprooted a newly completed granite reviewing stand and realigned it on the parade field so the cadets could perform proper maneuvers during drills and ceremonies. Although all these changes were for the good of the Academy, giving birth to them was more analogous to a drenching hurricane than the gentle showers that bring buds to dormant plants and turn them into beautiful flowers and majestic trees.

In times of tranquility, change requires leaders to stir things up and increase the level of stress. Most of us are less motivated to change during times of tranquility than during times of tumult, when people are eager for direction and when, for the most part, change is directed toward bringing increased order and reducing the level of stress.

Late in the fourth quarter of 2008, the world economy was on the verge of collapse. There was concern within IBM, and within most other companies, about how to weather the storm. As leadership was seen as one of the main levers to pull, I was asked to provide guidance on "leading in tough economic times." What follows is the essence of my response to that request.

Leadership is about tough times, economic or other. Name a great leader (e.g., Lincoln, Churchill, Gandhi, Mandela, Iacocca, Gerstner),

---

89 Cadet classes are noted in descending order: A Fourth Class Cadet is a plebe (freshman), a Third Class Cadet is a yearling (sophomore), a Second Class Cadet is a cow (junior), and a First Class Cadet is a firstie (senior). The Fourth Class System has evolved over the years, but at the time of General Palmer's arrival, it required plebes to perform menial tasks, recite definitions and facts, and be subservient to the upper-class cadets. In many respects, it was more hazing and a rite of passage than leadership development.

90 The Military Academy had a development system for all four classes prior to LTG Palmer's arrival, but he clearly revived and highlighted it.

and you will see that in most instances, dire circumstances were behind their ascent. Perhaps to say turbulence *creates* leaders is an overstatement, but it gives potential leaders the opportunity to lead—to show themselves and to become known. Michelangelo said that the purpose of the sculptor's hand is "to free the figures slumbering inside the stone."[91] Turbulence serves a similar function in awakening leadership inside latent leaders.

The answer to the question about whether a tree falling in the forest makes a sound if no one is there is no. Sound is the result of the physical stimulus—sound waves—created by the falling tree striking receptor cells in the ear of a person or some other creature. Without the sound wave *and* the receptor cells both being present, there is only the *potential* for a sound to occur. Likewise with leadership; it requires turbulence to strike a latent leader before it can manifest itself. So, the current tough economic situation presents the right set of circumstances for great leadership. Opportunities abound.

My hope was that throughout IBM people were thinking, "This is our time! These are the times when legacies are established and legends created. We will be the stories told by those who come after us, because our actions now will identify who we are as leaders and what IBM is as a company!"

However, to emerge as a leader takes more than being caught in turbulence. Just as a diamond requires carbon, heat, and pressure, leadership will come to the fore in tough times in people and organizations that are *capable*, *confident*, and *agile*. Exhibiting these attributes will generate a winning spirit throughout the enterprise. And that spirit will fuel the resolve to persevere in the face of the most demanding conditions. "[I]t will sustain the will to win should circumstances look hopeless and show no indication of getting better."[92]

---

91 Michelangelo Quotes, http://www.michelangelo-gallery.com/quotes.aspx.
92 *FM 6-22, Army Leadership: The Warrior Ethos* (Washington, D.C.: Headquarters Department of the Army, 1999), pp. 4–11.

Capable

Being capable consists of demonstrating *leadership competencies*, possessing *functional skills*, and having a *grasp of business acumen*. IBM has a comprehensive concept of *leadership competencies*.[93] A competency includes a person's motives, traits, assumptions, self-image, social role, and values as well as his or her knowledge and skills. IBM's view of competency is akin to the U.S. Army's longstanding "Be, Know, Do"[94] leadership framework. It is about who we are as persons—our motives, values, character; what we know; and what we do with that knowledge. Our character and knowledge will shape what we perceive and what we can and must do in any given situation, but leadership happens only at the point when we act.

IBM has identified nine leadership competencies. While all are essential, in tough times the following stand out as the most important: embrace challenge, continuously transform, help IBMers succeed, and build mutual trust.[95] *Embrace challenge* has to do with being energized by taking on complex challenges. It is about wanting to make the world work better, from daily breakthroughs to world-changing progress. So leaders focus on the future and welcome the challenges facing their teams, their clients, and their communities. Moreover, they see opportunity in complexity and take personal accountability for transformative outcomes. This well-grounded confidence in themselves and others generates an attitude that inspires others to take on the challenge with them.

Such confidence to embrace challenge was expressed by Kenneth P. Cohen, ExxonMobil's vice president for government and public affairs, when asked about how ExxonMobil would meet the challenge of the 50 percent drop in the price of crude oil that resulted from the economic collapse in the fall of 2008. Mr. Cohen's response was, "These

---

93 I will illustrate my thoughts using IBM; however, these ideas will also fit using other companies' competencies. Look at your own and see whether there are appropriate substitutes.

94 *FM 22-100, Army Leadership: Be, Know, Do* (Washington, D.C.: Headquarters Department of the Army, 1999).

95 IBM's nine competencies are to embrace challenge, partner for client success, collaborate globally, act with a systemic perspective, build mutual trust, influence through expertise, continuously transform, communicate for impact, and help IBMers succeed. For a description of each, go to Appendix I.

are uncertain and challenging times, and these are the times that our company is built to handle. We understand we operate in a commodity business. We understand that the cycle will go up, and it will go down. We don't get excited in the highs. We don't panic in the lows."[96]

The importance of instilling the desire to embrace challenge before crises arise can be summed up even more succinctly in the words of a Marine gunny sergeant: "In combat you don't rise to the occasion; you sink to your level of preparation."[97] IBMers are prepared to embrace challenge.

Leaders' desire and ability to *continuously transform* springs from their intellectual curiosity and spirit of restless reinvention, which are animated by a belief in reason, in science, and in progress. These attributes infuse the enterprise with energy and cultivate an environment of openness to new approaches and experimentation. Leaders rethink assumptions and ask probing questions to grasp new situations that tough times present and to unearth opportunities. When doing so, they engage others whose background, culture, language, or work style is different from their own. This willingness to embrace diversity is the heart of an individual and organization that can learn, adapt, and continuously transform to meet new challenges.

The third competency, *help IBMers succeed*, would apply in any organization, so think of it as *help others succeed*. This competency is about a leader's striving to bring his or her best self to the task at hand and helping others to do the same. Leaders are in the service of the success of others—ensuring that their people have resources, ongoing support, and clear milestones. Leaders take the time to share insights and discuss the challenges that lie ahead. They anticipate and remove obstacles and prevailing practices that might hold people back from making changes necessary to meet unexpected or unprecedented challenges. They also acknowledge others' contributions, champion

---

96 http://www.nytimes.com/2008/10/31/business/31oil.html?scp=1&sq=%22These%20are%20
uncertain%20and%20challenging%20times%20and%20these%20are%20the%20times%20that%20
our&st=cse.

97 Dave Grossman, *On Killing: The Psychological Cost of Learning to Kill in War and Society* (New York: Little, Brown and Company, 1995).

their ideas, and give life to an environment in which all feel a sense of personal value, purpose, and engagement—all of which heightens members' desire to act.

As will be noted a bit further on, in tough times nothing is more important than *building mutual trust*. People who know they have others they can count on to do their part and with whom they can think things through feel more assured and less troubled in the face of adversity.

While all of IBM's nine competencies are components of leadership, embracing challenge, continuously transforming, helping each other, and building mutual trust are the most essential for creating the passion and building the confidence needed for especially difficult times. These competencies create the environment that enables leaders to perform regardless of their functional responsibilities. But competencies are not all that is needed to lead in tough times. Functional skills and business acumen are also needed.

Whereas competencies are universal to leadership regardless of function, each function within any enterprise (e.g., sales, software, services, systems, HR) is differentiated by a delineated set of skills. A leader's duty, especially in tough times, is to ensure that people assigned to a particular function have the *domain knowledge and skills* to perform that function with excellence. Leaders need to ensure that even good workers continue to get better at what they need to do. Leaders and organizational members must know their craft and strive for eminence in their field. Without acquiring the level of knowledge and skill that defines functional excellence, the broader leadership competencies become less relevant—especially at lower leadership levels. Excellent leadership can improve the performance of any team, but tough times demand excellent leadership of a team of excellently skilled individuals.

In addition to well-developed leadership competencies and preeminent functional skills, there is a third set of complementary broad capabilities an organization needs to succeed in tough times. Those capabilities can best be described as *business acumen* (e.g., applying financial insights and cultivating client and other external relationships). Leaders need to ensure that they, and the people they lead, have all these capabilities.

To succeed in the worst of times takes more than a few exceptional leaders in senior management. Success in such times requires depth of leadership. Organizations need individuals dispersed throughout the enterprise—in every segment and at every level—who are capable and willing to engage in *acts of leadership*, regardless of their position in the designated leadership hierarchy, to make their part of the company work. For organizations to succeed, people must act based on commitment, not mere compliance. Every employee needs to be prepared to accommodate system-wide strategy to ground-level realities.[98] Senior leaders need to hold themselves responsible to create the environment in which this will occur.

A word of caution: In many organizations, people are familiar with the needed competencies, and their functional skills and business acumen have led to success in normal times. Normal times can breed complacency. Difficult times will reveal insufficiencies that might not surface in good times. To get through hard economic times, we do not need new competencies, different functional skills, or a greatly modified concept of business acumen. We need *strengthened* competencies and *elevated* functional skills and business acumen. Getting better at each of these components of capability requires effort; we need to engage in individual self-development as well as institutional programs. We need to reflect on what we are doing on the job and help others to do the same. Leaders' modeling and discussion of these components of capability will convey expectations to all organizational members. Along with corporate values, highly developed capability provides stability and clarity in the face of ambiguity and uncertainty.

Confident

In tough times, outstanding capability is indispensable, but what most differentiates leading in tough times from leading in good times is

---

98 John Gardner, *On Leadership* (New York: Free Press, 1999), p. ix.

the need for confidence—confidence in ourselves *and in each other*. To be effective in tough times, leaders must heighten motivation and build confidence—they must uplift the human spirit. And that process starts with individual leaders. Leaders are not immune to the anxiety, insecurity, and confusion that accompany tough times. They must prepare themselves to face those issues and keep them from undermining their confidence.

The bedrock upon which confidence is built is trust. Leaders must display integrity at all times. They must act according to clear principles and not just based on convenience or what works now. And, there must be 360 degrees of trust. In addition to trusting themselves and earning the trust of their people, leaders must trust their people and their colleagues. Fostering this 360 degrees of trust is necessary for a positive organizational climate and strong performance at any time, but the requirement for this level of trust becomes even more imperative during tough times—the very time when it is more difficult to achieve because the stakes are so high and the consequences of a misstep are greatest.

Leaders need to take an honest look at the level of trust in their organization. Leaders have a mandate to improve the level of trust that they have in their people and that their people have in themselves. As mentioned in earlier chapters, there are The 5 Trust Vital Signs that are characteristic of an environment in which trust can flourish. Leaders must have confidence that their people (and that they, themselves) know *what* to do, know *how* to do it, know *why* they do it, *care why* they do it, and *are enabled* to do it. Testing for these vital signs will not only help diagnose whether 360-degree trust exists but will also indicate what has to be done to strengthen them. Creating this degree of trust is no small feat, but gaining an authentic and credible trust in their people's capabilities boosts leaders' self-confidence and relieves them of the apprehension of facing challenges alone. In times when leaders face overwhelming challenges, they need confidence that *together*, they with their people can figure out what needs to be done and do it. This trust is essential to help people develop initiative, strengthen their judgment, and grow into better contributors.

Confidence is not just belief in ourselves and in each other but in the future. Leadership at its core is about optimism. Tough times attack optimism; leaders must protect optimism and keep it alive. People have to believe in their capacity to achieve great results. Leaders must ignite this enlivening belief. To do otherwise will breed dependency and pessimism, the consequence of which is "an incapacity to summon energy to make the necessary effort, an unwillingness to take risks, and a fatal timidity when the moment of opportunity breaks."[99] Leaders who communicate confidence, hope, and resilience to their people lift performance.

Leaders communicate confidence through *presence*. They must be *visible* and *available*.[100] Presence is not just a matter of showing up; it involves the image we project. Leaders set the tone by their example and conduct. In tough times, they must be particularly aware of what they say and do—even their physical appearance and the way they carry themselves will have intensified impact. They need to think about their demeanor. Being rested and physically fit will not only project a more positive appearance, but it will also enable leaders to perform more effectively under stress and in the face of inevitable setbacks. In the midst of turbulence, leaders have to take care of themselves. Sometimes the most important person to take care of is yourself. Leaders need to make consequential decisions, and a reasonably rested mind is better able to do so than one fuzzy from fatigue and racked with tension.

"*Visibility* [italics added] will take on special importance in that it sends the message [leaders] are engaged and actively involved in taking the measures necessary to resolve problems."[101] Leaders must be aware of their emotions as well as their physical appearance. People will watch their leaders' reactions to stress. Leaders must remain levelheaded. Leaders control their emotions; they are not controlled by them.

---

99 Gardner, p. 196.
100 Gene Klann, *Crisis Leadership* (Greensboro: Center for Creative Leadership, 2003), p. 52. I have taken these two words from Gene Klan; however, I have described *visibility* differently, and he gives no specific description of *availability*. He, too, used these words in terms of leading in difficult times.
101 Klann, p. 52.

Instead of outbursts of frustration or anger, or showing no emotions at all, leaders need to display the right amount of sensitivity and passion to tap into people's positive emotions. If leaders lose self-control, they cannot expect their people to maintain theirs. Leaders always have responsibility for controlling their own emotions and, to a degree, controlling those of others. Leaders have to convey that things are urgent without creating panic or hopelessness. They need to calibrate organizational tensions so that they stimulate positive emotions and energy as opposed to destructive stress. They have to be able to encourage their people to press on, even at the toughest moments when they see them faltering. More than ever, their people will be looking to them to set the example. Maintaining self-control inspires calm confidence in the entire organization.

Presence must be accompanied by information. Leaders must be *available*. People need information. They need to know the strategic intent and the business design that will allow them to execute. They need to know the information that applies directly to their duties as well as the context so that they understand what needs to be done. They need to know why. Effective leaders communicate the big picture; they provide the proper perspective on unfolding events. Employees will be more committed if their leaders keep them in the loop. Stick to the facts. We often have a tendency to think the worst. Communicating critical factual information allows people to gain a new understanding of the situation, controls rumors, and reduces anxiety. Timely information will allow people to determine what has to be done to accomplish their goals and to adjust to changing circumstances.

Open communication does more than share information. It communicates that leaders care about their people, and it builds trust. Informing people of decisions and the reasons behind them shows the people that they are appreciated and conveys that their support and input are needed. It helps them see how their work contributes to the organization's success. Leaders need to foster two-way communication. They must actively listen to their people. Information must flow up as well as down. Leaders must encourage their people to be forthright without fear of repercussions. Upward communication is the way senior leaders find out what their people are thinking, doing, and feeling. This upward communication may include employees' views of their leaders.

Tough times present everyone with developmental opportunities, and leaders need to spend their energy on self-development and development of their people and not waste time on being defensive, denying that anything is wrong, or analyzing the shortcomings of others. To quote John Gardner, "If messages from below say you are doing a flawless job, send back for a more candid assessment."[102] Leaders must benefit from what their people are telling them. They need to keep their fingers on the pulse of the organization; they need their people's ideas. Tough times are times for creativity and innovation, and what people tell their leaders can be of great assistance in planning and decision-making—and, at times, for the leaders' self-development. Leaders need to set up multiple means of communicating. Leaders have to find ways to ensure that they hear their people and that their people know their leaders are listening.

We all have an innate need to be valued and appreciated. Nothing builds confidence more than feeling that we are valued and contributing members of the group. Leaders need to find opportunities to recognize, affirm, and validate their people. Giving people more responsibilities sends those messages—as does acting on their ideas. Leaders need to enable their people to use their judgment by providing conceptual controls.[103] When leaders listen to their people's ideas, feed them responsibility, and enable them to use their judgment to make decisions, they increase their people's sense of empowerment. Doing so also increases their people's sense of engagement. Empowerment and engagement are the fuel that sustains all of us when things look bleak.

Empowering does not mean omitting checks or forgoing corrections. Disciplined execution is essential. Standards must be communicated and enforced. Proper supervision enables leaders to get to know their people better and prepare them for increasingly independent action. It allows them to know if their people are capable of doing the tasks

---

102 Gardner, p. 26.
103 Leading by conceptual controls is discussed more fully in Chapter 16, "Leading Kindergarten Recess."

assigned—do they know what to do, do they know how to do it, do they feel enabled to do it? Proper monitoring not only communicates to people that what they do matters—and that they matter; it also allows leaders to gauge whether plans are realistic and whether decisions have been wise. Leaders' ultimate obligation is to ensure their people have the necessary abilities, resources, and motivation to accomplish what they ask them to do.

Disciplined execution does not result from arbitrary orders, berating people on cadence calls, or demanding instant and blind obedience. Such behavior tends to destroy trust. Disciplined execution comes by providing feedback in a manner and tone that inspires a positive desire to perform. It must be coupled with respect for employees. Effective leaders instill discipline by setting high standards, seeing that their people are trained and resourced to meet those standards, and building trust and confidence among team members. Discipline also involves leaders taking care of their people and creating an environment in which they can learn and grow. When mistakes happen, as they inevitably will, leaders should help sort out what happened and why, but they must look at mistakes in a positive manner—to see what can be learned, not whom to blame. Leaders need to hold themselves and their people to high standards and refuse to cut corners, but also they must treat their people fairly, share their hardships, and use mistakes to develop, not to punish, them. Positive discipline results in teams that are self-empowered and self-disciplined and that have an infectious spirit that sees problems as challenges and not obstacles. When things go badly, positive discipline provides an inner reserve they can draw on to persevere.

Agile

To adapt, a leader must first sense the need. Leaders constantly scan what is going on in the work environment and mission. With awareness of the situation, they will be better able to recognize when circumstances have changed or when the plan is not achieving the desired results. Under the current global economic conditions, we need to be ready to address unanticipated events that will require us to replace plans with new ideas and initiatives. Leaders need to guard against clinging to nonproductive approaches. Our tactics must be flexible, but our goals must remain stable.

Being capable and confident sets the groundwork for being agile. In the new operational environment, the importance of workers lower in the organizational hierarchy making the correct decisions under pressure has taken on a new significance. Decisions and actions taken at the direct leadership levels can have major strategic impacts. Senior leaders need to communicate priorities, the current thinking on solutions, and what success looks like. They have to determine which decisions they need to make and which can and should be pushed to a lower level.

Inevitably, adjustments will be needed when facing unanticipated obstacles. In increasingly difficult times, leaders need to provide an environment in which their people can focus on and accomplish *critical* tasks. Leaders must minimize distractions. They need to ensure that additional tasks are within the team's capabilities. If the new tasks are not within the team's capabilities, line leaders need to seek relief by going to more senior leaders and clarifying the impact that the additional workload will have on the team or organization. Moreover, when enforcing standards, leaders should make sure the standards fit the importance of the task. Not everything can be the number one priority, and striving for perfection in relatively low-priority tasks would rob an organization of needed energy.

Effective leaders are good stewards of their own and their people's time and energy. They must anticipate cyclical workloads and schedule accordingly. They must make good decisions about when to push their people and when to ease back and narrow focus on the one or two most important tasks. Managing budgets and prioritizing other resources in an ever-changing environment is difficult. Especially in tough times, leaders must allocate resources judiciously. At times, leaders will need to make on-the-spot adjustments in the course of action to keep moving toward the designated goals. Leaders need to be more intent-centric than plan-centric, changing their tactics but not the strategic goal.

Leaders must recognize and address problems quickly. Getting and staying tuned into what is going on throughout the organization allows leaders to identify and solve problems before they escalate. Shared adversity is fraught with emotions; often those emotions strengthen bonds within a group, but the stress and pressure will inevitably create friction. Leaders' ability to reduce friction is critical. Failing to do so will cause divisiveness, which will dissipate energy, divert focus, and cripple efforts to achieve common goals.

Effective leaders think change. They prepare to be agile when the need or opportunity for beneficial change presents itself. Resisting reversion to a "command and control" style of leadership in tough times is difficult. However, necessity often *is* the mother of invention. Tough times stimulate innovation; leaders must not impede innovation by reflexively inserting an answer from the past. Developing agility in good times will prepare leaders to act quickly to take advantage of the opportunities adversities present. Leaders need to think creatively. New problems will arise, and old problems may require new solutions. People will need to develop new ideas and approaches, and they will have to do so under stress and amid chaos. Leaders should provide structure that will promote agile decision-making.

Clarity of purpose and well-understood organizational values help create such a structure. As Gene Klann from the Center for Creative Leadership has stated, "A viable vision communicates the direction the company is moving and what it will look like when it gets there. Values communicate what is important to the organization."[104] Clarity of purpose and well-understood organizational values provide reference points to people confronting ambiguity and uncertainty. They give us a sense of stability in times of chaos, confusion, and change. They give us a framework for our decision-making. This framework should be in place before crises arise. Leaders must constantly model and emphasize the organization's values and shared sense of purpose. Doing so binds members of an organization to each other—and will help hold things together when they seem to be falling apart.

Resiliency is essential to both confidence and agility. As mistakes and setbacks are inevitable, organizations need the character to bounce

---

104 Klann, p. 23.

back when things go wrong. Effective leadership will rally people to move forward despite setbacks. Gene Klann puts it this way:

> Leadership consistency is like the smooth ride of a well-engineered car—the car's suspension system adapts to the bumps in the road to protect passengers and to provide stability. In the same way, a leader who can handle change and difficulty with flexibility, courage, and optimism protects others in the organization, provides stability in a tumultuous environment, and inspires trust.[105]

Resilience *requires* confidence and *develops* confidence. Building resilience is difficult. Keep in mind, resilience is forged by setbacks and failures. We are never sure if we can get up until we have been knocked down. Many leaders at IBM and elsewhere have known mostly success. They must understand that their resilience may not have been fully tested. They must develop a reservoir of mental toughness to tap into when put to the test. Flagging in the face of setbacks can trigger a chain reaction throughout the organization that can lead to pessimism and paralysis. Leaders can encourage themselves by using positive self-statements, for example, telling themselves *something didn't work*—not that *it can't be done*. Leaders must encourage themselves and others. Setbacks must not be a source of self-doubt but of renewed resolve.

Leaders need to be critical thinkers. They also need to think on their feet. While continuing to execute, they need to interrogate the beliefs and assumptions underlying their actions. They need to develop the capacity to imagine and explore alternatives to their existing thinking and ways of doing things. Identifying assumptions is often difficult. Two proven techniques are *in-process review* (IPR) and *after-action review* (AAR).[106] An in-process review is a quality checkpoint on the path to accomplishing the mission. Assessment begins with taking a picture of the organization's performance as early as possible. Leaders anticipate in which areas the organization might have trouble and focus attention there. Once an organization begins a mission, successive IPRs evaluate performance as the mission proceeds and give timely feedback. Leaders

---

105 Klann, p. 57.
106 These techniques were developed by, and are in constant use in, the U.S. Army.

can use IPRs for major plans and operations as well as for day-to-day events. They will allow an organization to preempt problems.

AARs fulfill a similar role at the end of a mission. The AAR is a structured review that allows participating members to review what went right and what went wrong, to determine why things went well or badly, and to figure out how to repeat success and avoid failure next time. AARs are a good opportunity to develop people who did not participate in the mission but may have similar missions in the future. When organizational members share in identifying reasons for success and failure, they become owners of how things are done. Leaders need to be inquisitive and conduct regular assessments of themselves and their organizations and hold both to the highest standards. They have to be competent not only in planning, preparing, and executing but also in assessing. Once they complete an assessment and identify problems, they can develop appropriate solutions to address the problems. Open-minded reflection and corrective action are critical for performance in difficult times.

IPRs and AARs present invaluable opportunities to hear what is on people's minds. Agile adaptation requires broadening our perspectives. Leaders need to appreciate that they are faced not just with uncertain economic conditions but also the rapid intermingling of cultures. Large global organizations have become more culturally diverse, requiring employees and their leaders to deal with people from a wider range of ethnic, racial, and cultural backgrounds. Leaders must prevent misunderstandings arising from those differences. They must take into account that the economic challenges and any solutions the company might propose to meet those challenges may be viewed differently in different cultural contexts.

Leaders should model the desire to learn about people's cultural differences. By seeking to understand others' backgrounds, looking at things from their perspectives, and appreciating what is important to them, leaders demonstrate their respect for other people's cultures and sensitivity to differences among the various cultures. Leaders must understand that they have as much to learn from others as others do from them. Leaders need to be in touch with how company plans will play out on the ground and what the second- and third-order consequences of company decisions will be. The better able leaders are to see things from others' points of view and to understand others' feelings, the better they can live out the value of trust and the more quickly they will be to isolate problems, identify solutions, and take initiative to adjust during execution.

In turbulent times, leaders must adapt and exploit emerging opportunities. They must be flexible, innovative, and prepared to face the challenges at hand with the resources available. Navigating tough times will require each leader to learn, handle multiple demands, and shift priorities with agility. They will have to apply analytical problem solving, informed judgment, and courageous risk taking. Moving forward in such times will be exciting and daunting.

Leadership is hard. It requires major expenditures of effort and sacrifice—more than most people are willing to give.[107] But keep in mind that the future is shaped by leaders who believe in the future and in themselves and in their people. Leaders must have confidence that they can meet challenges. Leaders must reinforce the conviction that what is inside each of us is more than equal to the challenges we face. And leaders must recognize that although we will inevitably experience setbacks, we always have two choices: to give up or to get up and go on. Leaders choose to go on.

---

107 Gardner, p 3.

20

Leadership: It's Just Talk

The phone rang; it was Jane O'Donnell.[108] A few years before, she had participated in a program for high-potential vice presidents that the company runs once or twice annually. I had bumped into her several times since then but had not had much of a chance to talk with her. "Hi, Jack, I've just received an invitation to attend an Integration & Values Team Initiative.[109] Can you give me some idea of what I'm in for?"

"First of all, Jane, congratulations on becoming a member of the I&VT; that is quite an accomplishment. Did that just happen?"

"Thanks, Jack. Yes, I was notified a few months ago, and now I've just received this invitation to the I&VT Initiative. I'm a bit curious about what I should expect."

---

108 This is a fictitious name.

109 I&VT stands for Integration & Values Team, which consist of roughly 300 of IBM's most senior leaders. They are charged with integrating IBM by leading by values. In addition to leading within their business unit or function, they are to act as integrators across the matrixed IBM enterprise. The I&VT Initiative is an action learning activity that all member of the I &V Team eventually participate in, but it is also used to bring new members onto the I &V Team.

"Jane, the I&VT Initiatives are action learning activities that subsets of senior executives on the I&VT engage in as developmental experiences. There will be some longstanding members and some newer members, like you, involved—probably about thirty participants in all. The overall objective is twofold. First, Sam[110] will give the group a charter—a fairly substantial enterprise-wide issue to investigate—on which he will expect you to make recommendations. We usually run one or two of these initiatives a year."

"Any idea of what the charter will be?" Jane inquired.

"I don't know offhand; I think it's being determined in the next few days. However, it will be a critical enterprise-wide integration challenge, and the expectation will be that the solution will have a significant business impact."

"How long will we have in order to study the issues and come up with recommendations? And what if none of us has any expertise in the particular area?"

I sensed Jane was feeling a bit anxious. "I'm not sure of the exact timetable that you will have, Jane, but the initiative will be spread out over about three months. You will meet as an entire group three times, for about a week each. The first week will start with an orientation to I&VT membership, and then you will get immersed in the specific business challenge and plan the next steps. During the next four to six weeks, you as a group will gather whatever information you think that you need. You may benchmark with other companies and talk to external subject-matter experts and the like. Internally, you may do site visits and learn what you can from internal stakeholders and experts.

"Following the information gathering, you will meet again for a week to share your findings, insights, and questions and to determine what else the group needs to do. That meeting will be followed by another few weeks of data gathering and synthesis. Then you will return to headquarters, finalize your recommendations, and prepare your

---

110 Samuel Palmisano, IBM's chairman and CEO.

presentation to Sam. After making the presentation to Sam, you will integrate any feedback that he gives you, and then you will discuss your findings and recommendations with the operations team[111] to see what, if any, of the recommendations senior management wants implemented. You may also be involved in the ongoing implementation."

"That sounds pretty exciting, Jack, but you said there were two goals; what's the other?"

"Jane, the second objective is the main one, but many participants miss it. Investigating an enterprise-wide integration challenge and coming up with recommendations is of value in and of itself; however, it is really a means to an end—not an end in itself. The purpose behind this developmental activity is to build the sustainable leadership capability needed to integrate IBM in the future. It is about how the participants in the initiative, as a team, work *together* after the Initiative is over."

"Please explain that some more, Jack." Jane seemed a bit puzzled.

"Jane, remember one of the first things you asked was, 'What if none of us has any expertise in this particular area?'"

"Yes, won't we be pretty helpless and lost without some experts to guide us?"

"Jane, there is no question that in many situations experts help. It's great when there is a problem and someone has *the* answer and everyone falls in line to accomplish whatever they are told needs to be done to solve and fix the problem. However, both the marketplace and world are becoming increasingly complex and ambiguous, and more often than not, we need to decide among a number of possible answers, the consequences of which are not that clear. Leaders need to figure out what they should do when *they* feel at a loss and confused. Leadership is not about constant compliance and execution of well-understood missions; it's about determining the direction when the compass

---

111   The operations team is a small group of IBM's most senior leaders who meet with the chairman and CEO to make final enterprise strategy and strategic business decisions.

needle is spinning. Leadership is increasingly about the unfamiliar, the unexplored, and the unknown."

"Jack, that sounds a bit like the blind leading the blind! But I do see how dealing with unfamiliar events increases the chances that some new solution will emerge—but it feels pretty scary."

"Yes, Jane, increasingly something new is required, and we need to face the sense of disequilibrium, not try to escape it. It seems to be a pretty common reaction that we look for someone to save us and show us the way when we feel lost. There is nothing wrong with getting help from someone who has solved a problem before. At times, though, there is no one to reach out to or the problems are new, and we and our colleagues have to dig deep within ourselves to find the way out of our dilemmas and how to advance into the future without the help of someone who has mapped the escape route or the way forward before."

"So, Jack, you are saying we need to learn how to figure things out together."

"Yes. There is a professor at MIT by the name of William Isaacs. He wrote a book called *Dialogue and the Art of Thinking Together*.[112] In it, he states that too often 'we see our conversations as either opportunities to trade information or an arena in which to win points.'"

"I have to admit, many meetings seem like sparring contests between a few attendees, and the rest of us are in the role of spectator. But isn't sharing of information a good thing?"

"Jane, there is certainly a place for sharing information. People need to learn from one another; the difficulty comes with the extent to which we are so wedded to our points of view that we can't suspend them long enough to listen to others. Too often in meetings, people don't listen to one another. And, as you stated, too often most people in a meeting play the role of spectator. Thinking together occurs when people not only learn *from* each other but also *with* each other."

---

112 William Isaacs, *Dialogue and the Art of Thinking Together* (New York: Currency, 1999), p. 9.

"Jack, you are so right as far as listening—or the lack of it. If people aren't interrupting or talking over others, they are merely waiting for an opening to make a comment or give their opinion. It's like a tennis match: One person slams the ball across the net, and the other person instantly slams it back. There is often not enough real thinking going on—just people trying to score points, and many don't even participate. They just sit on the sidelines and wait to find out the outcome and what they are accountable for, and then they grouse about it in the hall after the meeting. It would be great if we could change that dynamic. A lot does seem to have to do with the way we engage in conversation with one another."

"Jane, the degree to which the I&VT or any other group of leaders achieves the ability to listen to each other and to learn with each other is the degree to which they transform from being a collection of dynamic leaders to a dynamic collective leadership force within the enterprise."

"Jack, I'm glad I made this call. This has been very helpful. I know that I would have not thought too much about how we relate and interact with one another. I would have just been heads down, trying to address the challenge—and frankly, pretty much hoping someone had the answer. I will be tuned into this more subtle outcome."

"It's been great hearing from you again, Jane, and do me a favor: Help your colleagues attend to these interactions as well. And again, congratulations on being selected to the I&VT; it is well deserved."

"Thanks, Jack."

The call ended, and I hoped Jane had a new perspective on the exercise in which she was about to participate. To many people, the concept of *collective leadership* is an oxymoron. We have deeply embedded cultural notions about leaders and leadership. We want someONE in charge—especially when times are ambiguous and difficult.

Although John Wayne died in 1979, even people who were not born at the time have an immediate understanding of not only who, but also *what,* John Wayne was. He could, and did, do it all. There was no mess too messy for him to clean up—and he did it with very little brooding. His hallmark was quick and decisive action. He was *a leader*—and, ah, if there were only more of him! The heck with "Where have you gone, Joe DiMaggio?"; our "lonely eyes" are not seeking Joe, they are desperately seeking John. But just like "Joltin' Joe," "The Duke" "has left and gone away."[113] And *we* are left on our own.

John Wayne was an actor; there was no mess, just a script, director, and multiple retakes. Yet, how often do we expect people who seek or occupy leadership positions to be a John (or Jane) Wayne? During Katrina, the overwhelmed New Orleans Mayor Ray Nagin was looking for John Wayne and expressed relief when Lieutenant General Russel Honoré, whom he referred to as a "John Wayne dude that can get some stuff done," arrived. As Mayor Nagin put it, "He came off the doggone chopper and he started cussing and people started moving!"[114] After Katrina, Representative Christopher Shayes of Connecticut, in Congressional hearings, berated FEMA's Director Michael Brown for not being Rudy Giuliani, who to some was the twenty-first century's reincarnation of John Wayne. How often do people who hold those positions expect that of themselves? In the interest of time, let me give you the short answer: too often.

We look for John Wayne when we feel lost, confused, scared—or lazy. He can take away our anxiety and uncertainty. But he also takes our sense of responsibility, our incentive to innovate, and our chance to grow. Similarly, leaders who believe that they must be John (or Jane) Wayne experience undue stress, miss out on the wisdom that surrounds them, and fail to lead as effectively as they otherwise could. Hollywood made Marion Mitchell Morrison into John Wayne; in the real world, it is just *us,* and we have to decide if we are going to lead—and if so, how?

In today's complex world and that of the future, one person cannot provide the necessary leadership that a complex organization needs to stay at the forefront of its field. Leadership must come

---

113 Paul Simon, "Mrs. Robinson," from the Academy Award–winning film *The Graduate*, 1967.
114 *Stars & Stripes*, "'One John Wayne dude' tackles relief efforts" (September 4, 2005), p. 1, http://www.stripes.com/news/one-john-wayne-dude-tackles-relief-efforts-1.37858.

from all involved—and all must be involved. Unlike traditional models of leadership, collective leadership is not about the personal characteristics and attributes of a few people at the top; rather, collective leadership results from a set of practices that governs the way people at all levels throughout the organization interact with one another.[115]

We generally equate leadership with influence. For example, we attribute good leadership to those who advocate and negotiate well. The sense of a collective leadership, however, begins to take hold when the question changes from "What do I have to say to convince the others?" to "What are the others trying to say to me?" "Why are they saying it?" "Do I really understand?" and "Is there something I can learn from what they are saying?" So, now the group members have gone from advocacy to inquiry and a mutual search for answers. Group members relax their grip on certainty, and they move from strongly speaking their own voice to being open to influence from others. As William Isaacs puts it, they state clearly and confidently what they think and why they think it, "while at the same time being open to being wrong."[116] It is at this point that individual participants begin to share the collective leadership task of creating the conditions in which mutual learning and understanding can take place. They confer legitimacy and respect for others' points of view and have an interest in understanding them—even if they ultimately do not agree. And they permit themselves to question their own assumptions as well as those of others.

Thinking together requires us to listen to ourselves as well as to others. We must be in dialogue with ourselves as well as with others. As William Isaacs puts it:

> One must listen in a serious way, not just to others' words, but to our own reaction to their words, and to the impulses that arise within us that make us want to react. As we do this we must also suspend our reactions and assumptions about what others say.[117]

---

115 Craig L. Pearce and Jay A. Conger, *Shared Leadership* (Thousand Oaks, CA: Sage, 2003).
116 Isaacs, p. 188.
117 Isaacs, p. 190.

Our ideas are a part of who we are, so when someone questions our ideas, even without hostility, we often feel threatened, which gives rise to the urge to defend. The feeling of threat and the urge to defend ourselves make it difficult for us to interrogate our own points of view and assumptions. We need to be vigilant for those feelings and use them as signals to open our minds for deeper inquiry rather than reflexively erecting barriers in defense of our current points of view.

When leaders create a psychologically safe environment in which there is a productive sharing of ideas and feelings and in which conflict is constructive, complex learning occurs as people explore and test their own as well as others' operating assumptions. The discovering and testing of current operating assumptions are what lead to change. Robert Kegan and Lisa Laskow Lahey, in their groundbreaking work on immunity to change, assert that within each of us there are deeply held beliefs that prevent us from making the changes we earnestly intend to make, and it is only through uncovering and testing the veracity of these beliefs that we are able to make lasting changes.[118]

Once this reflective dialogue is achieved, the conditions are set for a truly generative dialogue to occur. As group members gain new understanding of themselves and their colleagues, there is an ever-deepening sense of trust and openness in which the entire group assumes responsibility for the process itself as well as for the outcomes. As Pearce and Conger put it, "individuals experience the group or team as a connected web rather than as a set of individuals."[119] At this point, group members can energetically and nondefensively share not only their points of view but also their uncertainties, desires, and possibilities—and their appreciation for those expressed by others. They inquire into conflict rather than immediately attempting to quell it. The focus now is fully on the *common good*, and since "winning" presupposes opponents, the group moves beyond the accommodations of "win-win" to co-created and innovative outcomes.

---

118 Robert Kegan and Lisa Laskow Lahey, *Immunity to Change: How to Overcome It and Unlock the Potential in Yourself and Your Organization* (Boston: Harvard Business School Publishing Corp., 2009).

119 Pearce and Conger, p. 38.

Once we are listening to others and to ourselves, the whole becomes greater than the sum of its parts. The group's focus is on the facts and on how those facts relate to the achievement of commonly held goals. People are willing to let the facts lead where they lead and to accept the best ideas, whether those ideas were originally theirs or someone else's. The norm is "Let's look at the facts and figure this thing out." People understand that they are in the situation *together* and that the surest way to overcome obstacles and find the best way forward is to listen to and test each other's ideas and to support each other's participation in the process. As Ira Chaleff puts it, in effective organizations, "followers and leaders both orbit around the purpose; followers do not orbit around the leader."[120] In similar fashion, Michele Doyle and Mark Smith state:

> Where conversation has taken over, people run with the exchange and gain learning from that. It turns into a journey of discovery rather than a route with a fixed destination. For leadership this can be liberating. It means as individuals we don't have to know the answers. *What we need is to develop ways of being in conversation that allow those answers to arise* [italics added].[121]

When this type of leadership is being exhibited, people share ideas and *follow the conversation*, not any particular individual.

In spite of this chapter's title, leadership is more than talk. Leadership requires action. Thinking together, however, is the essential ingredient and catalyst for collective action. Thinking together generates a sense of collective ownership—and collective ownership involves the assumption of personal responsibility by every member of the organization. Owning an issue takes it from the routine to something deeply personal. When we own an issue, we invest ourselves more deeply in it. We give it more of our thought and energy. It is now *ours*, not someone else's, to resolve; we are not just complying with what the boss told us to do. We are doing what we believe should and needs to be

---

120 Ira Chaleff, *The Courageous Follower: Standing Up to and for Our Leaders* (San Francisco: Barrett-Kohler, 2009), p. 13.

121 Michele Doyle and Mark Smith, *Shared Leadership* (http://www.infed.org/leadership/shared_ leadership.htm), p. 9.

done. It becomes integral to whom we see ourselves as being. Collective leadership spreads ownership throughout the organization dealing with the issue. But within the collective, it remains *ours*, not the *other person's*.

Being a collective leadership force and *acting together* and *thinking together* usually do not involve every person in a worldwide organization. Collective leadership implies that the individuals who constitute the team take on the responsibility for leadership when their expertise, passion, and availability call for it. *Acting together* starts when some set of individuals identifies a challenge or opportunity and takes the initiative to self-organize to address it. They engage in *thinking together* to eliminate the sources of potential fragmentation, thereby enabling collective integrative action to occur. They identify stakeholders and make sure that all stakeholders have a chance to present their concerns. Their unity around the concern amplifies the sense of urgency within the enterprise and their unity of resolve builds confidence in ultimate success.

This group of concerned leaders, in concert with the identified stakeholders, constitutes a guiding coalition whose power is magnified by its breadth, consistency of message, and unity of effort. Moreover, the bonds formed and confidence built in each other foster a willingness to take informed risks and sustain the emotional strength necessary to persevere. Acting together requires exceptional leadership *and* effective management. An inspiring vision is followed not only by empowerment but by monitoring the execution and solving the inevitable problems that arise. Strategy and direction are coupled with planning and budgeting. And alignment is backed by the organizing and staffing required for implementation. Finally, successful approaches are institutionalized enterprise-wide so that they are repeatable and ongoing.

Collective leadership does not eliminate a chain of command or formal authority's accountability. A decision-making structure is essential. However, leaders in subordinate positions take responsibility and are enabled to act. They take shared responsibility for identifying issues, formulating solutions, and taking action. These groups are not leaderless; they are "leaderfull." When collective leadership exists, all members feel engaged and empowered. Leadership is defined by the quality of our interactions, not our position. Hierarchical distinctions exist, but as people at all levels of the hierarchy are involved in the leadership process, the hierarchical distinctions are less important than the interdependencies among members of the collective leadership group. Most significant is that in the face of ambiguity and uncertainty, the sense of security does not come from being told what to do or by being given the right answer. John Wayne need not appear. The sense of safety and well-being comes from the confidence we have in the community who is "in it" with us.

Leaders in Their Own Words

21

Leaders Are Full of Hot Air![122]

Bill came into my office. "You've got to hear this." His facetious grin signaled that I probably did not need to hear what he was about to say, but it would be fun if I did.

Flopping into the chair by my desk, he continued, "You won't believe it. I was there. I heard it with my own ears!"

"Heard what?" I asked.

"I wouldn't have believed it if I weren't there. Charles Addison,[123] the outside leadership guru to whom we pay big bucks to talk to our new executives, just told the group in the auditorium that 'leaders are full of hot air!'" The feigned disbelief in his voice was betrayed by the glee in his eyes.

"Really?" I said. "Tell me more."

---

122 In the interest of ensuring that I separate stories that happened from those that did not, I confess taking liberties with this one.

123 This is a fictitious person. If it coincides with any real person, it is only by coincidence.

"Well, he was talking about managing. He was saying that managing is about processes—about efficiency, best practices, and delivering state-of-the art products and services—all that stuff. Then he said, 'Leadership is about blowing white hot air across these processes.'"

"Then what did he say?" I asked. Charles Addison was an iconic retired senior executive who was well known for having turned around a major company that was on the verge of extinction and a respected authority on leadership. I had heard Addison speak a number of times, and it was apparent that Bill was delighted to have this opportunity to twist Addison's words to support his oft-stated opinion that a number of bosses—most notably his own—were full of hot air. I could not resist the opportunity to play along. And why miss the chance to test Bill's creativity?

"I don't know. I didn't stay. I had heard all I needed to hear, and I just had to come up and tell you. This is exactly what I have been telling you about my boss. He's full of hot air, and now Charles Addison has confirmed it. Most of these guys are just full of hot air. Maybe I should send them a memo telling them what Addison just said about them," Bill continued with no sign of letting up on the fun he was having word-clipping a noted speaker's statements. And, since it was Friday afternoon, what better way to end the week than to share some light moments with a friend and colleague? So I was not about to quit either.

"Well, Bill, I have heard Mr. Addison say that some executives 'swell up and others grow up,' but I don't think he had your boss specifically in mind, and I think you are missing the point."

"Well, I'm sure if Addison knew my boss he'd at least include him as a data point in support of his assertion that some executives swell up with all that hot air!"

"Well, you may be right, Bill, but I hope that the new executives Mr. Addison was speaking to understand that he was stating a fundamental truth about leadership: It always begins with passion—passion about a better tomorrow. Passion keeps people focused on the goal. It's what fuels leadership. It nourishes the courage to take bold action and supplies the emotional stamina and resilience necessary to persist when things get tough—and they always do.

"More important, passion is contagious. It energizes the entire organization. Keep in mind, leadership is about accomplishing things *through others*. Our own former CEO, Lou Gerstner, refers to passion as 'the electricity that courses through a well-made machine that makes it run, makes it hum, makes it want to run harder and better.'[124] Now, I admit, I'm not sure machines think about running faster and harder, but humans do. Bill, leaders don't just unleash employees' power and motivation; they create and increase it. Too few people in leadership positions realize that they have this responsibility.

"A few years ago, Mark Shearer, who is currently IBM's GM for System i, warned a group of new executives that 'one of IBM's core competencies is making exciting things dull.' As he put it, 'We turn it into skim milk.' Like Mr. Gerstner, Mark was conveying to them that there is a visceral component that is essential to leadership. Employees miss nothing in sizing up their leaders. No matter how eloquent leaders are in communicating the corporate strategy, if they are only half-committed to that strategy, the employees will know it. On the other hand, even if employees don't completely follow the leaders' logic or the details of what they say, the employees will feel the energy of their leaders' total commitment, and it will draw them in.

"Leadership is not just about passing on intellectual information; it's about infusing an organization with intellectual energy. Leaders need to get inside people's heads and *hearts*—and we can't fake it. John Kelly, IBM's SVP and director of research, exudes this kind of energy. A few years ago while talking to a group of new executives, someone brought up the then-new silicon germanium (SiGe)–based chip that was about 250 times faster than chips on the market at the time. Now, John could have responded by explaining that it ran more than 500 GHz— that is 500 billion cycles per second—and he could have provided other technical details, but he could hardly contain himself. His face immediately lit up and he blurted out, 'It's a real screamer!'

---

124 Louis V. Gerstner, *Who Says Elephants Can't Dance?* (New York: Harper Business, 2002), p. 238.

"Now, Bill, you know that I am part of IBM's affirmative action program for the technologically impaired. I don't know a silicon chip from a doughnut, but I knew whatever John was talking about was *really cool*—and I wanted to hear more. When John said, 'It's a real screamer,' he was giving voice to more than technological capacity. He was talking about *possibilities*—and everyone who heard him could *feel* it. And that rush of excitement is what ignites the imagination and sparks innovation. Bill, that's the 'white hot air' blowing across the organization that Mr. Addison is talking about. And Mr. Gerstner points out that it's the passion that is not only 'part of every top-notch executive's management style' but what personal leadership is all about.[125a] Tom Watson brought us THINK™. Lou Gerstner brought us *FEEL*! That's a winning combination. That's leadership!"

"Ah, moving soliloquy, Jack, but let me get a couple of things straight. I want to make sure that we have reached some agreement. You agree that Addison says that leaders emit hot air?" He hesitated for me to respond.

"Yes, Bill."

"And, furthermore, that John Kelly thinks screamers are great?"

"Yes, Bill."

"Well, Jack, hot air, screamer—that sure sounds like my boss to me."

"William, you have a way with words."

"Well, I just wanted to make sure we were clear."

"Bill, are you sure that we're clear?" I said with a smile, knowing his idea of clarity on this particular issue was likely a bit different from my own.

"Clear enough for me, Jack. I'd better leave before I get confused." Bob laughed as he stood to leave.

"Have a good weekend, Bill—talk to you Monday."

125a Gerstner, p. 238.

22

Crisis at 35,000 Feet[125b]

It happened years ago, but he remembers it as if it were yesterday. The pilot had begun the descent from 35,000 feet. The attendants were collecting the warm, damp towels that they had passed out to let the passengers freshen up after their long flight, and it had been a long flight—almost 20 hours. Fortunately, all had been routine. There had been no delays, and the skies had been unusually calm, but suddenly things did not seem just right. It was almost imperceptible—*but he felt it*. He looked up from the customs form that he was filling out and blinked to get himself more focused. The feeling was so fleeting, he wondered if he had felt it at all. He took a short breath and went back to the customs form. He was on the item that stated "List occupation," and there it was again—that feeling, ever so faint. This time he shrugged it off but for some reason skipped the item and went on to complete the rest of the form. No, he had no drugs. No, he was not carrying more than $10,000. And he signed his name, Dr. John Kelly III.

125b In this chapter, I am taking liberties to embellish on an actual event.

Then back to "List occupation." The feeling, though not overwhelming, was undeniable. "This is strange," he thought to himself. "In fact, it's silly. This is not a difficult question. Why the hesitancy—and what's it matter anyway?" He had filled out countless customs forms in the past. He knew the answer: He was an engineer. He had gone to the best schools; he had an undergraduate and a graduate degree in physics and a Ph.D. in materials engineering. He had worked for IBM for 19 years, mostly in technical positions related to the development and manufacturing of IBM's advanced semiconductor technologies. He had held positions in microelectronics and research and systems divisions and had been responsible for the company's most advanced research activities. He loved this stuff. Semiconductors excited him. He was an engineer—and a good one. So good that he had just been appointed general manager of IBM's Microelectronics Division and was now traveling around the globe to introduce or reacquaint himself with the employees and colleagues in the division.

So as the plane made its final descent, John started, as he had always done, to write "engineer" in the blank, but by the time he got to "g" he stopped. The discomfort had surged, and almost without realizing the nature of the internal debate, he crossed out what he had written and wrote in "manager." Now he felt something different—but more comfortable. "This is all VERY weird," he thought, shaking his head and smiling to himself. And he has never felt quite the same again.

So, why share this short anecdote? Well, because something important had happened. Healthy people continue to grow and change throughout their lives. Here a developmental transformation had taken place—an identity crisis, of sorts, was resolved, and it was an important one, an identity crisis that too many people in leadership positions fail to confront.

IBM's Leadership Framework defines a competency as any characteristic of a person that differentiates outstanding performance from the more typical. These characteristics not only include skills and knowledge but also other personal attributes, such as social role, values, self-image, traits, and motives. We use the metaphor of an iceberg to illustrate the relationship among these attributes. *Social role* is the layer just below the water-line—and we seldom think about it. But it has to do with the expectations others have of us and, more importantly, that we have for ourselves. So, if you see yourself as an engineer, your expectations of yourself are different than if you see yourself as a manager. Similarly, if others see you as an engineer, their expectations of you are different than if they see you as a manager.

IBM was no longer depending on John's degrees and what he learned in school. Rather, it was counting on what he had learned and how he had matured as a person as he had taken on successively increased responsibilities within IBM. IBM was now expecting John Kelly to be a *manager* and a *leader*—and he has proved to be a good one. He brought the Microelectronics Division back to profitability, went on to be the SVP and group executive of what was then called Technology Group, and now is IBM SVP for IBM Research Division.

Many managers continue to think of themselves as engineers, accountants, lawyers, or whatever their area of professional expertise was. They see their managerial responsibilities as secondary. However, when IBM puts people in those positions and gives them that status, it expects them to be leaders. It has placed a special trust and confidence in them and implicitly, if not explicitly, charged them to develop the human resources entrusted to them—and by doing so, multiply their impact on IBM. Leaders must take that responsibility seriously.

EPILOGUE

Your Leadership Book

Mark Hennessy, IBM's General Manager for northeast Europe, pointedly told a group of new executives, "There is a book being written on each of you. If you asked your people, would it be written the way you wanted it to be?" Mark's question is one each of us should ask ourselves. Would our autobiographies as leaders coincide closely with the mental, unauthorized biographies others are writing about us each day? Answering this question requires answers to several other questions. What would we want these stories to tell? What would we have to manifest in our day-to-day leadership to ensure that our legacy is one that will bring us pride and a sense of self-fulfillment? What motives and values would guide our behaviors?

A common practice in the Army is for officers to write and share their leadership philosophy. Brigadier General (ret) Maureen Leboeuf states, "This 'philosophy' ostensibly allows the supporting staff and soldiers to understand the leader's inner thoughts, beliefs, and expectations for organizational performance."[126] In a similar vein, Lieutenant Colonel (ret) Todd Henshaw states, "You need a leadership philosophy that's grounded in self-knowledge, and that begins with your purpose or passion. Why are you a leader? What do you intend to do as a leader, and how do you bring your values to that intention?"[127]

Each of us as leaders should be able to articulate our leadership philosophy—with an honest eye to both what our philosophy is and how well we are currently exhibiting it. This exercise is instructive not only to how we should lead but, more significantly, to *why we choose to lead*. Writing our leadership philosophy shapes not only the leaders we become but, more fundamentally, the people we become.

Over the years, I have continued to write my own leadership philosophy as it has evolved. I will now share it. Unlike those who have a gift for compressing their leadership wisdom ever so tightly into three to five profound, pithy maxims, I just keep extending the list as I continue to learn and hopefully to grow. If I were forced to be concise, I would say that my leadership philosophy is summarized in the first tenet listed below: People are the ends, not the means to an end. Leaders do not just want people to do something; they want people to *be* someone. That principle underlies all that follow; the others come in no particular order of prominence.

I make no claim that the listed tenets are unique insights. I am confident that others have reached similar conclusions. The purpose of spelling out a leadership philosophy is not to announce the discovery of new principles, though new insights may occur, but rather it is an exercise in self-discovery to illuminate for ourselves and others what undergirds and drives *our* leadership. It may also provide a mirror that reflects how far we have come, as opposed to how far we would like to have come, on the leadership continuum.

---

126 Maureen Leboeuf, BG (ret), "Developing a Leadership Philosophy," *Military Review* (May–June 1999), p. 28. A further note, BG Leboeuf was the first woman to head a department at the United States Military Academy. She was the "Master of the Sword" (head of the Department of Physical Education).

127 Wharton@Work, *Earning the Right to Lead* (August 2010), http://executiveeducation.wharton. upenn.edu/wharton-at-work/1008/earning-right-to-lead-1008.cfm.

The nineteen (and counting) tenets of my leadership philosophy follow.

- **People are the ends, not the means to an end. Leaders do not just want people to do something; they want them to *be* someone.** Leadership is often defined as some variation of "getting work done through others." Too often *work* is the operative word. The emphasis should be on *others*. The ironic but good news is that when we focus on others, we get better work and increased performance. More than enhancing individual and organizational performance, however, leaders elevate people's aspirations and help them achieve a deeper sense of self-worth. Leaders must see people not as the means to an end but as the desired end.

  The most memorable lines from the 1954 Academy Award–winning movie *On the Waterfront* come from Terry Malloy (Marlon Brando), a boxer turned dockworker, when he confronts his brother, Charley (Rod Steiger), a lawyer for the Mob-connected union boss, Johnny Friendly (Lee J. Cobb), who had gotten Terry, as he put it, "to take them dives for the short-end money." Charley protests and reminds Terry, "You saw some money." Terry's response makes clear that he expected more than money from Charley's leadership: "You don't understand. I coulda had class. I coulda been a contender. I coulda been somebody, instead of a bum, which is what I am, let's face it."

  Later in the film, Father Barry (Karl Malden) urges Terry to testify against the corrupt and murderous Friendly by appealing to Terry's need for self-worth, his need to become somebody.

  > Terry: If I spill, my life ain't worth a nickel.
  > Father Barry: And how much is your soul worth if you don't?[128]

  Ultimately, despite threats to his livelihood and life, Terry testifies and gains self-respect and the respect of his co-workers.

  Our identities are not fixed by our history; they can be shaped by what we strive to become. Charley and Johnny Friendly had used Terry as an effective means for generating wealth for

---

128 Memorable Quotes for *On the Waterfront*, http://www.imdb.com/title/tt0047296/quotes.

themselves and their organization. They had shared some of the gains with Terry and had given him cushy jobs, but they had left him feeling like a bum. Terry went from "bum" to "somebody" because Father Barry's persistent intervention gave him confidence that he could become someone and showed him how to get there.

Beyond helping others to accumulate wealth and improve skills, leaders must tap into people's deeper values and motivate them to become better people. Leadership requires more than rewarding others' efforts with "short-end money." The reward must be greater self-worth.

- **Leaders develop leaders, not followers.** Strategically, as leaders, we must continually remind ourselves, "I must decrease; they must increase." When an organization collapses after a leader leaves, people often point to the rapid collapse as evidence of the former leader's competence and the new leader's incompetence. Sadly, some "leaders" themselves take perverse pride in noting that the organization fell apart upon their departure. They fail to recognize that the collapse was their doing—their failure as a leader. As John Gardner states:

  > Some individuals who have dazzling powers of personal leadership create dependency in those below them and leave behind a weakened organization staffed by weakened people.[129]

A good leader's legacy is one of strength. As Noel Tichy puts it,

> The ultimate test of a leader is not whether he or she makes smart decisions and takes decisive action, but whether he or she teaches others to be leaders and builds an organization that can sustain its success when he or she is not present.[130]

When leaders leave their organization, if they have done their job well, the organization will be stronger under the new leadership

129 John Gardner, *On Leadership* (New York: Free Press, 1999), p. 36.
130 Noel Tichy and Eli Cohen, *The Leadership Engine* (New York: Harper Business, 1997), p. 3.

than it was before. One of a leader's critical tasks is to prepare a cadre of capable replacements so that upon the leader's departure, the new leadership will not have to spend time getting up to speed but rather will be in a position to accelerate forward.

- **The authority of one's ideas is more important than the authority of one's position.** John Gardner cautions that "we must not confuse leadership with official authority, which is simply legitimized power."[131] In this age of the knowledge worker, more than ever before, leaders must create environments in which ideas flow—in all directions. And people must listen to and rally around the most powerful ideas, not necessarily the most powerful individual. Work environments rigidly structured by lines on the organizational chart can destroy initiative and breed passivity. The best hope for vitality within large organizations is the willingness and ability of "a great many people scattered throughout the organization to take the initiative in performing leaderlike acts, in identifying problems at their levels and solving them."[132] Such a spreading of leadership throughout an organization will only occur if people's ideas are voiced, listened to, and championed. Only when people realize they are personally needed and expected to participate will they have the confidence to act.

- **Aspirations motivate! Leaders must awaken and harness other people's aspirations.** I quote John Gardner yet again:

  > One of the deepest truths about the cry of the human heart is that it is so muted, so often a cry that is never uttered. . . . We die with much unsaid.[133]

  Too many organizations are filled with people whose "I don't care" or "I don't want to" is a cover for "I don't think I can" or "What's the use?" Their aspirations have been smothered by routine and bureaucracy, and they have resigned themselves

---

131 Gardner, p. 3.
132 Gardner, p. 79.
133 Gardner, p. 186.

to doing assigned tasks rather than taking initiative or offering ideas. Disempowered people compound their disempowerment when they make their peace with the status quo and content themselves with the comfort that it can bring. Leaders should not allow themselves or their organizations to enjoy the peacefulness of routine. Louise Driscoll, in her poem "Hold Fast Your Dreams," urges us to

> Think still of lovely things that are not true.
> Let wish and magic work at will in you.
> Be sometimes blind to sorrow. Make believe!
> Forget the calm that lies
> In disillusioned eyes.[134a]

Leaders must send Ms. Driscoll's message to their organization. They must reignite "the wish and magic" and incite the "I can" and the "I will." If they fail to do so, they rob their organizations of the energy that pursuing aspirations generates and of the potential successes such energy often brings.

- **Leaders help people find meaning in what they do and acknowledge their contributions**. Helping people find meaning in what they do and acknowledging their contributions have been themes throughout this book. Viktor Frankl has stated that too often "people have enough to live by but nothing to live for; they have the means but no meaning."[134b] Humans are meaning making and meaning seeking. We want to matter and to make a difference. Frankl found that when working with people who were suffering from depression as a result of unemployment—people without means—if he could get them to volunteer to participate in some meaningful pursuit, their depression would lift. We are pulled by a sense of purpose as much as we are pushed by drives. A sense of purpose is what draws the human spirit to accomplish the most difficult endeavors. Man did not climb to the top of Mount Everest or rocket to the moon because

---

134a http://armymomhaven.com/driscolll/index.php.
134b Viktor E. Frankl, *Man's Search for Meaning* (Boston: Beacon Press, 1984).

we were forced to do so. We were drawn to those heights by a sense of discovery and a desire to do what we had never done before. While success may be its own reward, leaders have a duty to acknowledge the contributions of those who made the success possible. Saying thank you is one of the first lessons we learn, and it is often one of first we forget. Acknowledgment reinforces effort. It helps build mutual trust and admiration. It reenergizes people and makes them eager to look for and take on the next challenge.

- **Leaders inspire not only by identifying the gains a mission offers but the challenge it requires.** The Peace Corps' slogan, "The toughest job you'll ever love," and the Army's, "We do more before 9:00 A.M. than most people do all day," are more than catchphrases; these pronouncement challenge the target audience to dig deep inside themselves to see whether they "have what it takes." The slogans motivate not through the promise of extrinsic rewards but by the challenge of the work itself and the chance to see whether we "measure up."

  Shakespeare illustrates this inspiration of the challenge in his play *Henry V*. The relevant scene takes place at Agincourt in northern France on the eve and morning of St. Crispin's Day in 1415. In England, St. Crispin's Day was a day of rest when no work would be done, but for King Henry and his sick and weary troops, it would be no holiday. They were facing a well-fed, fully rested, and vastly larger French army. In the morning before the battle, the Duke of Exeter and the Earl of Westmoreland are lamenting their situation. The Duke complains, "There's five to one, besides they are fresh." And Westmoreland frets, "O that we now had here but one ten hundredth of those men in England who do not work today!"

  Overhearing these grumblings, Henry rallies his troops. He does so paradoxically by instructing Westmoreland to proclaim to his army that any who do not want to take on the challenge could leave, and that Henry would pay for their journey home:

  > "Rather proclaim it, Westmoreland, through my host,
  > That he which hath no stomach to this fight,

> Let him depart; his passport shall be made,
> And crowns for convoy put into his purse;
> We would not die in that man's company
> That fears his fellowship to die with us."

For those who stay, Henry does not offer wealth—or, for that matter, victory. He admits that they all may be "mark'd to die." His rallying point is the glory of taking on the challenge. Rather than lament being outnumbered, he exclaims, "The fewer men, the greater share of honour."

Henry makes clear that the tangible rewards of success are not the motivation but rather the intangible rewards of taking on long odds:

> "By Jove, I am not covetous of gold.
> Nor care I who doth feed upon my cost;
> It yearns me not if men my garments wear;[135]
> Such outward things dwell not in my desires."

So, why stay? Because the challenge offered something that could not be coerced and that money could not buy—honor.

> "But if it be a sin to covet honour,
> I am the most offending soul alive.
> God's peace! I would not lose so great an honour."

He assures his men that live or die, the names of those who stay and face the challenge would become household words and that from that day "to the ending of the world," remembering them would be part of celebrating St. Crispin's Day.

Henry ends his exhortation by focusing his men's attention not on victory but on the heroism of the fight, regardless of the outcome:

> ". . . Gentlemen in England now-a-bed
> Shall think themselves accurs'd they were not here,

---

135 When Henry speaks of "feed upon my cost" and someone wearing his clothes, he is referring to the practice of stripping those killed of all their valuables.

And hold their manhoods cheap whiles any speaks
That fought with us upon Saint Crispin's Day."

History records a great victory for the English Army that day.
Leaders reach in and grab hold of that indomitable spirit—the
desire to stand tall—that resides in each of us, and they do not let
go.

- **Sacrifice must be shared, justified, and acknowledged.** In
1940, Winston Churchill was elected Prime Minister of England.
When he went before his Cabinet for the first time, he told them, "I
have nothing to offer but blood, toil, sweat, and tears." He went on
to make clear that others would have to give the same:

> "We have before us an ordeal of the most grievous kind. We
> have before us many, many long months of struggle and of
> suffering. You ask, what is our policy? I can say: It is to wage
> war, by sea, land and air, with all our might and with all the
> strength that God can give us; to wage war against a monstrous
> tyranny, never surpassed in the dark, lamentable catalogue of
> human crime. That is our policy. You ask, what is our aim? I can
> answer in one word: It is victory, victory at all costs, victory in
> spite of all terror, victory, however long and hard the road may
> be. . . ."

He then continues by justifying the need for the terrible suffering
and struggle ahead.

> ". . . for without victory, there is no survival. Let that be realised;
> no survival for the British Empire, no survival for all that the
> British Empire has stood for, no survival for the urge and impulse
> of the ages, that mankind will move forward towards its goal."[136]

Churchill continued throughout the bombing of London and the
entirety of World War II to provide both encouragement and

---

136 Winston Churchill's first speech to his Cabinet (May 13, 1940), http://www.winstonchurchill.org/
learn/speeches/speeches-of-winston-churchill/1940-finest-hour/92-blood-toil-tears-and-sweat.

justification for the shared sacrifice. England and the English prevailed, and though dear the cost, the outcome was worth the price.

Sacrifices are seldom as dramatic as those Churchill called upon the British people to make, but in today's do-more-with-less workplace, people are working exceptionally hard. In large global companies, what used to be metaphorically seen as running a marathon has turned into a never-ending, three-hundred-sixty-five-day-a-year sprint. It is even impossible to find a comfortable pace. Before asking someone to pull some data or to do a study, leaders need to ask some questions of themselves. "How vital are these data?" Too often "nice to have" or "I want them just in case" data pulls are demanded with a quick turnaround and with a lack of appreciation for the work involved. "How much are we willing to invest in this project?" Too often people do studies or work on whitepapers that almost all involved know will go nowhere, yet the urgency of the request causes people to work long hours and to get behind on other priorities. How often have we received a request to put some thoughts together or provide some data on a Friday, with the due date on Monday, and when we ask for feedback on Wednesday, the boss says, "I haven't had time to look at it yet!" (How often have you given that response?)

Leaders should also be mindful that the demand for an employee to make a sacrifice often means that his or her family and others share the sacrifice—outings missed, special dinners gone cold, kids and other family members deprived of conversation and human attention. On the occasions when we must ask others to sacrifice, we should make clear the necessity of the request, and we should acknowledge that we understand that the request might have unintended collateral consequences on the employee and the employee's family.

The most valuable thing we can give others is our attention, yet most of us live lives of continual distraction and inattention. Even when we are physically present, our thoughts are often on the job. Leaders should spend as much time thinking about "What do we need to stop doing?" as they do about "What do we need to get done?"

- **Fun and happiness are not the same. Happiness often comes from looking back on the gut-wrenching, bone-tiring, nerve-wracking effort that went into accomplishing a worthwhile mission**. Admittedly, many might not see the distinction between fun and happiness as a leadership principle. Maybe I have listened to too many senior executives close their talks to emerging leaders and new executives by declaring, "The most important thing is to have fun!" And I sit there silently shouting, "No! No! That's not true."

The most important thing for humans to do is to accomplish a worthwhile mission well. The effort required to do so often is anything but fun. However, the accomplishment stands a good chance of instilling a deep and lasting sense of satisfaction and fulfillment that the momentary and fleeting thrills of fun will not. The English soldiers at Agincourt were not having fun; fun was what the folks on holiday back in England were having. Most likely on St. Crispin's Day 1416, the gentlemen who had been "a-bed" in England the prior year could not remember what they had done that day, while, as King Henry had predicted, the veterans of the Battle of Agincourt were likely showing their scars and telling their neighbors about the "wounds [they] had on Crispin's day." And as they remembered "with advantages" the feats they had done that day, the names of "Harry the King, Bedford and Exeter, Warwick and Talbot, Salisbury and Gloucester" were "in their flowing cups freshly rememb'red." As Vince Lombardi put it:

> I firmly believe that any man's finest hour, the greatest fulfillment of all that he holds dear, is the moment when he has worked his heart out in a good cause and lies exhausted on the field of battle—victorious.[137]

Raising a difficult, wayward child into a mature and productive adult is far from fun, but it is worth more than anything else to the parents who have succeeded in doing it. I spent much of my adult life preparing young men and women to be Army officers,

---

137 Thinkexist: Vince Lombardi, http://thinkexist.com/quotation/i_firmly_believe_that_any_man-s_finest_hour-the/173395.html.

all the time knowing they could end up in an Iraq, an Afghanistan, or some other war-ravaged place trying to stay alive and whole while fighting so others could have a better life. I found the task intensely meaningful in that I was preparing them to be competent, ethical leaders, which I hoped would save lives, but nothing about war is fun.

Do not get me wrong. In spite of my Puritan heritage, I do not think fun is bad. Wholesome fun is good, but happiness is not the sum total of all the parties we attend or the trinkets of material wealth we accumulate. Too many people search for happiness by relentlessly pursuing fun. Fun fades quickly; happiness is enduring. If the most important thing is to have fun, we cannot succeed in the serious business of achieving difficult, lofty goals. Leaders focus people's efforts on satisfaction that will last.

- **Leaders must encourage people to care not only for the mission but for each other.** Leaders understand the importance of fostering intimate bonds. Leadership involves groups of people accomplishing tasks *together*. Leaders must not only ensure that people have the job-related skills but also that members of the team will work well together. Success requires competent teams, not just competent team members. We cannot simply put a bunch of top-notch people together and expect good things to happen; the team itself must have the appropriate social and emotional skills to work well together.

  Shakespeare's King Henry V built bonds when rallying his army before the Battle of Agincourt. At no point does he demand loyalty to himself as King or to England. He does not speak to his men as their king; he is a fellow soldier with all who stay and fight with him; he calls them brothers.

  "We few, we happy few, we band of brothers;
  For he today that sheds his blood with me
  Shall be my brother."

He is no longer a king leading nobles and foot soldiers. Those who stay and fight are a noble brotherhood. No matter what their background, those who go into battle that day are noble:

". . . be he ne'er so vile,
This day will gentle his condition."

It is well understood that soldiers in combat courageously persevere not so much for the Constitution, which they have sworn to "protect and defend," or for a national ideology; foremost in their minds is the person next to them, whom they will not let down. Leaders do not have to be in uniform to create an environment that fosters similar bonds.

Forming social bonds is part of normal human development. New parents learn quickly that if they put their finger into the hand of their newborn, the baby will grab hold. If they touch their newborn's cheek, the baby will turn toward them; babies react this way only to the human touch. Babies will smile if we look at them and cry to get our attention. They naturally—and quickly—emotionally attach to their caregivers. The bond requires more than meeting physical needs. Studies have shown that even if infants get their physical needs met, they can fail to thrive, go into depression, and possibly die from lack of affectionate attention.[138] We are hardwired to be part of a group and to form intimate bonds. The pleasure of affectionate attachments has side effects. Once we acquire these attachments, we begin to experience the discomfort of *separation anxiety* and *stranger anxiety*. In spite of these anxieties, we continue to show interest in others—and the more secure our attachments are to those closest to us, the more likely we are to explore and expand our relations with others.[139]

If members of work groups do not have healthy emotional connections to each other, the group will lag in its ability to function effectively. With the greater dependence on long distance, virtual interaction, the increase in diversity within global corporations, and the greater need for quick and smooth interdependent action, the formation of the requisite social and emotional bonds within groups has become both more challenging and more necessary. Leaders must foster an organizational climate

---

138 Rene A. Spitz, "Anclitic Depression: An Inquiry into the Genesis of Psychiatric Conditions in Early Childhood, II," *Psychoanalytic Study of the Child, 2* (1946), pp. 313–342.

139 Carol K. Sigelman and David R. Shaffer, *Life-Span Human Development* (Pacific Grove: Brooks/Cole, 1991).

in which individuals recognize an affirmative duty to nurture the community of which they are a part.

- **Leadership requires integrity. Only integrity that is lived matters.** I confess to a philosophical point of view that leadership is about ideas and values. It is about bringing out the best in others and getting "good" things done through others. There are tyrants, demagogues, and other people with variants of selfish, misguided, and evil intent who wield power, manipulate, terrorize, and get things done through others. I am not so naive as to deny that Hitler, Stalin, and the like have effectively organized nations and movements and have had global impact, but I do not count them as leaders. I categorize them as tyrants and demagogues, perhaps skilled and clever but selfish, misguided, and evil people who make bad things happen.

  Integrity is a broad concept. It involves consistency in terms of ethics, honesty, unselfishness, genuineness in relationships, and transparent authenticity. Leaders with integrity not only say the right things, but they also "walk the talk." We can believe in and trust them—and not be disappointed, disillusioned, or hurt as a consequence. They know themselves, are not egocentric, are concerned for the well-being of others, and devote their efforts to improving lives and people.

  Studies[140, 141] indicate that people value integrity in their leaders. In one study that lists eleven traits, 95 percent of the respondents rate honesty and integrity as the most important qualities of leadership. The respondents rate these attributes significantly higher than a leader's knowledge, skills, and abilities.[142]

  Robert Moorman and Steven Grover have asked the question, "Why does leader integrity matter to followers?" Their answer:

  Leader integrity matters because it plays a significant role in the decision process used by followers when deciding who they

---

140 James M. Kouzes and Barry Z. Posner, *The Leadership Challenge*, 4ᵗʰ Ed. (San Francisco: Jossey Bass, 2007).
141 Hal Quinely, *National Leadership Index 2005: A National Study of Confidence in Leadership* (http://www.usnews.com/usnews/news/features/051022/22leaders.pdf).
142 Quinely.

will follow, who they will trust, to whom they will be loyal and committed, and ultimately for whom they will perform. Leader integrity's importance may lie in its positive influence on the leadership process and the positive organizational outcome it achieves.[143]

I would add to Moorman and Grover's answer that leaders' integrity matters because it is the greatest protection that their constituents have against being exploited, and it ensures that their energies and talents will be directed toward the common good and not used in service of another's selfish interests. Without integrity, leaders will lose their legitimacy in the eyes of their constituents. No organization, institution, or society can operate effectively if the leadership has lost legitimacy with the relevant constituency and if the leadership and its constituency no longer share values.

- **Being successful and being good at what you do are not always the same. If you need to choose, be good at what you do.** "Successful" in this context means "getting ahead," climbing the corporate ladder, or moving up the chain of command. Although being a good leader is generally key to being successful, in this context a good leader is not always successful.

  Outstanding performance, in terms of making numbers or accomplishing an assigned task, is not always the best measure of leadership. Some executives may accomplish short-term goals at the expense of longer-term outcomes. By the same token, the successes of those who take a more strategic view may be attributed to persons who succeed them and are in charge when the long-term strategy pays off but who had little to do with shaping the favorable outcomes. Likewise, the negative consequences of those who have gone the route of short-term success at the expense of solving long-term problems may be attributed to that person's successor after the person who took the short-term view has moved on—or up.

---

143 Robert H. Moorman and Steven Grover, "Why Does Leader Integrity Matter to Followers?" *International Journal of Leadership Studies*, Vol. 5, Issue 2 (2009), pp. 103–114.

Without being cynical, we can assume that some people have gotten ahead in their careers by currying favor with superiors, playing it safe, taking ethical shortcuts, being a merciless tyrant, or satisfying the demands of the moment, knowing full well that the short-term "solution" will cause or compound problems in the future. Other executives may be incapable of acting with a systemic perspective and may make decisions to meet an immediate need oblivious to the problems they are causing in the future. When viewed from the perspective of history, these executives' "accomplishments" may look less impressive, but they may have already reaped the benefits of their apparent successes.

Still other people get ahead because they fit the existing corporate mold. They make no waves, they are quick to validate superiors' ideas and decisions, and they may be very capable of current best practices but not *next* practices. They have been good at execution but not at innovation, and they "go along to get along." They excel at knowing and providing what people want to hear and not what they need to hear. Senior people may be comfortable with them and prefer them to their more "annoying" colleagues who question the status quo, which the current leadership may have created.

The hallmark of organizations that have performed well over time is that senior management recognizes that leadership is about the long term, not the short term, and about change, not the status quo. While on occasion shortcuts may pay off, competent leaders do not take them, and while at times going up against the status quo may be risky, most of the leaders of successful organizations took that risk.

- **Leaders must purposively instill, protect, and promote organizational norms. Leaders must live them.** Norms and values are different. Norms are values put into action. Values are personal beliefs. Norms are the unwritten, socially imposed standards of behavior in any group. Norms are generally the outward manifestation of the group members' shared values. All groups have values and norms; the question is, whose are they? Without shared norms and values, an organization lacks an identifiable character that sets expectations for the conduct for its members and establishes its reputation in the outside world. A great organization is a dream lived in the minds of its members. It is shared values, norms, expectations, and purposes.[144] These intangibles are what transform a gaggle of people into a team, a community, or a society.

Group members tend to adopt the norms and values of their leaders. It is imperative that the leaders be clear and intentional in what they communicate. People in positions of leadership can escape being leaders, but they cannot escape being role models. Their status amplifies both what they do and what they do not do. Group members will infer, to the best of their ability, what leaders want and feel is important. Leaders have two competing responsibilities. Because of their influence on the group norms, leaders must be the exemplar of the organizational norms—a source of stability during the times of volatility and uncertainty that inevitably occur. Leaders, however, must also be the change agent when changes in values and norms are needed. The revitalization of values and norms to align with new realities is a fundamental leadership function. Confronted by the widening diversity inherent in our globalized world, people find this function to be more important and challenging than ever.

- **Leaders manage paradox. Both diversity and a common cause are vital to organizational effectiveness. Justice and mercy must coexist—so, too, stability and change.** Leaders always have to deal with conflicts and contradictions. Often it is valid to support opposing actions.

During a Sunday service, a chaplain at West Point told the following story—one I suspect history cannot confirm. A young soldier in Napoleon's army had fallen asleep on guard for a second time. The sentence for such a failure of duty was death. The soldier's distraught mother approached Napoleon, begging him to show her son mercy. Napoleon replied, "Madam, your son does not deserve my mercy." To which the mother responded, "If he deserved it, it would not be mercy." Napoleon was persuaded that

---

144 Gardner, p. 13.

mercy rather than justice was the better course and spared the young soldier.

Leaders often straddle the thin line between too rigid adherence to a policy and leaving organizational members confused as to "What really is the policy?" The letter of the law and the spirit of the law have to be reconciled. Few things are black or white; the color spectrum in our worlds is much richer and more nuanced. Even polar opposites need not be mutually exclusive. For example, corporate policy may be to "cut cost" and to "increase investment" or "to speak with one voice" and "to distribute decision-making." Both actions may not only be justifiable but necessary.

Paradoxes cannot be removed. Sometimes we must pursue them simultaneously. At IBM, we are "dedicated to every client's success."[145] But any company's dedication to the client has to be balanced with a competing need to make a reasonable profit. Reconciling paradox requires that leaders create a shared understanding among organizational members of the organization's competing goals and a commitment to a balanced pursuit of those goals so that all members are thinking and acting from a common systemic perspective. It helps to include leaders from all parts of the organization in setting the balance. Having a broad range of leadership wrestle with the contradictions and dilemmas will require the leaders to anticipate the impacts across all constituencies, which will enable them to see the end-to-end view and to understand the underlining pattern that integrates the seemingly disparate courses. Having this knowledge will give the leaders a deeper appreciation of and commitment to the ultimately agreed-upon course of action, and it will allow the leaders to communicate the agreed-upon action to their organizations more convincingly. Skillful management of paradox enables an organization to act wisely while boldly taking the right risks.[146]

- **Leaders help others achieve their goals.** Leaders are unselfish. They must put the interests of those they lead ahead of their own.

---

145 IBM's corporate values are: (1) Dedication to every client's success; (2) Innovation that matters to our company and the world; (3) Trust and personal responsibility in all our relationships.
146 One of IBM's Competencies is "Act with a systemic perspective." See Appendix I.

Leadership is about unleashing human potentialities in service of the common good.

An attribute that is not linked to leadership often enough is altruism. While we focus on influence, providing direction, and motivating, putting others first is at the heart of leadership. Putting others first does not entail a total renunciation of self-interest, but leaders must put the interest of their constituents ahead of their own. Members of an organization entrust leaders with power for the common good of the organization—not for the leader's personal aggrandizement or gain. Great leaders do "the right things, in the right way, *for the right reasons* [italics added]."[147]

To the degree that these leaders "devote themselves to serving the needs of organization members, focus on meeting the needs of those they lead, develop employees to bring out the best in them, coach others and encourage their self-expression, facilitate personal growth in all who work with them and listen well to build a sense of community and joint ownership,"[148] they resemble Robert Greenleaf's servant leadership. However, these leaders are leaders first. They help shape the community interests. They do not blindly adopt the will of the people whom they lead most directly or automatically advocate for their desires. Their immediate constituents' will may well be influenced by a desire to avoid personal sacrifice or to shift it to others. Leaders must sometimes call for mutual sacrifice for the long-term good of the organization as a whole. The United States and much of the world currently find themselves in need of such leadership with regard to the economic crisis that began in 2007. All agree that sacrifices are needed, and all agree that others should bear them. Many government leaders have suggested solutions that would minimize the sacrifice of their most immediate constituents and would shift the burden to others. They have muddied the issues

---

147 Joanne B. Ciulla, "Reflections on Why Leaders Abuse Entrusted Power," p. 4 (http://docs.google.com/viewer?a=v&q=cache:5nq6GO5FewAJ:www.nd.edu/~ethics/wcConference/presentations/Ciulla/Ciulla%2520Why%2520Leaders%2520Abuse%2520Entrusted%2520Power.doc+altruistic+leadership&hl=en&gl=us&pid=bl&srcid=ADGEESjMWJ0XXw0Ae5IIwoQSznVh37WugHxWbHxqpeNEzILRlBIP-4FfjUs-aqLoeqtQGhSZi4OOFWj5hreqBm8ElrI1naxHtXy-f3WkBlU-jxYCK3ecgdMlkA3eW0FK1PeBCYdtGh5G&sig=AHIEtbTaiDuQfH_cx3Ryc_zjk3bfLOBjJQ).

148 Mitch McCrimmon, Servant Leadership (http://www.leadersdirect.com/servant-leadership, 2006).

and polarized the nation rather than uniting the people in a mutual commitment of self-sacrifice.

People must trust their leaders to advocate actions that put the organization's or community's interests ahead of their own. Only then can the leaders unite those they lead to do what needs to be done, even when the proposed course of action requires widespread sacrifice.

- **Leaders cannot lead people they do not trust or who do not trust them. Trust requires confidence in both integrity and capability.** On September 11, 2001, terrorists flew planes into the twin towers at the World Trade Center, killing thousands of people and disrupting the U.S. economy—which was their main aim. Since then, some high-profile business leaders have done far worse damage to the U.S. economy; they have undermined people's trust in the business world. They have betrayed their shareholders, their employees, and their customers.

  For any organization to function effectively requires trust. James Kouzes and Barry Posner state that "without trust you cannot lead."[149] Organizational members must not only have confidence in their leaders, but leaders must have confidence in those they lead—and all involved must have confidence in each other. I refer to this reciprocal trust as 360 degrees of trust.

  Trust enables the cooperation and collaboration that a group needs to accomplish complex tasks. Trust not only requires that leaders and all organizational members have reliable confidence in each other's integrity and good intent but also in their abilities and motivation to achieve organizational objectives. Without such trust, leaders will have to spend much of their time tightly supervising and micromanaging projects, and those charged with execution will lack motivation and question the use of their time and energy. Leaders will not have time to do the more strategic tasks necessary for ongoing success, and the other organizational members will become passive and compliant; they will not take initiative or engage in the creative thinking that fosters

---

149 James Kouzes and Barry Posner, "Without Trust You Cannot Lead," *Innovative Leader*, Vol. 8, No. 2 (1999), http://www.winstonbrill.com/bril001/html/article_index/articles/351-400/article385_body. html.

innovation. Without a community of trust in which members at all levels trust each other and themselves, people will not be able to tap into their reservoirs of boundless energy or realize their full potential to create and to be as wonderful as they can be.

Michael Reuter is the director of the Center for Leadership Development in the Stillman School of Business at Seton Hall University. He always starts my week on a high note by sending me his "Three Minute Leadership" message. In a recent one, he recounted a story told by Mark Lewis in his commencement speech at the University of Texas in 2000. Dr. Lewis talked about Jean Francois Gravelet-Blondin, more commonly known as "The Great Blondin."

The Great Blondin was a daredevil tightrope-walker. In 1859, he came to the United States and repeatedly performed a variety of stunts while walking on a rope eleven-hundred feet long and three-and-a-half inches in diameter one-hundred-sixty feet over the Niagara River Gorge just above the falls. Among his stunts were doing a back flip midway across the gorge, walking the tightrope blindfolded, and crossing while carrying his manager, Harry Colcord, on his back. As Michael wrote:

> Just as [The Great Blondin] was about to begin yet another crossing, this time pushing a wheelbarrow, he turned to the crowd and shouted, "Who believes that I can cross pushing this wheelbarrow?" Every hand in the crowd went up. Blondin pointed at one man. "Do you believe that I can do it?" he asked.
> "Yes, I believe you can," said the man.
> "Are you certain?" asked Blondin.
> "Yes," said the man.
> "Absolutely certain?"
> "Absolutely certain."
> "Thank you," said Blondin. "Then, sir, get into the wheelbarrow."

Do the people that we lead have enough confidence in us to get into the wheelbarrows we are sometimes forced to maneuver on tightropes over steep gorges? Do we have confidence that the people that we ask to get into the wheelbarrow will not throw us off balance halfway across? As Dr. Lewis went on to point out, there are going to be times in our lives when "in order to succeed [we] will have to trust";[150] people will have to trust us, and we will have to trust them. We will have to jump into each other's wheelbarrows.

It is important to note that The Great Blondin did not expect people to accept the risk on blind faith. He had repeatedly demonstrated his capabilities—and he was sharing the risk. Leaders cultivate organizations in which they and the people that they lead have a reciprocal trust that enables them to cross gorges on tightropes together.

- **Never demand of people that which you do not empower them to accomplish.** A vital task of leadership is to do all we can to ensure that people can succeed when given responsibility to accomplish a task. Ensuring that people can succeed does not mean that we cannot ask people to undertake missions with long odds. For example, we continue to urge medical scientists to search for cures for various cancers even though we know that best efforts have failed in the past and that total success is unlikely in the near future. What ensuring that people can succeed does mean is that leaders have a responsibility to see that bureaucratic obstacles are removed, essential resources are made available, any necessary coaching and training are provided, and people have the appropriate level of decision-making authority to succeed.

  When assigning tasks, leaders should be clear as to how those tasks fit into the ultimate goal. Without knowing why tasks are important, people often view them as meaningless activity. This feeling of lack of purpose saps motivation and makes people overly reliant on management for direction. People must understand how they are contributing to important outcomes, and they need to have some flexibility in how they achieve their piece of a project. Only then will they feel a sense of ownership that will stir their creativity. Updates on progress should be

---

150 Michael Reuter. "The Three Minute Leader: Jumping into Wheelbarrows" (July 4, 2011, email). Quoted with permission.

occasions for determining achievement of milestones, assessing the need for additional assistance, and celebrating successes—not for browbeating and assigning blame. Positive reinforcement of effort fosters an environment of deepening commitment; berating and blaming fosters an atmosphere in which the fear of failure makes people reluctant to take risks.

People who are given the tools to succeed at the task they are assigned become more capable and enthusiastic about seeking and assuming increased responsibilities. This empowerment sets in motion a virtuous cycle of ever-increasing excellence.

- **Never confuse leadership with status, position, or power. What makes a leader is the act of taking on the responsibilities these attributes confer on us**. Leadership is not determined by a person's status, position, or power but by the degree to which the person deserves those attributes. Leadership is a special trust that organizations, institutions, or communities confer on individuals, and it carries with it responsibilities and obligations. We frequently see people appointed to high-level jobs, such as an ambassador, simply because they filled the coffers of the political party in power. They have status, position, and power, but they are not necessarily leaders—though they may turn out to be. Most of us have also been victims of government or corporate bureaucrats who may not have status but have power. We would not classify these persons as leaders, although without their signature nothing happens—we cannot get our license or the document we need.

In 2010, IBM launched a new set of competencies. These competencies replaced two prior sets: a set of *leadership competencies* and a set of *foundational competencies*. The former provided guidance and set the aspirational direction for those IBMers designated as managers or executives. The latter provided guidance and direction for the rest of the company. In looking at what was required to be a premier globally integrated enterprise, the company determined that it needed a broader definition of leadership to align with that strategy. Leadership could no longer be seen as residing in upper hierarchical positions, the responsibility of a few. Rather, regardless of position, job category, or career aspirations, *all IBMers* needed proactively to identify problems or opportunities and take responsibility for undertaking the tasks and making the decisions necessary to address these problems or opportunities in a timely manner. All had to engage in acts of leadership. The new competencies did not eliminate IBM's hierarchy, but they did expand the power and the responsibility to lead—and redefined what it means to be an IBMer.

- **Leaders must give and take feedback. Leadership development is the outcome of extended experiences of feedback in positions of increasing responsibility**. Leaders need to be lifelong learners, and they need to encourage others to be such as well. The most important person to know is yourself, and the most difficult person to know is yourself. We have built up all kinds of internal defense mechanisms to shield us from the more unpleasant aspects of ourselves. To penetrate these defenses, we need feedback, and we need to be willing to listen to it. Leadership development is never-ending. As the world changes around us, there are many things that we need to learn—and unlearn.

  Although all leaders are born, there is a great deal of evidence that they are not born leaders. We learn leadership from experiences. Leaders must be willing to expose themselves to new experiences and to find opportunities for others to be exposed to such experiences—and the risks involved. We need to engage these experiences in a way that allows us to convert them into lessons learned. To learn how to learn from experience, we need to practice listening to feedback without reflexively giving an explanation or immediately trying to assess the accuracy of it. Just listen. When providing feedback to others, we should describe our specific observations and the reaction we had—both positive and negative. We must also be willing to interrogate our assumptions and to help others reflect on theirs. Doing so increases self-awareness. The more self-aware we are, the greater our potential to learn and develop. Organizations that display self-awareness become learning organizations.

- **Leadership is not binary, nor is it a steady state. We need to earn it every day**. Being a leader is not either/or—something one is or is not. Leadership is measured on a sliding scale from day to day. The end point on that scale is infinity. We can never fully master it, but we can always get better. Even if we are at our best today, our potential is to be better tomorrow. Morgan McCall, in his book *High Flyers*, states:

  > Potential [for leadership] . . . is not the demonstration of acquired assets but rather is *the demonstration of the ability to acquire the assets needed for the future situation*. . . . In a world of rapid change, the real measure of leadership is the ability to acquire needed new skills as the situation changes [italics added].[151]

  Leadership needs constant renewal. The potential for tomorrow is to be either better or worse than today. There is no *final* exam or certification—no leadership tenure. The measure of our leadership is taken daily.

  *****

  I started this book by declaring that it was a book any leader could write and that all leaders should write. Each of us lies somewhere on the leadership continuum. The next sentence in your leadership story is being written right now. What do you want it to say about your values, your goals, how you go about achieving those goals, and your impact on others? Put it into words. Put your words into actions. Lead.

---

151 Morgan W. McCall, Jr., *High Flyers: Developing the Next Generation of Leaders* (Cambridge: Harvard Business School Press, 1998), p. 5.

APPENDIX I

IBM's Leadership Framework[152,153]

The IBM Leadership Framework (Figure 1) depicts how a leader's behavior ultimately affects business results through the people he or she leads, all of which is infused with an ethos of IBM's values and corporate responsibility. It is a dynamic model that starts with the leader's behavior. The leader's behavior plays a significant role in shaping the climate of his or her team. People in formal positions of leadership have been given a special trust and confidence by the enterprise and are responsible for shaping the conditions that enable IBM to achieve its strategy and enterprise-wide goals. Research has demonstrated that the leader behaviors described in the IBM Competencies and the IBM Derailment Factors are significantly

---

152 Copyright International Business Machines Corporation, 2010. Reproduced with permission from IBM.

153 I would like to acknowledge all the people who have worked to create this Leadership Framework and those who subsequently articulated the IBM Competencies. I will do so in alphabetical order. For the Leadership Framework: Sharon Arad, Jack Beach, Sergio Bernardi, Tuan C Ch'ng, Michael Crespo, Richard DeSerio, Steve Gray, Sofia Lamuraglia, Christopher T. Rotolo, and John Wattendorf. For the Competencies: Sharon Arad, Jacqueline Bassett, Michael Bazigos, Jack Beach, Sergio Bernardi, Michael Crespo, James Curtis, Tayna Delany, Richard DeSerio, Mary "Angela" Duffy, David Felicione, Vicki Flaherty, Amanda Harthausen, Sofia Lamuraglia, Chia Y Li (Yvonne), Reetika Montwane, and Erin Vialardi.

correlated to the climate created by the leader. The climate, in turn, produces the level of employee engagement, which ultimately affects the business results.

Figure 1: The IBM Leadership Framework

IBM Competencies

IBM has deciphered nine IBM Competencies, which provide guidance and set the aspirational direction for all IBMers. They state what IBMers need to know, do, and be if we are to accomplish all we are capable of achieving. IBM's corporate strategy requires a broader concept of leadership. Leadership can no longer be seen as a position or the obligation of a select few. All IBMers, regardless of position or job role, need to proactively identify and take responsibility for what needs to be done, to do so in a timely manner, and to do so in alignment with corporate intent. All IBMers must create the conditions in which this can and will happen.

Partner for clients' success: IBM's worth depends not just on what we imagine but what we deliver. IBMers go above and beyond what is expected to achieve our clients' current and future aspirations. We deliver client value. We act as their partners and derive great pride from their success. We invest the time to understand their situation and unmet needs, seek market and societal insights, and make connections across the whole of IBM to serve them. We work alongside our clients, co-creating approaches, solutions, and ultimately their success—which in turn transforms whole industries, economies, and society.

Embrace challenge: IBM is in the business of taking on complex situations and challenges. The mission of IBMers is to make the world work better—from daily breakthroughs to world-changing progress. So, we focus on the future and embrace the hard challenges facing our teams, our clients, and our communities. We see opportunity in complexity and are skilled at identifying the central issues and charting a path forward. We take personal accountability for transformative outcomes, and our belief in progress inspires others to rise to the challenge with us.

Collaborate globally: IBMers are global professionals and global citizens and must therefore be skilled at collaboration. We think and work shoulder-to-shoulder with others—across the boundaries of teams, disciplines, organizations, countries, and cultures—to achieve the right outcome. As the human dimension of a globally integrated enterprise, we build our own networks of experts, and we encourage our colleagues to use the collective intelligence of their network not just to get work done but to identify what needs to be done and to take collective action. We see our networks of global citizens not just as collections of individuals but as a collective leadership force creating the full promise of IBM to transform the marketplace, society, and the world.

Act with a systemic perspective: IBMers are systems thinkers. We help our clients, our colleagues, and the world understand and design the essential dimensions of any system—how it senses, maps, and analyzes information; detects underlying patterns; and translates that knowledge into belief and action. We help others see this end-to-end view, synthesizing information from many dimensions, whether the system in question is technological, economic, societal, cultural, or natural. This systemic view allows us to frame problems properly and to take the right action in the right way at the right time. It also lets us anticipate the impact of our actions on others. Knowing all this, we act wisely while boldly taking the right risks.

Build mutual trust: IBM's business model requires getting different constituents to work together to solve problems and open up opportunity, be that inside IBM, among organizations, within our clients, or in the case of world-changing work, with many communities. IBMers are skilled at building 360 degrees of trust across this full spectrum of IBM's constituents, finding common ground for those with different objectives, aspirations, constraints, and cultures. We build these kinds of relationships by acting with integrity, assuming positive intent, and ensuring that openness and trust are maintained, even when agreement is not achieved. We trust in the skills of others, that they know what to do and how to do it and are motivated to achieve the result. And if we see trust eroding, we take accountability to remedy that quickly.

Influence through expertise: IBM's value proposition and business model are grounded in delivering expertise, so we continually deepen our own and our colleagues' knowledge and eminence as professionals, as collaborators, as leaders, and as fully realized IBMers. We develop our skills and careers through feedback, coaching, mentoring, and challenging assignments within IBM and in the communities where we and our clients live and work. And we take personal responsibility for developing IBM's thought leadership, both inside and outside our organizations.

Continuously transform: IBMers are committed to building the future—a better world and a better IBM. This is what IBM has done for 100 years. Our intellectual curiosity and spirit of restless reinvention, animated by a belief in reason, in science, and in progress, infuses the enterprise with energy. Today, in a world where the future is far less predictable, IBMers actively seek what we do not know and haven't yet imagined. We cultivate an environment of openness to new approaches and experimentation. We rethink assumptions and ask probing questions—to grasp new situations, unearth opportunities, and create new markets. We engage others whose background, culture, language, or work style is different from our own. This is the heart of an IBM that can learn, adapt, and continuously transform.

Communicate for impact: IBMers communicate to find mutual understanding and to build a sense of shared outcomes. That starts with listening; we ensure people's ideas and concerns are heard. We bring deep expertise and perspective, which are the ingredients to communicating clearly and simply, especially in complex situations. We interpret and synthesize disparate concepts, strategies, and intent. We leverage our understanding of others' perspectives—the ones they can express, and the ones they cannot yet—to tailor what we say and how we say it. We communicate authentically, in a timely way, in the most effective manner, even when conveying an unpopular opinion.

Help IBMers succeed: The IBM brand is about IBMers and how we show up in the world—not just client-facing IBMers, but all of us. So we each strive to bring our best selves to our work. And we are in the service of the success of others, ensuring they have resources, ongoing support, and clear milestones. We take the time to share insights and discuss the challenge in front of us. We anticipate and remove obstacles and prevailing practices that are holding people back. We acknowledge others' contributions, champion their ideas, and help each IBMer find his or her own motivation. We create an environment in which our colleagues feel a sense of purpose and engagement and which draws on their own strong desire to act.

Derailment Factors

IBM has identified thirty derailing behaviors organized into eight Derailment Factors. Derailment Factors refer to a set of behaviors that, if exhibited in the workplace, can decrease your leadership effectiveness and interfere with your overall performance. Demonstration of these behaviors is often the result of "blind spots" (areas about which one is uninformed, biased, or uninterested; behaviors that unknowingly cause negative impressions), over-reliance on a personal strength, or character weaknesses.

Even the most effective leaders occasionally exhibit behaviors consistent with these derailment factors. The key is to identify the derailment behaviors you tend to exhibit and learn how to best manage them. Managing your derailment behaviors is as important to effective leadership as is developing your leadership capabilities. Moreover, it is important to note that IBM wants every IBMer to have the opportunity to advance to positions of leadership and expects all IBMers to engage in acts of leadership regardless of formal authority. Therefore, these derailment factors apply to all IBMers.

IBM Derailment Factors for Leaders

Lack of Self-Awareness: Lacks the ability to accurately understand his/her strengths and weaknesses or the impact of his/her behavior on others.

Lack of Self-Control: Lacks the ability or willingness to control his/her emotions, including negative impulses or moods, or has difficulty effectively handling stressful situations and being resilient in the face of setbacks.

Lack of Interpersonal Acumen: Is insensitive to or lacks the ability to understand other people's emotions and nonexplicit communication, or does not demonstrate care for other people's needs and problems.

Lack of Organizational Acumen: Lacks the ability to build consensus or resolve conflicts; can be uncooperative and fails to build effective relationships with others.

Lack of Backbone: Appears indecisive; complies with authority or popular opinion; is unwilling to state a point of view or avoids responsibility.

Lack of Adaptability: Lacks the ability or willingness to adapt to change and learn from experiences; does not appreciate others with different perspectives or skills.

Lack of Trustworthiness: Fails to build trust; can be inconsistent in what he/she says and does or in keeping commitments; fails to take care of important details.

Lack of Broad Perspective: Lacks the capability or willingness to think strategically or broadly and can be overly focused on details, which in turn can decrease his/her effectiveness in leading his/her team.

The derailment factors were created by examining literature outlining the more common behaviors leaders exhibit that may potentially decrease their leadership effectiveness and interfere with their overall performance in role. These derailment factors have been internally validated with high-performing IBMers, and this internal study has determined that the derailment factors are highly negatively correlated with the organizational climate.

Employee Experience

Leader behaviors—the IBM Competencies and Derailment Factors that leaders display—are means to an end. The end goal is the impact they have on others, or the Employee Experience. As depicted in IBM's Leadership Framework, the Employee Experience consists of two major elements: Organizational Climate and Employee Engagement.

Organizational Climate

Organizational Climate is people's perceptions of what it is like to work in a particular work setting. More to the point, *how easy is it to do to good work here*. It has to do with employee performance. Global focus groups of high-performing IBM teams helped to identify seven organizational dimensions that directly influence employees' ability to perform. These seven dimensions are as follows:

Clarity: The degree to which members understand IBM's strategy, the goals of the organization and work group, and how their role contributes to these goals. Clarity also refers to the degree to which members understand the interdependencies between their work group and other parts of IBM.

Empowerment: The degree to which members feel they are trusted and have the freedom to make the decisions necessary to perform their work well. Moreover, it refers to having work they find meaningful and challenging, which in turn inspires purpose and instills an increasing sense of competence and self-confidence.

Support and Enablement: The degree to which members feel they get the support, resources, and organizational flexibility they need to do their work well. It also refers to the level of buffering provided by management toward bureaucracy and conflicting priorities.

Opportunity and Development: The degree to which members feel that their workgroup, as well as the larger organization, supports their professional development and provides them opportunities to grow their skills and their careers in IBM.

Reward and Recognition: The degree to which members feel valued and recognized for the work they do. This dimension also pertains to the extent to which members feel the rewards in IBM are consistent with IBM values as well as related to job performance.

Teaming and Collaboration: The degree to which members are bonded to each other and a common sense of mission. They share information and resources in service of achieving common goals. They take ownership and willingly pursue these goals even in the face of obstacles.

Innovation: The degree to which members respect and value others' ideas; provide each other feedback and share their knowledge; and encourage each other to try new ways of doing things and to take risks in service of achieving outstanding results.

Employee Engagement

Organizational climate is the key determinant of *employee engagement*. In other words, groups that display high-performing organizational climates, as described by the seven climate dimensions, have employees who are fully engaged in their work. Therefore, employee engagement is an outcome of organizational climate. IBM defines employee engagement as *a psychological state in which employees are intellectually and emotionally involved in their work, and are positively connected with both their co-workers and the larger organization. This state of mind fosters a sense of pride, a willingness to apply discretionary effort, and, most importantly, ignites energy that would not otherwise exist.*

A deeper look at employee engagement reveals two sub-dimensions: *energy* and *pride and belonging*. *Energy* refers to the degree to which organizational members are energized by the work itself. Their work is more than a job, it is a part of their identity; and the more they achieve, the better they feel. *Pride and belonging* refers to the degree to which members gain a sense of community and pride from the work they do and from being an IBMer.

As indicated in IBM's Leadership Framework, employee engagement has a direct influence on business results. Furthermore, employee engagement has been shown to have a significant impact on client satisfaction and retention, product and service quality, innovation and efficiency, turnover, and sales performance.

APPENDIX II

U.S. Coast Guard Principles

1. **The Principle of Clear Objective** directs every operation toward a clearly defined and attainable objective.

2. **The Principle of Effective Presence** requires that the right assets and capabilities be at the right place at the right time.

3. **The Principle of Unity of Effort** describes the performance of cooperative operational objectives by working in concert with different Coast Guard units and coordinating these efforts with a diverse set of governmental and nongovernmental entities.

4. **The Principle of On-Scene Initiative** involves Coast Guard personnel being given latitude to act quickly and decisively within the scope of their authority, without waiting for direction from higher levels in the chain of command.

5. **The Principle of Flexibility** describes how the Coast Guard pursues multiple missions with the same people and assets by adjusting to a wide variety of tasks and circumstances.

6. **The Principle of Managed Risk** involves two dimensions: First, the commander is obligated to ensure that units are properly

trained, equipped, and maintained; and second, the commander is obligated to assess the crew and equipment capabilities against the operational situation to determine whether and how to execute a mission.

7. **The Principle of Restraint** reflects the obligation of the Coast Guard personnel to act with good judgment and treat American citizens and foreign visitors with dignity.

APPENDIX III

U.S. Coast Guard Values

Honor. We demonstrate uncompromising ethical conduct and moral behavior in all of our personal and organizational actions. We are loyal and accountable to the public trust.

Respect. We treat each other and those we serve with fairness, dignity, respect, and compassion. We encourage individual opportunity and growth. We encourage creativity through empowerment. We work as a team. We value our diverse workforce.

Devotion to Duty. We exist to serve. We serve with pride. We are professionals, military and civilian, who seek and revere responsibility, accept accountability, and are committed to the successful achievement of our operational missions and organizational goals.

Index